Robert Browning and His World

Robert Browning

and His World:

Two Robert Brownings?

[1861-1889]

BY MAISIE WARD

CASSELL · LONDON

CASSELL & COMPANY LTD
35 Red Lion Square, London, WC1
Melbourne, Sydney, Toronto
Johannesburg, Auckland

S.B.N. 304 93424 0

Printed Photolitho in Great Britain by
Ebenezer Baylis & Son, Ltd.,
The Trinity Press, Worcester, and London
F. 569

For two granddaughters

Mary Jo in England

Elizabeth in America

Acknowledgments

I am most grateful to John Murray Ltd. for allowing me to see the holographs of Browning's letters to George Smith and for general permission to quote from all Browning material, published and unpublished, of which they own the copyright.

For passages from *New Letters of Robert Browning* my thanks go also to Kenneth Leslie Knickerbocker and the Yale University Press; from *Letters of the Brownings to George Barrett* to Paul Landis and the University of Illinois Press; from *Henry James and H. G. Wells* to Professor Leon Edel and the University of Illinois Press; from *The Swinburne Letters* to Professor C. Y. Lang and Yale University Press; from *Henry James: The Conquest of London* to Professor Edel and Rupert Hart-Davis; from *Monckton Milnes: The Flight of Youth* to James Pope-Hennessy and Constable and Co. Ltd.; from *Alfred Tennyson by his Grandson Charles Tennyson* to Sir Charles Tennyson and Macmillan; to Baylor University for the Curtis diary and Milsand's letters to Sarianna Browning.

I am grateful to Balliol College, Oxford, for permission to quote from Browning's letters to his son; to Trinity College, Dublin, for a letter of Browning's to an unknown correspondent; to the Alexander Turnbull Library, Wellington, New Zealand, for letters of Alfred Domett and Robert Buchanan; to the New York Public Library (Henry W. and Albert Berg Collection, Astor, Lenox and Tilden Foundations) for passages from letters of Elizabeth Barrett Browning to her sister; to the University of Texas for letters of Browning to his son, "Pen," his son's tutor and his art teacher, and to the Rev. J. R. Williams; to Wellesley College Library for one short Browning letter and a passage from a Christina Rossetti letter; to the Henry E. Huntington Library for letters 92 and 135 (Browning-Furnivall). I thank Dartmouth College and the trustees of the James Estate for permission for quotations from several unpublished letters of Henry James.

In Florence, Conte Bernardo Rucellai most kindly allowed me to copy passages from the holographs of Browning's letters to his grandmother, Mrs. Bronson. His sister, Marchesa Fossi, had stores of her mother's memories of the poet and introduced me to her lovely house in Asolo where Browning used to visit.

My warm personal gratitude goes especially to Professors Robert Langbaum and Edward McAleer, to the Rev. William Whitla and Saul Maloff all of whom read this volume in manuscript. I owe much to their careful scrutiny and suggestions and in addition have been greatly helped by Professor Langbaum's treatment of Browning's poetry—both in *The Poetry of Experience* and in various articles especially that on Browning and Myth.

Professor Edel sought out allusions to Browning and his son in unpublished Henry James letters and generously lent me his own copies of them to quote.

E. V. Quinn, librarian of Balliol College, Margaret Scott at the Alexander Turnbull, Veva Wood and Dr. Herring at Baylor, Mrs. Szladits at the Berg Collection, have all helped in every possible way. Indeed I have found every library quite astonishingly liberal in copying material, and assisting me to make the best possible use of their treasures. Finally, my thanks go to Ruth Ames but for whose assistance I should have despaired of finishing my book.

Contents

Illustrations

Concerning the Title

THE over-all title of this book is *Robert Browning and his World*—and Browning's world in the English years was above all the world of people and of his poetry. We must see him in relation to his contemporaries whether friends, enemies, critics or casual observers—and in the context of the surrounding world, social in two senses, political and deeply personal. It is of course difficult to keep the right proportion. A colorful contemporary may, like a minor actor, hog the scene for a while; one can only do one's best to keep him within limits. But those most involved with Browning must stand out in any study of him—and perhaps still more those who themselves wrote about him.

Among these Henry James comes first. He was especially fascinated by the contrast between the Browning who had written the poems and the Browning one met socially. It was a near impossibility to believe that the poet's high speech had originated from the assiduous diner-out in white waistcoat. He was always, says James, "loud, cheerful and copious." And the novelist plays with the notion from which the title for this volume is taken, *Two Robert Brownings?*

In a short story entitled "The Private Life" James develops the idea, not just of a man with two sides to his character, but of two men using one persona—or mask—on the stage of life. He is *at the same time* absorbed in contemplation in his room and chatting on the terrace below. How James works this out will be discussed when we have seen enough of Browning between his wife's death and his own to feel for ourselves what drove James to fantasy for a solution.

Introduction
by Way of a Catalogue

G ENIUS will turn up in the most surprising places: it is present in Sotheby's nostalgic catalogue of the six-day Browning sale of 1913—the arrangement and descriptions of the material, the alluring quotations and illustrations.

Elizabeth Barrett Browning had died in 1861, Robert in 1889, their only son, Robert Wiedemann Barrett Browning (universally known as "Pen"), in 1912—just after the centenary celebration of his father's birth. Now his collection of books and pictures, his father's and his mother's treasures, once the central object of his life, were to be scattered: the picture of Hope End, Elizabeth's childhood home, was there; the tapestries that had glowed on the walls of the Casa Guidi, birthplace of Pen and center of his parents' sojourn in Italy, were reproduced. The love letters were there and Mrs. Jameson's record of the honeymoon journey from Paris to Pisa. Elizabeth's autograph letters, published and unpublished, became that week the prized possession of colleges and collectors, and in their vivid pages we can read today the story of her never-forgiving father, her slowly relenting brothers, and the friendships and enthusiasms of almost fifteen years' happy married life. We are shown the Casa Guidi with its heavy furniture picked up in Florence and occasionally even put together by Browning, his large desk and Elizabeth's tiny one. There was her writing case, too, with the local newspapers inside it from which, to the end, she so eagerly absorbed the news of the making of Italy.

And then, going back again in time, there were the books from

Browning's own and his father's libraries, and copies belonging both to him and to Elizabeth of the classics, Greek and Roman, love of which they shared. There were Latin, Greek, and Hebrew Bibles; there was even their childhood reading (of which few would have been capable at such an early age). One is struck at once by the astonishing likeness in the education of the child of the bank clerk and the child of the rich slave owner—and then one recalls that Browning, too, had the Jamaican slave-owning background which his father had repudiated, choosing to slave himself in a bank rather than rule in a compound.

The array of learned books is formidable, but no less impressive are the autograph letters to both husband and wife from Carlyle, Ruskin, Tennyson, Dante Gabriel Rossetti, Leigh Hunt, Monckton Milnes, Swinburne, Meredith, Oscar Wilde. Mrs. Gaskell describes the Brontë background, Dickens invites Browning to hear him read—a whole world comes to life, quotations being skillfully chosen to whet the appetite of purchasers.

Never I think was a catalogue with such quaint touches as a "lot" made up of "Pencil drawing of Joanna Southcote, the Prophetess, two photographs from a picture of Byron, and a flower from Shelley's grave." This chance mingling is fascinatingly indicative of two elements in Browning: his reverence for his fellow poets and an abiding curiosity about things strange or weird, balanced in him, though not always in Elizabeth, by a passionate sanity.

Browning's two problems—his wife's eager belief in spiritualism and her dependence on morphine—go unmentioned; but the catalogue, taking us through their elopement (as Elizabeth hated to hear it called) and their life in Italy, goes on to Pen's childhood: the many books inscribed to him help us to picture it in all its stages.

The Casa Guidi is photographed from the drawing commissioned by Browning after Elizabeth's death—with all the furniture neatly marked in "lots." And then we see the widower returning to England with one conscious object only—the education of the twelve-year-old son on whom his life now centered. What he made of that life, how Pen developed, and what the atmosphere and people were like to which they had returned, after the long exile in Italy, is the subject of this second volume of *Robert Browning and His World*.

Robert Browning and His World

1 A Time of Loneliness

So, let him wait God's instant men call years.

THE RING AND THE BOOK

BROWNING had often kept vigil while his wife coughed or slept fitfully; now as she lay dead he spent a last night at her side: "The future is nothing to me now," he wrote to his sister Sarianna, "except inasmuch as it confirms and realizes the past. . . . I shall leave Italy at once. . . . Pen has been perfect to me: he sate all yesterday with his arms around me; said things like her to me. I shall try and work hard, educate him, and live worthy of my past fifteen years' happiness. I do not feel paroxysms of grief—but as if the very blessing, she died giving me, insensible to all beside, had begun to work already. . . . Don't be in any concern for me, I have some of her strength, really, added to mine. . . . How she looks now,—how perfectly beautiful!"[1]

It was, Ruskin declared, the Italian battle for nationality that had killed Elizabeth Browning, "while smooth English propriety maintains the Austrians at Venice and the Pope at Rome and the devil everywhere."

But Ruskin lay under the same condemnation by his fellow countrymen as both Brownings for preferring, as Kingsley had put it:

> . . . popish Appenines,
> Dirty stones of Venice
> And his gas-lamps seven;

We've the stones of Snowdon
And the lamps of heaven.

Ruskin went to and fro between England and Italy; the Brownings had been forced by Elizabeth's health to make their home abroad where the Italian skies and sun—not stones, lamps, or even mountains—had prolonged her life.

There is a sharp contrast between the English criticism of Browning as Italianate and the long-resisted pull on him of what can only be called homesickness. He was to an unusual degree a man of two countries, longing for his homeland yet loving Italy, his poet's imagination afire with its beauty, variety—and strangeness. And you have only to read *Aurora Leigh* to realize that, with all her enthusiasm for the Italian cause, Elizabeth's roots, too, had been elsewhere. Only their son "Pen" could say, with no reservations, "*Sono italiano*"— yet even he had had for playmates the English and American children of his parents' friends. As we have seen, their intimate circle was that of fellow expatriates. It was in the little Protestant cemetery that Elizabeth was buried. "The service," wrote Browning to Sarianna, "will be that of the Ch. of En., that I may hear those only words at the beginning." The "words" were "I am the Resurrection and the Life." It was to his American and British friends—the William Wetmore Storys and Isa Blagden—that Browning turned in his grief. William Story was indignant at the lack of feeling in the "fat English parson" who "blundered through the burial service in a brutally careless way . . . she was consigned by him to the earth as if her clay were no better than any other clay." But Browning's eyes were turned toward "the dear and noble Italians" who "honored themselves by honoring her," to the newspapers that proclaimed her great both as poet and friend of Italy, to the shops shut up, the hearse passing "thro' the streets, which is never allowed—with crowns on it, laurel and white flowers." These he did not realize Story had brought—and Kate Field was indignant that not more Italians were present. Browning was oblivious to all but the grief that met his, the tribute of those who did come. He wrote of "Italian men crying like children, Villari the historian, Dall'Ongaro the Poet—and many others unknown to me."

The black and white in Browning's own feelings, and in his views of others, can be bewilderingly interchangeable, but never did they meet and melt into gray. He was miserable or blissful. And as Edmund Gosse was later to point out, he approached the world around him with a confidence that turned into amazed resentment against any who disappointed him.

In any record of these first months of loss a note of dreariness is inescapable. When two have become one flesh, one mind, one spirit, the breaking of this composite being brings not only acute pain but at least a temporary emptiness. The man left feels only a half man. Browning would build again; but many years later. Now in the black of his loss he took comfort in the white of Elizabeth's glory. "One must not think about oneself," wrote Ruskin to Burne-Jones; "it is all the earth's loss." And to Browning himself a little later, "When you care to see me, or hear from me, I shall thankfully come." There was no one, he felt, "who regards her loss with a more grave and enduring bitterness . . . —not the acute, consolable suffering of a little time, but the established sense of unredeemable, unparalleled loss, which will not pass away."

Browning was in desperate haste to leave Florence. A letter to his brother-in-law ended: "Dear George, I must write no more letters like this. . . . All brothers and relatives *must* forgive my not attempting to write to them—I am absolutely alone,—with much help of another kind, and every sort of offered assistance, but I cannot yet go over this again and again in letters. I hope I shall see you in England. Peni is quite well and very perfect in his goodness. I hope to get off in another week."

It could not be quite as fast—but speedy this packing and dispatching of business certainly was. Small wonder that in addition to the outpouring of his grief Browning broke down at moments physically. After a blackout—and choking from what he calls "closings of the throat"—he told Isa Blagden "things necessary to be known for Peni"— just in case. "You must not blame dear warm-hearted Isa," he wrote to Sarianna, "who got needlessly frightened." Needlessly perhaps, but not unreasonably! Isa herself as I have told in my first volume spoke of the weeks that followed as her "apocalyptic month," in which the exalted speech of the poet broke into a sheer cry of human desolation: "I want her, I want her."

The hour of fresh grief is the last one at which momentous decisions should be taken, large changes made. But it is the hour when one feels most determined to make them. How live on in scenes that thrust perpetually the happy past into the agonizing present? There were obvious arguments for going to Browning's only living relatives, or for taking Pen to his mother's family. Paris, near his own father and sister, was a possible home; but Pen and his education were the paramount consideration. And Pen, concerned to comfort his father, was "like an angel to me—inspired all at once."

Browning wrote later to Story: "The staying at Casa Guidi was not the worst of it: I kept in my place there like a worm-eaten piece of old furniture looking solid enough, but when I was *moved*, I began to go to pieces." As to Italy, he would always be pulled in different directions, with a dread and a longing, summed up in another letter to Story: "I do not call the week or whatever it may be which I suppose I shall have to spend in Florence a return to Italy, any more than Father Matthew called taking the sacrament wine-drinking."[2]

The immense difficulty of Browning's task in educating his only son, now the motherless child of an overdevoted mother, is illuminated by Nathaniel Hawthorne, who was no less observant than his wife when they had all visited the Casa Guidi three years earlier:

> I never saw such a boy as this before; so slender, fragile and spirit-like,—not as if he were actually in ill health, but as if he had little or nothing to do with human flesh and blood. His face is very pretty and most intelligent, and exceedingly like his mother's. He is nine years old, and seems at once less childlike and less manly than would befit that age. I should not quite like to be the father of such a boy, and should fear to stake so much interest and affection on him as he cannot fail to inspire. I wonder what is to become of him,—whether he will grow to be a man,—whether it is desirable that he should.[3]

Hawthorne went on to say that the father's task must be to develop the more "earthly" qualities and capacities in such a boy—and this Browning had already been endeavoring to do, while allowing his wife to have her way in such matters as dress. Riding, swimming, and regular lessons had always been insisted on, and now the shearing of the curls and the adoption of ordinary boy's dress was perfectly natural and need imply no criticism of the past. "Pen," he wrote to Sarianna, "the golden curls and fantastic dress, is gone, just as Ba is gone: he has short hair, worn boy-wise, long trousers, is a common boy all at once: otherwise I could not have lived without a maid. I can now attend to him completely myself."[4]

Isa Blagden accompanied them to Paris, and in London they were "pleasantly smothered" with Arabel Barrett's hospitality. Browning seemed able to think only about Pen and his education, asking advice from George Barrett, Robert Lytton, and others. Letters are printed in Robert Lytton's correspondence[5] querying whether to send Pen at once to a public school, about which he, of course, knew much more than Browning. "Too abrupt an initiation into the rough rules at such an establishment," the father concluded, "might disgust the poor little fellow too much; I shall begin with a private tutor—and use him to the academical harness first of all. . . . I don't mean to hurry any of the stages." A tutor should come first, then possibly (he told George Barrett) "Eton or Harrow when qualified for the Upper forms, thus saving him many of the early troubles." Yet in November, still undecided, he writes to Story that he is told a private tutor is much better at bringing boys on than is a Public School; " 'the advantage at Eton is *not* of getting scholarship, but of-of-of'—why, getting aristocratic connexions and friendships, which in England is the chief end of man! In a week or two, I shall decide."

Meanwhile came a long and complete holiday for which St. Enogat in Brittany, not yet absorbed by Dinard, was chosen. In a letter to Isa Blagden, Browning writes of its success. Pen and his grandfather had become the best of friends: "They sketch together, go home and paint etc., and Pen's loud merry laugh is never out of my ears." It had in fact amazed Browning that Pen could suit himself so well to new circumstances, that with no boy companions "he *never* was so happy and so cheerful" as with aunt and grandfather. No doubt there were, as with every child who has lost mother, father, or brother, the passionate tears at night, gone with the day and the occupations it brings. There was swimming, with a good teacher—and pony rides accompanied by Browning for two hours daily. "I walk myself to death by his side— there not being a single horse to be hired here or in the neighbourhood."

The pony, escorted of old from Siena to Rome, was with them until Pen grew too big to ride it. But how to bring it home from St. Enogat? Misinformed as to the time of the transport train, Browning insisted that the pony must accompany them on the express. "I was upwards of two hours [he told Story] in this weary work of battling with them— 'It *could not* be!'—but at the last moment, literally, it *was*." A horse box was attached to the train "which there was no time even to pay for" and off they went, having missed the original express "which was run into by another train at Amiens," a dozen passengers killed, more than a score injured.

At the station at Amiens, Browning saw Tennyson and pointed him out to Pen, but pulled his own hat down over his eyes to avoid recognition. Associated with his grief was a shrinking from the friends he would later find so valuable. Anne Thackeray (Lady Ritchie) saw him in Kensington Garden "coming towards us along the broad walk in his blackness through the sunshine," and felt when he visited them that "he was in a jarred and troubled state, and not himself as yet."[6]

He told the Thackerays of "the house he had just taken for himself and his boy"—his brief attempt at living in rooms to avoid housekeeping problems being as impracticable with a small son to educate as had been the idea of a home in Paris. A house was taken in Warwick Crescent, almost a continuation of Delamere Terrace, where Arabel Barrett now lived—and where Pen could row on the nearby canal. A Mr. Gillespie was engaged as tutor and a woman teacher for drawing and music.

This was a honeymoon period between father and son, but the amiability and adaptability which were Pen's characteristics made it rather specially difficult to decide if he had any marked bent. He seemed ready to be happy anywhere and with anybody—and with any occupation. He enjoyed playing the piano just as he enjoyed drawing and did both rather well. He learned to fence and to skate. He boasted later of having taught his father to swim and in one of these seaside summers he helped a swimmer to rescue and resuscitate a drowning man—dismissing incompetent assistants with the remark *"allez au diable"*—("So you see," comments Browning, "he promises.").

The degree to which Pen and the plans for Pen loomed in the letters made Isa anxious and Browning reassured her; he would never become a "monomaniac" on the subject of the boy's education—"nor do I ever put my hand to the machine a minute after it is really working by itself." But the famous Master of Balliol, Benjamin Jowett, meeting him four years later, wrote: "Of personal objects he seems to have none except the education of his son, in which I hope in some degree to help him."

The correspondence with Isa was a regular one and especially intimate. The close friend of both husband and wife, at his side in the days of his loss, she was now overseeing the arrangements in Florence for the placing of a tablet to Elizabeth on the Casa Guidi. It was characteristic of the delightful Italian people that, though the inscription uttered a truth in their intense gratitude to the "noble poet" who had espoused their cause, delay followed delay in the arrangements and Browning felt that only through Isa was the inscription at last put up. She was perhaps his closest friend—certainly the one with whom his intercourse was the least inhibited. They could quarrel and forgive, they could exchange gossip about the people and places both knew so well. And of all his friends she came nearest to sharing his loss. They decided to write to one another on a fixed day every month: she on the twelfth, the day of the Brownings' marriage, he on the nineteenth, the day they fled to France.

In September 1862 he wrote:

with respect to Florence, I cannot tell how I feel about it, so do I change in my feelings in the course of a quarter of an hour sometimes: particular incidents in the Florence way of life recur as if I

could not bear a repetition of them—to find myself walking among
the hills, or turnings by the villas, certain doorways, old walls, points
of sight, on a solitary bright summer Sunday afternoon—there, I
think that would fairly choke me at once: on the other hand, beginning from another point of association, I have such yearnings to be
there! Just now, at the approach of Autumn, I feel exactly like a
swallow in a cage,—as if I *must* go there, have no business anywhere else, with the year drawing in.—How thankful I am that all
these foolish fancies never displace for a moment the solid fact that
I can't go but have plain duty to do in London,—if there could be a
doubt about that, I should drift about like a feather: at times (to
give you a notion of what I might do if free to be foolish) I seem as
if I should like, by a fascination, to try the worst at once,—to go
straight to the old rooms at Casa Guidi and there live and die! But I
shake all this off—and say to myself (sometimes aloud) "Don't be
afraid, my good fellow, you'll die too, all in good time."

When at last Isa could tell him that the tablet was in place, Browning wrote on November 19 that he had found her letter hard to answer
"so strangely did it affect me ... I can't tell you the thrill of pain and
pleasure I feel about it; the presence of Her is now habitual to me,—
I can have no doubt that it is my greatest comfort to be always remembering her,—the old books and furniture, her chair which is by mine."
But above all came "the deepest gratification at this act, determined and
carried into effect. ... I shall love the dust of Florence, the letters which
make up its name, every man, woman and child it holds."
　　A correspondence with William Story also takes us back to Italy
"every minute of those last six months in Rome would *melt up* into gold
enough for a year's use now, if I had it ... Dear Story, tell me what
you can about the studio—let me smell the wet clay once more, and
hear the birds and the goat thro' that dear little door to the left."

These letters tell of Browning's sudden rise in the eyes of literary
London. Only a few months after his return he was offered the editor-
ship of the *Cornhill* and was half tempted—by the salary "which Pen
might find something to do with." And "They count on my attracting

writers,—I who could never muster *English* readers enough to pay for salt and bread!" His request for a clearer idea of terms and conditions, which was, he told Isa, tantamount to a refusal, went unanswered. But as he wrote to Story, "people are getting good-natured to my poems. There's printing a book of 'Selections from R.B.' (SCULPTOR and poet) which is to popularise my old things; and so and so means to review it, and somebody or [other] always was looking out for such an occasion, and what's his name always said he admired me, only he didn't say it, though he said something else every week of his life in some Journal. The breath of Man! . . . Reviewers will have my heart in their rough hands for the next month or two."

By 1863 Chapman was holding back *Dramatis Personae* only to allow selections (two had appeared, a third was talked of) and the new complete edition of poems to have their run. Browning was busy, too, with the publication of Elizabeth's early work, anything and everything that could keep her memory alive in England. "Nothing," he told Isa, "that ought to be published, shall be kept back." But there had been a threat that some of her private letters would be printed, in a biography which Browning had refused to authorize, and with characteristic violence he commented on all who would attempt such profanation: "what I undergo with their paws in my very bowels, you can guess and God knows! . . . it shall not be done if I can stop the scamp's knavery— along with his breath . . . the law protects *property*—as these letters are."

It has been noted that Elizabeth had written to Miss Mitford of the value of correspondence in a biography and had maintained that writers should not shrink from the idea of such a future use of their letters. But when Browning told Isa it was something Elizabeth would have "utterly writhed under," he was vividly aware of what (whatever her theories) his wife's feelings had been. Of Miss Mitford's indiscretions in her *Recollections of Literary Life* Elizabeth had written: "She has pulled out the very heart from me, to hold it up to the world with its roots still bleeding."

While Isa meant Florence, Story meant Rome, which without the poignancy of Florence brought back the days "when I used really to live." His friends there "are all like portraits in the one habitable room of a house. I go in among them many a time in the course of the day and night."

To Story, who kept begging Browning to resume social life, he had written in January 1862: "I make up my mind from week to week, *next* Monday I will begin and call on my friends." And in February: "I go out a little . . . mean to accept all invitations henceforth: am just made a member of the Athenaeum by the committee." But a year later he is still feeling: "You throw bits of porphyry and marble pavement from Rome, and I have only London mud, that's the fact." And when, becoming more engaged socially, "I do seem to know that you understand my first satisfying people outside—and then sitting down quietly with the inmates of my soul's little house."

And, surprisingly, in November 1863:

O Rome, O Story, my master!—I have just finished the fitting up my little studio, lying waste since you saw it—there is clay in, and modelling-tools, and I shall set to work at once—letting the memories curl around me while I preposterously meddle and make! I seem as if it would solace me beyond gin and water—some people try *that*. Our clay is white, not the rich Roman *brown*.

We hear no more of an attempt that can have brought only disappointment. The old days in Rome had meant instruction given and emulation awakened, ambition stirred by the surrounding atmosphere, above all the endless talk in which Browning delighted. None of this he had in his solitary little studio in London. And the long sunny days in Rome contrasted painfully with the pressure he now felt.

"I never had so much to do," he had written to Story soon after his return, "or so little pleasure in doing it."

With the presence of Mr. Gillespie, Pen's lessons were off his hands, but there were endless proofs to be corrected—his own reprints and Elizabeth's—work to be done for Story on his book *Roba di Roma*, concerning which Browning renders long accounts of his stewardship. There was a correspondence of which we are still learning the extent. Above all came the publication in 1864 of *Dramatis Personae* and the first beginnings of *The Ring and the Book*.

2 Dramatis Personae and an Interesting Friendship

It is the glory and good of Art
That Art remains the one way possible
Of speaking truth, to mouths like mine at least.

THE RING AND THE BOOK

IT SEEMS impossible to be certain how much of *Dramatis Personae* was written in this period, how much in Rome. "Most of them," Browning wrote to Isa, "were written long ago—some were seen by Ba." Some can, however, be placed in the seaside holidays of Pornic and Croisic, and several are clearly affected by the atmosphere of thought in which Browning had found himself on returning to England. While his contemporaries sought inspiration from the ages of chivalry, it was the intellectual life around him, or the past *in its effect on the present*, which inspired Browning to write, whether in agreement or vehement dissent.

A reaction was under way—not only against the High Church movement, to which he had always been opposed, but against the main Christian dogmas by which so much of his poetry was inspired. *Essays and Reviews*, published in 1860, was a manifesto of the theological Liberalism Newman so greatly feared, and among its writers was Benjamin Jowett, soon to become one of Browning's intimates. Jowett was not yet the Master of Balliol—he was only an exceedingly able classical tutor with the power both of imparting knowledge and of gaining a permanent influence over his pupils, whose mentor he often enough remained for life. It was courageous of him to get involved in the controversy that raged over *Essays and Reviews*. Visiting a pupil's father he might well hear himself denounced from the pulpit of the village church. Nor was this only by High Church or evangelical commentators. Carlyle remarked of Jowett's essay "The sentinel who deserts ought to be shot"; Leslie Stephen felt that he said nothing which "might not be consistently admitted by Renan, or even by Voltaire," and that the intelligent youth adopting him as a guide might well feel "as though his master had pushed him over a cliff and advised him to fall softly or perhaps assured him that he was not falling at all."

Actually it was not so simple. Many discoveries were being made in an almost unexplored field and it would take several generations to realize that such things as the incorporation of earlier documents in the Bible, the later dating of the Pentateuch, the composition of the Psalter and of Isaiah by many writers, need not vitiate their divine message either for Jews or Christians.

A deeper question was of course the spirit in which these researches were undertaken, and the faith or unfaith of the searchers in the fundamental dogmas. To Pusey it seemed idle when Jowett's supporters spoke of his belief in " 'the best form of Christianity'. . . . A Christianity without the supernatural, without immortality, and without 'a personal God' seems to be merely an alias for morality." The following year came Colenso's *Commentary on the Epistle to the Romans* and in 1862 his *Critical Examination of the Pentateuch*. In 1863 Renan published his *Vie de Jésus*. Before writing *Christmas-Eve and Easter-Day* Browning had read Strauss; now he passed on to Renan's book, which he criticized as "weaker and less honest" than he had expected. It is agreed that "A Death in the Desert" was largely inspired by the wish to strike a blow against the destructive power of Strauss, and perhaps of Renan too. C. H. Herford (in *Browning and the Christian Faith*) has said that this poem "did no manner of harm to Strauss," who had to be met on grounds of scholarship—and he dismissed it as a "smart pamphleteering device" giving Browning's "otherwise noble verse a disagreeable twang of theological disputation."

But who today remembers scholarly writings against Strauss—or even reads Strauss himself? And who cannot still feel the inspiration of Browning's aged Apostle, seeing the rise of the first doubters and foreseeing not Strauss alone but the ever-changing succession of critics? John reaffirms his memories: "What first were guessed as points, I now knew stars/ And named them in the Gospel I have writ." And the glimmering twilight in the cave suggests how a world grown blind might be led from its shadows into the light of the revealing Christ. "Outside was all noon and the burning blue."

"The evidence of divine power," Browning said, "is everywhere about us; not so the evidence of divine love. That love could only reveal itself to the human heart by some supreme act of *human* tenderness and devotion; the fact or fancy of Christ's cross and passion could alone supply such a revelation." But is Humanity, loving so weakly and poorly, capable of such a fancy? The Apostle has known:

> ". . . that Life and Death
> Of which I wrote 'it was'—to me, it is";
> —Is here and now: I apprehend naught else.
> Is not God now i' the world His power first made?
> Is not His love at issue still with sin,
> Closed with and cast and conquered, crucified
> Visibly when a wrong is done on earth.

The line "Closed with and cast and conquered, crucified" was omitted in later editions. Elizabeth used to entreat Browning invariably to cancel his own alterations. She told a friend that he never altered without damage. Were his first thoughts always his best?

It is surprising to find no single poem about Italy in *Dramatis Personae*. The high spirits of *Men and Women* have gone, the reflective note is more dominant. There is less characterization. "Rabbi ben Ezra" is a poem about life and death, time and eternity, but hardly a dramatic monologue. "Abt Vogler" expresses the spirit of music more than the personality of a musician. But "Mr. Sludge, 'the Medium'" (already discussed in Volume I) is a triumphant Dramatic Monologue—and so is "Caliban upon Setebos"[1] which depicts natural theology, unlike Revelation, as intensely anthropomorphic. "Shakespeare, Darwin, and Browning," remarks William DeVane, "join hands most strangely here." And Scripture too, in the title motto "Thou thoughtest that I was altogether such a one as thyself."

Bernard Shaw, at a meeting of the Browning Society, contrasted Browning's conception with Shakespeare's. "Shakespeare," he said, "being a dramatic poet, has never labelled any work of his dramatic; Browning being essentially undramatic, has called this Caliban poem a dramatic monologue." In highly Shavian fashion he wrote up his own comments for the report of the Browning Society (April 25th, 1889).

> Browning's *Caliban* is a savage, with the introspective powers of a Hamlet, and the theology of an evangelical Churchman. I must confess that I cannot conceive an evangelical Churchman possessing the introspective powers of a Hamlet. (Great laughter.) Although this character of Caliban is very interesting, and is, in fact, one of my Browning favourites, I am compelled to say that it is unnatural, impossible, and radically undramatic.

It is significant that at this date Browning should have put into the same volume Caliban with his anthropomorphic view of religion and St. John, writer of *the* spiritual Gospel. And he ends the volume with an assertion of Christ's ever spreading influence, believing perhaps that it will need no longer those elements which "Divide us, each from other, me from you—": "the walls / O' the world" will displace the Temple, the "Levites' choir, Priests' cries, and trumpet-calls." But

> That one Face, far from vanish, rather grows,
> Or decomposes but to recompose,
> Become my universe that feels and knows.

"Abt Vogler" shows music taking the place, as it did in Browning's London, of the pictures and scenery of his Italian life. DeVane is of opinion that in *Dramatis Personae* he is speaking "more often than before" from himself; even when the words are uttered by an imaginary character, "the disguise has worn thin." This certainly seems true of "Prospice," "Rabbi ben Ezra," "A Death in the Desert," and even more "Abt Vogler" where the music brought help

> To me, who must be saved because I cling with my mind
> To the same, same self, same love, same God: ay, what was, shall be.

"Rabbi ben Ezra" is perhaps the most popular of Browning's poems, certainly one of the most quoted. It has been hailed as giving the reply of hope to FitzGerald's hedonistic but despairing *Omar Khayyam*. I heard so often how Frederick Le Roy Sargent had arranged the two poems as dialogue that I sought and found a copy of his rare little book. It is a brief musical playlet with eight characters: Omar the astronomer-poet of Persia, the Rabbi, four singers representing the seasons, a Youth and a Maiden.

The songs are all taken from the *Rubaiyat,* while Omar tempts the youth with wine and the maiden tries to draw him back toward the Rabbi. But the duel between Omar and the Rabbi for this soul is played out in speeches taken from one poem or the other. For long, Omar has the advantage. All the songs are his, the wine cup is in the hands of his attendant singers. The picture is powerful, of helpless clay vessels turned out awry by the shaking hand of a "divine" potter—generously forgiven by His unhappy creatures. Can the Rabbi answer? Browning believed he could—and this bringing together of two sharply contrasted uses of the same metaphor ends in his triumph. Although this is interesting there is everything to be said for reading the poems separately—the playlet adds little to one's understanding of either.[2]

I have called the first years of the century's sixties and Browning's fifties lonely—in contrast both with the quieter life of close love and intimacy never to be replaced, and the abounding, at times overwhelming, social existence which followed during his last two decades. He declared at this time that he would never stay in a country house if invited by the angel Gabriel. He told Isa of refusing eight invitations on the first anniversary of his wife's death. His gradual return to social life came at first through literature and his wife's family. William Rossetti boasts of being among the earliest acquaintances to penetrate the self-inflicted solitude. Browning lunched with Dante Gabriel and Allingham, he was seeing Matthew Arnold, dining with Dickens, Wilkie Collins, and Forster at Greenwich. Always pulled in two directions, he needed solitude, he needed society; and in these first years, after some months of resolute isolation, engagements were still limited, invitations often refused or grudgingly accepted.

I wish I could form a picture of Arabel Barrett. One of the rash vows Elizabeth had described her husband as so often making was to give the first £50 their poverty could afford to the "ragged school" that was her sister's chief interest. They both admired her intensely, and had given her poetry when they had nothing else to give. Now Browning had chosen to live as close to her as possible, visited her daily and went with her each Sunday to Bedford Street Chapel, where the Welsh preacher Thomas Jones greatly impressed him. "It was a fancy of mine," he wrote later, in the preface to a posthumous volume of Jones's sermons, "that, in certain respects and under certain moods, a younger Carlyle might, sharing the same convictions, have spoken so, even looked so."

Browning must certainly have talked over with Jones the ideas in *Essays and Reviews,* but I doubt whether he could have had any fruitful talk with Arabel. Resembling in some respects her sister, she lacked the swiftly darting mind, the intellectual equipment, which had made the dialogue with Elizabeth fruitful and enriching.

Besides Arabel and this younger suggestion of Carlyle—and Carlyle himself—the Pre-Raphaelites and newer disciples, Browning formed in this decade a friendship with a young woman, Julia Wedgwood, great-granddaughter of Josiah, so illustrious in the world of artistic china.

Their exchange of letters is interesting, carrying a curious faint shadow of a still living past. One sees what drew Browning to Julia and made him tell her how perfect a friend Elizabeth would have found her![3] She was, as Elizabeth had been, a solitary young woman, aged now about thirty, shut by deafness into a world of books, thought, letter writing. She, like Elizabeth, had lost her very dear brother—he was ill when the correspondence with Browning began. It was Julia who opened it. She had long admired his poetry and drawn spiritual help from it, and her brother's death brought from her a touching allusion to this help. But again, as with Elizabeth, he had constantly to assure Julia that he did not visit her merely to do *her* good. It had been by the chance of circumstance that, "in the meeting of our hands, mine has seemed somewhat to lift, rather than be lifted by, yours. . . . I value your friendship for me, as you shall know, if you will but wait." And while he feels annoyance at her desire to sit at his feet, she refuses to consider the friendship as "a figure of 8."

Like Elizabeth, Julia lived in a highly conventional world. But— very unlike Elizabeth—convention had eaten into her, and she was tormented by the thought of having acted unconventionally in writing first. "A woman who has taken the initiative," runs an early letter, "in a friendship with a man, as I have done with you, has either lost all right feeling or has come to a very definite decision on the issue of all such friendships." This rather blue-stocking eldest sister in a family of six was a niece of Darwin, and had won her uncle's approval as one of the rare critics who "understood my book perfectly."

To Browning, she felt she could speak as "spirit to spirit. Nay, why do I justify myself, for I have no fears of your misconception. . . . The knowledge of you was a cordial in this swoon of life that is not likely to recur . . . a consolation exactly at the moment when I imperiously needed it."

"Three years ago, in this very week," wrote Browning by return of post, "I lost my own soul's companion. . . . I dare believe that you and that I shall recover what we have lost." And to her his "hope of the future amid the complex suggestions of intellecual doubt," is of far more value in the "darkness of my mind than the conventional assurances of those who have felt no doubt."

To Browning it seemed that God "for probational or educational purposes to ourselves," did not in this life give more than "rare flashes of momentary conviction . . . in the habitual dusk and doubt of one's life . . . the yearning we *have* and the corroborative facts, which by various processes I think we *may* have . . . you should *live* step by step *up* to the proper place where the pin-point of light is visible . . . and then, your part done, God's may follow, and will, I trust."

The fact that Julia needed his help was a big element in the friend-

ship. Browning needed to be needed: the overconcentration on Pen
was a symptom, as were the visits to Arabel, and later the daily reading
aloud to Lord Leighton's sister Alexandra Orr. Elizabeth had compared
herself to the ivy on the oak, and however much Robert proclaimed his
very real need of her she could not have lived at all but for his support.
There was one element in the years with his wife which this new
friendship partly supplied: a meeting of minds. Pen was too immature
even if he had shared his father's intellectual interests. And while it is
hard to assess a correspondence of which only one side is available,
reading the letters to Isa and to Story one feels overwhelmingly that
Browning did not expect or receive much intellectual response from
either. Both gave him, Isa especially, affection, sympathy, admiration,
but this was all. There is discussion of politics with Story, there is much
inquiry about and news of friends and acquaintances with both: Browning is obviously racking his brains for a few more items for Isa, is eager
to bring back the life at Rome with Story. The Wedgwood letters are
very different, with their references to books, casual Latin phrases,
discussion of ultimates. Browning is at home in these letters—that restful and stimulating feeling one gets only with people who themselves
are at home in a library and can toss ideas to one another as readily as
gossip. And while there is on Browning's side no faintest note of
patronage there is on hers not the least subservience.

In one exchange Julia expresses her doubts of Browning and others
"who hold that one may fetch fire from Heaven or Hell so that one's
torch burns brightly. No, I know you don't exactly say that, but the
artist mind demands intensity above every thing else, and there are
some things you can't set square with that Gospel."

"As to what you say," Browning replies, "of my Devil's Gospel—
I cannot disagree with you altogether." And after some wholly irrelevant remarks, he adds, "How funnily and contemptibly one does good,
when that happens," going on to tell a story of how he had cured a
family from belief in Sludge. "I hope," replies Julia, "you will escape
assassination, I am so weak and mean (as I m afraid you'll think it)
that I have a little pity for poor Mr. S.—I don't mean for this last
business, but for the poem."

Criticizing "James Lee" (in later editions called "James Lee's Wife") she felt it was "an artistic fault" to put them "into such a proletarian, to use the horrid new slang, background. Those are not the feelings of people who are earning their bread." But no, Browning replied, they were not proletarians—"I meant them for just the opposite—people newly-married, trying to realise a dream of being sufficient to each other, in a foreign land (where you can try such an experiment) and finding it break up,—the man being *tired* first—and tired precisely of the love:— but I have expressed it all insufficiently."

This poem, like "Youth and Art," is one of the many pictures of failure which Browning so often drew as contrasted with his own success. "Youth and Art" falls into his more familiar pattern—a fear to take the plunge into a penniless marriage. Sculptor and singer have failed both in their love and in the reality of their art:

> But you meet the Prince at the Board,
>   I'm queen myself at *bals-paré*,
> I've married a rich old lord,
>   And you're dubbed knight and an R.A.

> Each life unfulfilled, you see;
>   It hangs still patchy and scrappy:
> We have not sighed deep, laughed free,
>   Starved, feasted, despaired,—been happy.

Browning never appears annoyed by Julia's contradictions and criticisms; both are refreshed by the exchange of ideas—we are refreshed by overhearing it. The score of years between them having been emphasized by Browning, Julia threatens a commentary on his works. But "I think I must wait till you are dead before I venture on that, and as you are so old it will not detain me long. Reading it will probably form your occupation in Purgatory." Yet she, she reminds him, is not so *very* young and he replies, "I will not be older than you like, or you younger than I want. I daresay nothing but good will come out of it all for you and me."

Browning relates (against his critics?) the story of Rabbi Perida, who patiently repeated the same lesson four hundred times—and when it still went uncomprehended by one pupil repeated it four hundred more. Whereupon his class begged heaven for another four hundred years of life for him "and if he was a schoolmaster all the time, I heartily pity him."

"You are always and have been always," says Julia, "perfectly intelligible to one reader . . . I will promise you to make no outcry to Heaven that you should live till the 'Saturday' understands you as well as I do. However it (the 400 years) might be a wholesome contingency to contemplate, for I think you would bear clarifying."

In the letters that follow, Browning pours forth gossip and literary discussion much as he did in the period of his Love Letters. Of the books he has taken with him on his holiday, and of his visit to the Pas de Roland, where a kick of Roland's boot let Charlemagne's army through. Of Tennyson, in whose dedication to his wife Browning rejoices, "loving Mrs. Tennyson singularly." Of how he himself would have written *Enoch Arden* differently—with a little smile at Tennyson's view that the conclusion, "And when they buried him the little port/Had seldom seen a costlier funeral," was "a very pregnant one." Of Helen in music, "the seed of beauty . . . scattered all over the world is infinite." Of Landor's death, "the grand old solitary man, beset by weaknesses just as, in his own words, 'the elephant is devoured by ants in his inaccessible solitudes.' Bless us, if he had let the world tame him and strap a tower on his broad back, what havoc he would have made in the enemy's ranks!" Of the "sacred place" of his wife's memory, where Julia is never "in my way . . . so far as you go, I like walking with you. Nobody else goes many inches over the threshold of it." Of Keats and what he suffered from criticism: "don't believe a man of average sensibility is ever insulted by a blackguard without suffering enough: despise it? yes, but you feel the slap in the face, too: and, in this case, to feel anything unduly was to spill the fast-lessening life."

Above all came, on October 3, the momentous announcement "I have got the whole of that poem, you enquire about, well in my head, shall write the Twelve books of it in six months, and then take breath again."

Much in these letters was called out by comments, questions, criticisms from Julia, whose summer was spent traveling from one house to another of friend or relative, some so narrow that she fears even her very small hoop will stick in the strait gateway—houses where it would be perdition to open a newspaper on a Sunday, others where the time is occupied entirely by prayers and meals. Small wonder that the arrival of a letter made the day bright, that a friendship throwing open so many doors on a larger world became intoxicating and a trifle dangerous.

Yet there was from the first a strange element in her letters suggestive of a neurosis akin to "the death wish." She told Browning at the beginning she felt sure their friendship could not last; he will find worthier friends, but she trusts he will never draw back "from mistaken kindness to me that you had feared to inflict a pain against which I am shielded by the deliberate decision of my mature life."

By Victorian standards she was an old maid, though the man who married Elizabeth could hardly be expected to think so: definitely she wanted him to believe she did not intend to marry.

Browning was aware of a double problem, which he noted quite early, writing in June 1864: "It is for you to determine when it is right that I should see you. I thought myself too plainly a sort of tombstone, to be scribbled over when so many blank walls spread on every side: yet a friend of yours and mine did, out of fun, write a silly name on me some months ago, which was read and repeated by various people."

And again a month later:

You know the difficulties will begin soon enough: my visits will seem importunate, be remarked on, the usual course of things must be looked for. And then, *you,* yourself, now, let me speak plainly— keep in mind, for justice' sake, exactly what my claims are—arising from your own free gift, but understood in their largest sense,— and do not let them presume to obstruct what may, ought to be claims paramount: don't cut, in that royal way, your palm-tree to the heart, that the poor traveller you delight to honour may have a draught of palm wine, "after which," says Xenophon, "the whole tree withers." A better than I, God knows, should have the whole palm tree in its season. There, that's said. Meantime grow and be happy, and let me sit under the branches to my day's end, come what will.

Extraordinary as it would seem today, the poor girl had already suffered from the kind of talk they feared. She answered:

It was so horrible to me to find my attitude towards you looked upon as it was for a time, that this infused something of hesitation towards you—if one who loved and knew me well (neither my father or mother) could hint "a pear left basking over a wall, etc."—the doubt was sometimes in my mind whether this aspect was possible from your point of view, but thank God that is past.

You will repay me, will you not, for that glimpse of Hell you will entirely trust me? . . . What you charge me not to do for you, I have been trying to do for everybody (Xenophon's palm-wine) and my Ten thousand did not want my wine very often.

Ah no, dear friend, do not you be afraid of or for me. I am sheltered in the happiness of a very definite allegiance in my own house, which I would not surrender under a greater pressure than losing the luxury of our intercourse. It would be a loss—but not an intolerable one—oh, I have said all that before. But in truth I do not think I shall be tried. You saw me under the perturbation of that insult, as I must call it though it came from a noble nature, but that was something purely accidental and passing, and will not return.

Hell? Insult? The words seem absurdly strong unless the verses were actually quoted and the title mentioned of the poem "A Light Woman," of which she gives one line only. Surely even in that strange era and stranger class no old friend could have been so savage. But if the friend only recalled that one line, Julia certainly remembered more:

> And she,—she lies in my hand as tame
>   As a pear late basking over a wall;
> Just a touch to try and off it came;
>   Tis mine,—can I let it fall?

With no mind to eat it, that's the worst!
Were it thrown in the road, would the case assist?
'Twas quenching a dozen blue-flies' thirst
When I gave its stalk a twist.

Browning does not in his reply refer to the insult at all but he returns to the palm wine and to the man who one day will want "his whole tree," and requests for himself a "pin-head-sized drop." Both had spoken of their relative age as though protecting them from comment, but the paragraph that follows is a pleasing challenge to any reader clever at crosswords or other puzzles:

And now, the good of saying this is, that I can add with a safe conscience, "what wine you can afford, my own friend, I am quite thirsty enough for, and not a drop shall be spilt, do believe!" And then—do you want some of the uses of my age? Well, I *know*,— shall I say?—the signs and tokens, by this time, and how palm-wine is not proof-spirit, of which I am not without the experience of certain thimble-fulls: oh, the *vivandières* will press *le petit verre* on us old grey *moustaches*, "for love," if we flaunt a *chevron* or two, and have arms presented to us by the sentinels! And now, doing you this homage, let my own turn come, nor let mistake be feared, when I tell the pure truth that you are most dear to me, and will be ever so. I can live in very various spheres of activity, like those insects that people dry up and keep for years in a pill-box—something that had the sea to swim in once: I can't get *that* again, but any globule of your palm-wine will set me free within its circumference.

After this came the long summer correspondence, prolonged through autumn and winter. Julia lingered on at various country houses, then Browning was unwell and did not want to spread his bad cold, then Pen had measles and Mrs. Wedgwood preferred he should stay away, fearing he would infect various young relatives constantly in and out of the house.

During this gap came Christmas and with it a letter to Browning's older and more intimate friend Isa Blagden.

Yes, dearest Isa, it is three Christmasses ago—*fully* now: I sometimes see a light at the end of this dark tunnel of life, which was one
blackness at the beginning. It won't last for ever. In many ways I
can see with my human eyes why this has been right and good for
me—as I never doubted it was for Her—and if we do but re-join any
day,—the break will be better than forgotten, remembered for its
uses.

Browning had often spoken of feeling Elizabeth's presence: in this
letter he distinguishes "the natural working of what is in my mind"
from "vulgar external appearances," and bestows a passing kick on "the
stupid people who have 'communications.'"
    There is of course much about Pen in the letter, but the heart of it
shows him absorbed in the great work he had begun that summer.

I could no more take root in life again, than learn some new dancing
step. On the other hand, I feel such comfort and delight in doing the
best I can with my own object of life,—poetry,—which, I think,
I never *could* have seen the good of before,—that it shows me I have
taken the root I *did* take, *well*. I hope to do much more yet: and that
the flower of it will be put into Her hand somehow.

We know nothing of any visits to Julia for several months, which
does not prove there were none. The letters become shorter and mostly
speak of hopes or postponements of Browning's visits. It is quite certain
that *he* had not the faintest intention of making any break, when, with
extraordinary suddenness, on March 1, 1865, Julia asked him to come
no more:

I have reason to know that my pleasure in your company has had an
interpretation put upon it that I ought not to allow. . . . You have
only accepted a position into which I invited you—remember, I invited you. Your attitude has been response from the beginning. . . .
You are to me the friend of years, I only of months to you. . . . You
know in some degree how dark it was, in what a delirium of sorrow

I turned to you; you know too, I hope, how fully you satisfied that need.

She trusts he will realize, not necessarily that she is correct in her view, but that, holding it, she is right in her decision, "that you are *with* me in it."

Browning accepted:

I left you always to decide . . . I still leave it to you. But I would remark—as common sense must, I think—that to snap our outward intercourse off short and sharp will hardly cure the evil, whatever it be: two persons who suddenly unclasp arms and start off in opposite directions look terribly intimate. But you know all the circumstances. . . .

I kept away when measles were to be apprehended: . . . I minded worthy folks' fears: here is a fear of another juvenile ailment, and I may have to keep away long, longer and longest: what then? The old clothes will end in being burned, and then we will shake hands again. . . . God bless you, my dearest friend.

Was he smiling a little as well as grieving?—for he certainly missed these visits. Would the outcome have been different in the long run had this very Victorian young woman acted by other standards? For the story is perfect in its Victorianism—even to the lost letter confiding in her friend, Julia Stirling, whose answer has survived: "your heart must be torn out by the roots . . . what a real effort you must have made in your appeal to him to conceal the fact that your heart had betrayed you. If he guesses the truth, he certainly most honourably ignores it—and makes the path easy to you which you now have chosen."

3 Three Generations

Browning's affection for his son was "almost painful in its intensity and absorption."

GEORGE SMITH (BROWNING'S PUBLISHER)

THE TIDE of Browning's fate with the public had turned, though continued bad reviews made him slow to realize it. *Dramatis Personae* was his first book to reach a second edition—and within the first year of publication. A new generation was the chief factor. The younger Oxford men were putting forward his name for the Poetry professorship and he would have been willing, he said, for Pen's sake, "Had they wished me to blacken their boots instead of polish their heads." But "the Council," he told Isa, thought it unfair—and he considered them perfectly right. "I should not have liked, had I been one of the members of the University, to be ousted of my chance by an outsider." But he much liked the kind ways and attentions of the undergraduates. Visiting Jowett at Balliol he saw (he believed) the best of them.

"It is impossible," wrote his host, "to speak without enthusiasm of his open, generous nature and his great ability and knowledge. I had no idea that there was a perfectly sensible poet in the world, entirely free from vanity, jealousy, or any other littleness, and thinking no more of himself than if he were an ordinary man. His great energy is very remarkable, and his determination to make the most of the remainder of life." "A perfectly sensible poet?" (Yet Jowett was a friend of Matthew Arnold's!)

To Isa, Browning wrote toward the end of 1866: "Next Michaelmas if God please to help us—Pen goes to Balliol. And what am I to do? . . .

I have my poem to mend and end in the gaps between Greek and Latin."

But early in 1867 Jowett, who had Pen to stay, "said he was up to mark in Latin, hardly in Greek." A delay was decided on and Jowett arranged for the boy to live at Oxford and learn something of undergraduate life while studying for matriculation. Meanwhile Browning himself was given by diploma the degree of M.A. in preparation for a greater honor. In November 1867 he reported of Pen: "the experiment turning out exactly as I hoped: the impulse gained by a glimpse, or rather good gaze into the life of young men with a purpose to study, has done him great good. He writes me often,—enjoys himself much, having his own boat there. Indeed, people are only too kind to him, and the magnates have him to breakfast etc. in an unusual way. Did I—no, I did not tell you of the honour conferred on me . . . I was elected last month as Honorary Fellow of Balliol,—admitted to all the privileges,—*minus* the emoluments of course. This is a very pretty compliment to me,—Pen at the College of which I am Fellow, is it not? I really don't know what makes folk so kind all at once!"

But to Jowett he wrote of " 'emoluments' through which I shall be wealthy all my life long."

Owing to the religious tests Browning had, as we have seen, been excluded in his youth from the two great national universities, Oxford and Cambridge. Observing him "identifying" with Pen one wonders how deeply he had felt this. Now he found himself in possession of a Fellow's rooms at Balliol, honored by the college which seems of all Oxford colleges to awake the strongest loyalties in its sons. It is fascinating to observe the poet at fifty-two beginning to enjoy a second youth. It was not of course Oxford only; but the honorary degree, and still more the Fellowship, set a seal of academic approval on his work which Browning much appreciated, besides throwing him into congenial society. Visits to Oxford, he claimed, helped him to cast off colds and minor ailments—he was never so well anywhere else. He soon gave up the rooms, feeling it was not fair to keep them just for an occasional visit, but he could always be Jowett's guest, especially when Jowett became Master.

Meanwhile, there was the momentous question: When, if at all, would Pen be ready?

A curious fate has overshadowed the story of Browning's relations with his son. Victorian convention forbade the publication of intimate family details, and one has only to compare the published *Letters of Elizabeth Barrett Browning* with the Kenyon typescript, which gives these letters in full, to discover the intensity of Browning's interest in Pen, the degree of love given to the boy concerning whom, *before his birth*, the poet had shown no interest (asserting indeed that he had "no paternal instinct"). Another test of the new insight given by the more human method of printing all letters in their entirety is to contrast Mrs. Orr's *Life and Letters of Robert Browning* with the *Letters of the Brownings to George Barrett*, with *Robert Browning and his American Friends, Learned Lady,* and *Dearest Isa* all published in this century.

For Mrs. Orr's biography, like the two volumes of Elizabeth's letters, belongs to the period of selective editing: omission of indiscreet letters and indiscreet passages. There *are* disadvantages in the modern practice of putting in everything, with at times overabundant notes, but for the biographer trying to understand a man and to draw him with all his lights and shadows it is sheer gain.

To George Barrett and to Isa, Browning is writing on a subject in which their feelings also are engaged. There are in the index to *Dearest Isa* 213 mentions of Pen under seven separate headings. The daily events of his life are chronicled (buys own books, figures in coat and white tie, resembles his mother, writes poetry, etc.), his health gets thirty-three mentions, his height seven, his character nineteen, his studies twenty (drawing, music, Euclid, German, Greek, and Latin), his diversions forty-three (dancing, fencing, idling, reading, riding, rowing—steers Christ Church boat—shooting, skating, swimming). The rest are "Other References"—and one does not wonder at Isa Blagden's anxiety lest Pen loom too large in the new life Browning was building for himself in what he certainly felt, in these first years, to be dreary fog-ridden London.

Intensely what is called a family man, Browning was trying to re-create an atmosphere which without wife and mother is impossible of complete achievement. He had given up the idea of living in Paris near his father and sister as impractical, with a son to educate; but the long summer holidays in Brittany at St. Enogat, Ste. Marie, Pornic, Croisic, included, besides Pen, his father and sister, whom he visited also in Paris. Home meant Pen again—and the daily visits to Arabel Barrett. But as this decade drew on, these bonds would break or loosen.

The loss of his father came first. It would be hard to exaggerate the place he had held: his teaching, his library, his example and support. I doubt indeed if there was any real imbalance in the picture painted by Mrs. Orr, by Griffin and Minchin, in their well-known biography and by others who have shown it as paramount, despite Browning's deep affection for his mother. Intellectually the son had gone far beyond the father, but the memory remained—and the love—as he gathered in gratitude the fruits of his father's planting.

A vivid picture of old Mr. Browning in his eighties is given by Henriette Corkran in *Celebrities and I*.[1] Established in Paris since his breach of promise case,[2] he lived with his daughter Sarianna in a small flat close to the Invalides. Among their chief friends were the Corkran family, with whom they dined about twice a week and went on expeditions to the country. Over seventy when they first knew him, he had lost none of the educational enthusiasm poured out on his son so many years earlier. He taught both children, Alice and Henriette, with rhymes and pictures, asked them questions from the Bible and ancient history, and rewarded them for successful answers.

Mr. Browning would wander off by the hour along the quays, picking up bargains from the fascinating bookstalls. Fond of prints as well as books, he had some remarkable Hogarths, which he would show them as a special treat. Sarianna, as he grew older, took charge of his finances, limiting him to small sums for his absorbing pursuit of bargains. But this was just an added excitement in the game—the only irksome thing was the incursion of real life. Meals, engagements were forgotten as he pored over his treasures.

Henriette remembers a train missed as they waited for him at the station. Another day he did not return to lunch. Sarianna was alarmed: he had been away for hours already, he knew no French (the bargaining must have been done with fingers—or coppers), and he had no sense of direction. The police were furnished with a description and Mr. Corkran had spent many hours in the search when he found the old man in the Jardin des Plantes sitting calmly reading on a bench. He tapped him on the shoulder, he shouted at him—but like someone in a trance Mr. Browning continued to read. At last looking up he called on his friend to rejoice with him, for he had found what for years he had been seeking: "*The Letters of Junius*, a perfect copy, only a few sous." And he hugged the book. Mr. Corkran, busy Paris correspondent of an English newspaper, endeavored to make him aware of the anxiety he had caused.

"So sorry," he said absently, and then with a triumphant smile, "but at last I have found this *Junius*—now it is mine"—again hugging the volume—"splendid print, what a find"—trembling from excitement.

Besides the classics he delighted in "tales about mysterious murders; indeed he had a detective's interest in crime and criminals." The missing of the train was due to his discovery of *The Manning Murders*— with a picture of the kitchen where the body was buried—"only five sous" and nearly as intoxicating as *The Letters of Junius*.

Sarianna, already a middle-aged woman, the Corkrans remember as witty and amusing, with a dramatic sense so strong that her story of a visit to a dressmaker became a first-class comedy. She would stand to tell her tale—and being very small, usually on tiptoe. "No one could interrupt her flow of words." She had one weakness from which her father was wholly free: a snobbery which made her dislike some of his memories. "When I was a clerk in the Bank of England . . ." he would begin—and Sarianna would tread on his toes. Whereupon he would get confused and apologize—"making things far worse" comments Henriette, who would watch, with mischievous amusement, the expression of annoyance on the daughter's face. "She loved to talk about the grandees who visited her illustrious brother and sister-in-law . . . but these were spots on the sun . . . she was a splendid character, a staunch friend . . . not expansive or demonstrative; indeed there may be a lack of *outward sympathy*; she does not caress or purr but . . . thoroughly reliable . . . a truly delightful companion." So she had been to her mother and father, would be to her brother—and finally to her nephew, living with Pen until her death at ninety.

The Brownings were a long-lived family and Henriette speaks of the old man's "grand health" and "vivacity and freshness of mind." He was now (1866) in his eighty-fifth year—and when the end came it came quickly, from "exhaustion caused by excessive loss of blood: there is an internal tumour." So Browning wrote to Pen, having been summoned hastily to Paris, where two doctors in consultation could not determine "of what nature" the tumor was.

"He is in the most complete peace of mind," wrote his son to Pen. "[He] takes it all in his habitual entirely-confiding way [with] no sort of doubt as to his future state, 'having the promise of One who cannot lie.'" He would ask Sarianna to read to him from the Bible, indicating chapter and verse.

There was pain in plenty—for the immense strength of the old man's constitution resisted powerfully: "He was entirely conscious the whole time,—up to the very last, understanding and answering to whatever I said." He asked to see Joseph Milsand (Robert's old friend and his) once more "just to shake hands with him," made Sarianna go to bed —she was worn out after sitting up two nights. Her father said to both his children, "If we do not meet again, I hope we shall meet in Heaven," and in the very agonies of death he told Browning, "I'm only afraid of tiring you." All that night the son watched over him. It was on the next day that he wrote to Pen: "It is over at last, and he is with God. I am most thankful that you were not here to be distressed by the useless sight of pain you could not relieve: I persuaded Sarianna, even, not to witness the last struggle."

Of the passages read to him Mr. Browning had chosen as especially suited for "a person in my circumstances" St. John's Gospel XIV to XVII, the discourse of Christ at the Last Supper. Browning wrote telling Pen the day of the funeral:

I wish you particularly to row as usual,—it is good for your health and right: but if you please, in memory of what is going on here, read by yourself in the morning those last chapters which he had read to him a few hours before his death. . . . It can do you no harm to hear what an extraordinarily learned and able man like Nonno, who might have been a great man had he cared a bit about it, found a comfort to him in, I suppose, the greatest sufferings he ever underwent in his long life.

To Isa Blagden Browning repeated that his father's:

powers natural and acquired would have so easily made him a notable man, had he known what vanity or ambition or the love of money or social influence meant. . . . He was worthy of being Ba's father—out of the whole world, only he, so far as my experience goes. . . . My sister will come and live with me henceforth. You see what she loses,—all her life has been spent in caring for my mother, and, seventeen years after that, my father: you may be sure she does not rave and rend her hair like people who have plenty to atone for in the past,—but she loses very much.

Clumsily enough, as so often in his prose, Browning is uttering here a supreme truth about man's life—about his own life. To give abundantly is to receive richly. His own grief when his mother died had had in it a root of bitterness springing from memories of himself as a selfish, unheeding boy "The wise person of my perfect remembrance and particular dislike." Far greater had been the loss of Elizabeth, far deeper the grief, but there had been in it no least sting of remorse: theirs had been as flawless as finite love can be; he had given his all, he had received more than he gave. And so, by the inexplicable paradox of a deep love, had she.

How strangely Arabel's death two years later mirrored her sister's. Again Browning was more anxious than the doctor's view warranted; it was he who asked for a second opinion. Both doctors agreeing that there was no danger, he left her in the evening: "there was super-abundance of female attendance." But Browning was summoned at six in the morning by Arabel's servants. "I found her in a deplorable state." Yet another consultant was due at three and the first doctor reiterated that there was certainly no immediate danger. "So he went, and, five minutes after, I raised her in my arms where she died presently. . . ."

"George, the useful brother, was away touring it in Ireland," so Browning had again to handle all the sad business and finally to meet George at the station at 4:30 one morning to tell him that his sister was already buried: "He is alarmingly susceptible and may find the blow too much."

Five years earlier Arabel had shown her agitation over a dream in which she saw Elizabeth and asked her "When shall I be with you?" to be answered "Dearest, in five years." Browning had made a note of the date (July 21, 1863), had fancied mistakenly that only three years were passed, and now insisted to Isa that it was "only a coincidence, but noticeable."[3] Arabel died on June 11, 1868.

Coincidence? The result of Arabel's fears? Or that strange thing "psi" or extrasensory perception of which we have still so much to learn? "I am not superstitious," Browning emphasized—yet he had made a note of this old maid's tale.

The loss of Arabel was a heavy one: we find Browning, who would not, after his father died, spend the summer months where they had spent them together, shrinking now from passing the house where Arabel had lived. So it had been with his mother's loss, so supremely with Elizabeth's. He had fancied he could "take the sacrament" of a brief visit to Florence, but in fact he could never face it.

There is a curious note in the letters to Pen about his grandfather's death: the suggestion that he should read the Bible passages, the exhortation to manhood, seem to carry overtones not wholly consistent with Browning's enthusiastic mentions of the boy to his various correspondents, although heard occasionally in the letters to Isa. It could, of course, mean that Pen was now going through the adolescent measles of skepticism or other troubles of mind or body, but I fancy it was at once less definite and more profound. For five years Browning had been congratulating himself and praising Pen, but it looks as though a shiver had just gone through him.

I have described Pen earlier as seen by the many eyes which almost turned him into an exhibition piece. But Elizabeth's unpublished, and therefore unexpurgated, letters to Arabel reveal a problem that this physically sick and terribly overstrung woman was refusing to face.

When Pen was barely three she wrote of fears that he was not long for this world. No apparent childhood's illness but a strange sort of hysteria beset him: "he struck out violently with his arms and legs," and did not appear for some minutes to recognize Wilson (his mother's maid and his nurse) or even his mother. The doctor, hastily summoned, found him in a deep sleep. Next morning he came again, ordered castor oil and belladonna. But neither in this nor in a later experience could he discover anything physically wrong, and Elizabeth was puzzled that a child apparently very ill could recover so suddenly. The doctor said he was overexcitable—and advised them to keep him quiet. Nor was this only a medical opinion. Elizabeth's description of Pen's sayings and doings brought from her sisters the same urging against overstimulation. Wilson entreated her not to talk to him about God. "He does nothing night and day but talk of God ... and I'm sure he ought not to have any ideas put into his head at all. He has far too many ideas as it is."

Then there was the spiritualism. Elizabeth's jocose description must have horrified Arabel. "Dear little Spillet," Pen had begged, "do write something for Penini? Do please Penini and write *Napoleon*." The spirit obliged, Elizabeth declares: "On which the pencil moved and *Napoleon* was written,—'Sant you dear little Spillet.' "

The amount about Pen in these letters is so immense, the ink so pale, the paper so thin that, concentrating for my first volume on husband and wife, I did not attend sufficiently to Pen. Now I read them again.

There seems to have been a strange but perhaps not uncommon mixture of unconscious forcing combined with delayed development. When he was probably about eight Pen had, Elizabeth wrote, been put in Robert's dressing room to sleep, disliked his "exile," and insisted the door be left open. "He really gets too old," she justly observed, "for sleeping in our room." But "he is younger than his age in some respects."

The hysterical fits did not go on for long, but something similar was apt to recur if he was scolded or thwarted. A graphic letter describes one of Elizabeth's rare attempts at discipline. She had doubled Pen's lessons for loitering and dawdling, "upon which he fell into one of his old fits of passion and despair . . . said he would kill himself . . . 'Where's the knife?' . . . said I had a very hard heart and that if I saw him *dead at my feet*, I would only kick him . . . knocked his head against a chair . . . and then fell down exhausted, crying out that his legs were trembling and his heart was beating all over his *stomach* and he was very ill— 'O God make me better!—O Jesus Christ!!' "

Elizabeth did this time insist on the lessons, but later in the day he begged for (and shortly after got!) the gift of a rabbit, urging that he was so lonely without brothers or sisters—"I haven't even a little green fairy like Mr. Patmore's child." Every post, one comes to feel, was for Pen a winning post. "I am not a child like other children *is*," he urged, " 'and when I feel a thing I feel it in *my heart*'—clasping his side with both hands."

Pen was probably high strung, most certainly very intelligent, while his mother describes him as "made of heart." Writing to Wilson, whose baby delighted him as the gift of a younger brother, he signed his letter "Your affectionate and everlasting Penini"—and he did take both her and her husband to live with him in their old age.

But how deep did his affections go? It is hard to tell. The mother's letters overflow with examples of his getting anything he wanted by a sufficient display of feeling. But when she wrote "Oh my child *he* shall be a worker—if prayer and struggle can avail me," when she told of his two and one-half hours' piano practice and of giving him the chance *not* to be an amateur but an artist—in music, painting, or words—did she sometimes tremble? After two days in which he paid attention to his lessons she wrote to Mrs. Eckley: "I have felt less like the tortoise carrying the world on his back."[4]

The abbé who was tutoring him seemed almost as weak as the mother against Pen's blandishments: he did occasionally complain of inattention—but said also that the boy *could* do anything. At his music, taught by his father, he was attentive—indeed apparently enthusiastic. And, although one sees in Browning almost as much as in Elizabeth the idealizing parent of an only child, occasions when he was out of the house, or safely away in his study, appear to have been chosen by Pen for his emotional displays. If the father did realize the position, what ought he to have done?

"Other people's children," an old saying runs, "are easy to rear," and criticisms of Browning's treatment of his son are more commonly offered than practical alternatives.

Both parents approached the idea of school as against home education with an unusual bias. Elizabeth had had absolutely no school experience, Robert only a few unhappy—and, he felt, wasted—years. They could not but realize that they had both imbibed far more culture at home, than most of their school-educated friends. They were giving Pen what Robert had had—teaching in music and languages, swimming and riding. Then too Elizabeth could not live in England: could Browning have sent Pen away from her? And in any case, they could not afford it until the Kenyon legacy was paid.

Pen was only twelve when his mother died and, as we have seen, the advice given by friends was by no means unanimous. At that date it certainly was not universally held that school was a "must" as against a private tutor and specialized masters.

The year of his grandfather's death showed Pen presumably ready for Balliol, but Jowett, as we have seen, had advised a postponement, and arranged for him to stay in Oxford with special coaching until the following year. The boat his father had given him, the many invitations, cannot have promoted his studies. But his failure for the Balliol entrance exam was probably an illustration of his character. For Jowett had complained in the preparatory period that he would often answer the hard questions well and muff some of the simplest: Browning put this down to nerves, Jowett to carelessness. And Jowett did not want anyone for Balliol but men who would bring scholastic or other fame to the College. He had, says Geoffrey Faber (in *Jowett: a Portrait with Background*), "a little difficulty in distinguishing between the interests of Balliol and the interests of the universe." With all his affection for Browning, the decision must have been a relief to him that Pen should try for a less high-pitched standard. But the father felt vindicated when he passed easily (on January 15, 1869) for Christ Church. "Two dozen *postulants,*" he wrote triumphantly to Isa, "and eleven recipients only, as these ritualistic asses would say."

College life began propitiously from Pen's point of view—for he coxed the Christ Church boat, which "bumped" five times that May, and Browning and Sarianna were there: "Pen was never seen by either of us to such advantage." At Lady Ashburton's house, Loch Luichart, in August "Pen has got what he wanted—shooting and deer-stalking: ... shot a splendid stag-'royal'; the head of which will glorify his rooms at Ch. Ch."

These notes of joy were sounded for Isa's benefit, but an undertone of worry distressed her, and Browning wrote in September: "My 'worry' is increased to pretty nearly the last degree, but there is no need to put it down on paper yet,—or perhaps ever—so, only be prepared to 'comfort' me when there is absolute need."

The last happy letter for many years on the all-absorbing subject of his son was in February 1870 when Pen had "once more broken out in violent poetry! . . . a very welcome proof indeed of what may be still in him." But on June 17, 1870, Browning wrote to George Barrett: "Pen has failed again: he did his best in the country, I believe,—but two months of labour were not enough to overcome nine years of idleness." Another chance *might* be allowed—but was it worth it? Pen was costing about £170 a term. "He cannot be made to see that he should follow any other rule than that of living like the richest and idlest young men of his acquaintance. . . . So dear George, *what do you advise?*"

The diplomatic career, the army, each would offer even more temptations. "Or will it all end in my pensioning off the poor fellow to go and rot in the country?" Clearly there had been a row of some magnitude, for Pen had told his father, in the presence of his Uncle "Occy," that "he would not have consented to be at Ch. Ch. at any less expense than he had been incurring, and that he considered getting a first class no brilliant thing at all."

The letter to George miscarried. Writing again two weeks later Browning was more moderate in tone, more sympathetic toward "the poor boy," who "had made a real and important effort for the previous ten weeks,—I believe, *working*—so as to deserve the expression for the first time in his life." His tutor was clearly puzzled, reporting him as "quite able, should he do his best, to pass" and "now exceeding, now falling below the mark." He had, the tutor felt, a mistrust "in his own power of learning." The estimate of his last term's expenses the father now puts at £150 to £160. "Multiply that by 4, add seven months of holidays to be provided for, and you will judge whether I am justified in trying to go on with the experiment. On the other hand, I am quite at my wits' end and hopeless of doing anything to the boy's advantage. He is unfit for anything but idleness and pleasure,—each as harmless, as such indulgences can be."

Browning asks the question what shall be tried now: diplomacy, the army, the law:

> You may imagine what would be his requirements for the next five or six years as an *attaché* at Paris or Vienna in the company of the sons of men of fortune. This exquisite stupidity being unconquerable, applies even in greater measure as a disqualification for the only other career that he would like,—that of a "cavalry officer": I will not hear of a life,—first of all, hateful to his Mother: next, as hateful to me,—finally, involving all the worst temptations to every sort of weakness. It is all miserable to contemplate. The poor boy is simply WEAK—not bad in any way. . . . Had you been still a barrister—to give you an instance of the influence *anybody but myself* can exercise over him—he would have cheerfully worked under your eye, had you allowed it, and *worked well,*—I, at least, would have made the experiment. What do you suggest? I know your kindness, to me, to him, to his mother: help us all if you can.

The first strange thing in these letters, written of course in an intensity of emotion by a very emotional man, is the balancing *between* a further period at Oxford and a future career—for surely one was merely the preparation for the other. Not even Browning could have dreamed of Pen as a don, but had he, or Pen himself, only *now* begun to consider what would follow Oxford? Even stranger is the suddenness of Browning's realization that *he* had failed with Pen when he dreamed he was succeeding. "I am merely the manger at which he feeds," the father cried bitterly, "nothing is more certain than that I could do him no greater good than by dying tonight and leaving him just enough to keep him from starving."

But the remark that Pen had recently been "working—so as to deserve the expression for the first time in his life" was absurd. Browning's letters to Isa and to William Story had been filled with praise of Pen's diligence over a period of years. Moreover it had been a terribly crowded timetable: Italian, German, music, "Drawing, Dancing and other matters as much as he can properly bear," besides the Greek, Latin, and mathematics required for the university.

Once at Oxford, Pen, set free from his father and his private tutor, had been spending his time with great success on more congenial activities. He was a good oarsman, a first-rate shot, and an exceptionally good billiard player. Browning, not himself given to these pursuits, did not realize how much time must be spent in acquiring skill at them; he had perhaps never heard the aphorism "To do well at billiards is a sign of a misspent youth."

The other reason of his past blindness is, I think, expressed when Browning says that Pen is "singularly engaging to his friends with whom he is as popular as possible, and quite docile and amenable to reason with a comparative stranger." So no doubt his tutor had found him—and been puzzled at his failure. But so too had Browning felt— the half-hearted rebellion was as much a mood in Pen as the anger was in Browning. No less than his friends was Browning charmed by his son. But the verdict appeared, alas, a true one: "There is something infinitely pitiable in this butterfly-nature with no fault in it but what practically is the worst of all faults,—weakness: a restive horse may be broken of his vice and made win a race against his will,—but how can you make a butterfly cross the room [for] his life?"[5]

At the University of Texas I found autograph letters to Gillespie, Pen's erstwhile tutor, showing an immense appreciation of what he had done; immediately after the Christ Church failure Browning wrote: "so end the hopes in which you sympathized entirely: we must try and entertain new ones with reference to new aims. Ever most affectionately yours." And to Gillespie's son he wrote fifteen years later: "I shall always hold in affectionate reverence the memory of that admirable man your father." Here as elsewhere he speaks for Pen, who certainly did not abound as did his father in correspondence.

But the first year after Pen's Oxford failure must have been an uneasy one. At Christmas 1870 the father was writing to Lord Houghton (the Monckton Milnes of London Breakfast Parties)[6] refusing an invitation to stay for Christmas—"but shall I be bold and add something": Pen too had been invited and "If it would suit you to receive him by himself, few circumstances would delight me more. I begin to mistrust my own notions about him; the matter is too interesting to me and I stand too close." And in a later letter: "Pen will enjoy Christmas nowhere better than with you. . . . Don't trouble yourself about any thought of a youth quite able and willing to amuse himself—make him play to the young ladies, if they like music, for one thing." Making a refusal easy he added that Pen was away at the moment with a tutor and he did not even know his plans. But the visit took place and Browning wrote again, dating the letter Old Year's Day. "I expected you and your family would be kind to Robert, but you have been miraculously kind he says. . . . He is a grateful and loyal boy and sure to remember you all gratefully through life."

Lord Houghton loved to fill his vast, cold Yorkshire house with an incredible variety of guests. Pen might have met there youthful aristocrats, playmates of the Milnes children Amicia, Florence and Robert; he might have met Swinburne or Richard Burton the traveler; he might have met just country neighbors. Often a mixed party of twelve to sixteen sat down to dinner while each morning at small round tables in the breakfast room the host would "wander from group to group with a book in his hand, talking and joking away as briskly as at his breakfast parties in London."

We can imagine too the more youthful groups around the piano of an evening, or engaged at the billiard table—Pen's performances at both being much above the average. We can imagine him too in Lord Houghton's astonishing library, where he might meet an even more mixed company than the living guests. Theology, English poetry, the French Revolution, magic and witchcraft, crime and its punishment were all represented—including a whole series of books on school punishments. Pen had not been subject to these, nor probably had he read the strange book companioning his father's childhood: Wanley's *Wonders of the Little World,* in which punishments are so gruesomely described. One does not know how great his intellectual curiosity was, but if he did explore the library he must have viewed with interest the "piece of Voltaire's dressing-gown folded into a fine edition of *La Pucelle* . . . Richard Burton's passport to Mecca and the Visitors' book from Burns' cottage at Alloway."

We do not know either whether the section of this library called by James Pope-Hennessy "all too celebrated" was available to the casual browser. "He is *the* Sadique collector of European fame," wrote Swinburne delightedly, and Pope-Hennessy comments: "His collection of erotic books, engravings, etc. is unrivalled on earth—unequalled I should imagine in heaven. Nothing low, nothing that is not good and genuine in the way of art and literature is admitted. There is every edition of every work of our dear and honoured Marquis."

It is much more probable that the visit meant for Pen a delightful social occasion than a chance for literary discovery, of however strange a nature. The picture of Fryston with its charming hostess and gay children as "a sinister Yorkshire mansion filled with Sadic literature and presided over by a 'feline' and malicious host" is, as Pope-Hennessy notes, utterly absurd. Later on the Frenchman who had painted it himself changed his view, but alas "his first interpretation of Milnes' character has persisted with all the desperate vitality of ill repute. . . . To prudish and illiberal persons his name has become a bogey, to the prurient a decoy."

The introduction of the young Swinburne to Richard Burton was, whether accidentally or intentionally, fraught with danger, but Pen was not suitable material for dangerous experiments. He was just an attractive ex-undergraduate a little older than Amicia, and the only question was whether he was a social asset to the younger members of the party. One would gather from Browning's letter and what we know of Pen that the answer was yes: he never had any problem about houses to stay in, though we do not actually know whether he was invited again to Fryston.

Even when troubled about himself and his human bondage Browning seems not to have realized how much of his troubles with Pen were due to the world that he himself had chosen.

The sons of this "crowd," as he called them in a letter to Isa, were Pen's companions at Christ Church, it was their daughters who clustered around him as he played the piano, who danced with him at Oxford and in London, admired his prowess at billiards and shooting. The poet had enough strength of character and enough experience to keep some life apart, but his son had not. The great experiment of making Pen an all-round personality—musical, artistic, sufficiently learned, had indeed failed—and failed largely through the overdevelopment of his social side. He was becoming the sort of young hanger-on at country houses, the good shot, the convenient extra to be bidden at the last moment, the pleasant, popular, amiable and useless individual whom one met everywhere, whom everybody liked but nobody took very seriously.

4 The Ring and the Book

His poetic creations crowded out the real world.

EDMUND GOSSE

BROWNING later, says William Rossetti, told him that at the Pas de Roland he had in 1864 "laid out the full plan of his twelve cantos (or books), accurately carried out in the execution." It was already four years since he had begun to think of it as he read the record

> . . . in a Latin cramp enough
> When the law had her eloquence to launch,
> But interfilleted with Italian streaks
> When testimony stooped to mother-tongue.

Since then he had offered the subject to two friends—but in September 1862 he had asked Isa Blagden to get him a second MS "which I am anxious to collate with my own collection of papers on the subject." And a month later: "I am going to make a regular poem of it . . . a strong thing, if I can manage it."

The summer near the Pas de Roland, in glorious scenery that took him back to Tuscany, he wrote to Isa once more of "my new poem that is about to be; and of which the whole is pretty well in my head,—the Roman murder story."

Carlyle commented: "all made out of an Old Bailey story that might have been told in ten lines and only wants forgetting." But Carlyle too had written a detective story, *The Diamond Necklace,* and Browning might have made with far greater validity Carlyle's claim:

One many-glancing asbestos-thread in the Web of Universal-History, spirit-woven, it rustled there, as with the howl of mighty winds, through that "wind-roaring Loom of Time." . . . O Brother! is *that* what thou callest prosaic; of small interest? Of small interest and for *thee?* Awake, poor troubled sleeper: shake off thy torpid nightmare-dream; look, see, behold it, the Flame-image; splendours high as Heaven, terrors deep as Hell: this is God's Creation; this is Man's life!— . . . Such being the intrinsic quality of this Time, and of all Time whatsoever, might not the Poet who chanced to walk through it find object enough to paint? What object soever he fixed on, were it the meanest of the mean, let him but paint it in its actual truth . . . an indestructible portion of the miraculous all,— his picture of it were a Poem.

The Florentine lawyer who had put the old yellow book together described it as *A Setting-forth of the entire Criminal Cause against GUIDO FRANCESCHINI, Nobleman of Arezzo, and his Bravoes, who were put to death in Rome, February 22, 1698. The first by beheading, the other four by the gallows. ROMAN MURDER-CASE. In which it is disputed whether and when a Husband may kill his Adulterous Wife without incurring the ordinary penalty.*

Today anyone can read this, and the "secondary source," and a third document discovered later, which Browning probably had not seen, all translated and edited by Charles W. Hodell, in Everyman's Library. One is struck by the closeness with which Browning follows large sections of the record, in the lawyers' speeches especially, with their Latin tags and their stilted arguments. Yet even in them he has created characters who stand out: the fond and greedy father in the one, the cold, ambitious careerist in the other. "Half-Rome" and "The Other Half-Rome" are drawn from the pamphlets issued to attract public opinion.

Many volumes have been written for and against Browning the "historian" in his treatment of his material—largely provoked (as long ago with *Paracelsus*) by his own determination to believe he had subordinated the genius of his creation to a faithful following of the facts.

But the main facts of this story were not in dispute so much as what they signified.

An old couple named Comparini, with a certain amount of property, had for heiress an only daughter, Pompilia. Count Guido Franceschini, far above them in rank, having failed to get in Rome any lucrative position, was trying to repair his shrunken fortunes by a wife's property. Violante Comparini arranged his marriage with Pompilia, then only thirteen, concealing the fact from her husband, but both parents accompanied the child to the Franceschini estate at Arezzo. There they found an old and tyrannical mother, a clerical younger brother, a cold and miserable house, insufficient food and watered wine. Guido had deceived the Comparini parents—and it later transpired that Violante Comparini had deceived him. Pompilia was not her child: unknown to her husband she had bought the baby from a woman in the slums of Rome.

Very soon the Comparinis could stand Arezzo no longer; back they went to Rome, leaving the poor child-wife at the mercy of a cruel husband and his lascivious younger brother. Pompilia appealed vainly and repeatedly both to the Governor and the Archbishop against her husband's cruelty, only to be sent back to him with good advice. In despair she entreated Giuseppe Caponsacchi, a young canon, to take her back to her parents in Rome since she was utterly friendless in Arezzo. They were caught by Guido on the journey, were brought to trial and sent, the one into temporary exile, the other to a convent whence she was later transferred for the birth of her child to the Comparini home. Once they had her back, the mother confessed the truth about her parentage, thus driving Guido to the last extreme of blind rage. Using the name of Caponsacchi to win an entry, he brutally murdered the Comparinis and wounded Pompilia fatally, was caught in his flight, tried, and condemned to death. Having received minor orders he claimed the privileges of a cleric, but the Pope refused to change the verdict and he and his four accomplices were all executed.

It was open to Browning, as to all Rome, to choose whose testimony he would believe where they conflicted and to make his own reading of the various characters. This was what he claimed in his simile of the

Ring: the pure gold of fact came to him in the Book, but it needed the alloy of fancy, the shaping under the hammer. Pure gold alone cannot become guinea, coronet, or Ring.[1]

But Browning had done more than he admitted. Pompilia is in the Book a slightly ambiguous character: innocent certainly, and so declared in the final judgment that followed her death, but improbably the saintly and deeply wise child-woman of the poem. Caponsacchi, something of a "play-boy," may have been transformed by her influence and his own defiance of evil into a heroic character—we simply cannot tell. Does it matter with Browning any more than with Shakespeare? The oddity is Browning's insistence on his own factual truth, which provoked various replies—a distinguished lawyer defending (after the mode of all specialists) the men of his own craft, a priest attempting to prove the lack of value in the confessor's testimony to Pompilia's spotlessness, etc.

This speech from myriad lips, spelling out man's weakness and God's strength, is perhaps the peak utterance of Browning's philosophy, and he, so often blamed for his excessive optimism, gives to evil in this poem more voices and louder than he gives to good. As the poem neared completion he resumed his correspondence with Julia Wedgwood and found himself on the defensive on this very score. The four-year gap had done her no good: her tone had become more distinctly that of the old maid, not to say the prude. She complains of hearing Browning's own voice with lamentable clarity even in his evil characters —and he confesses to a weakness he recognizes in himself: "I believe I do unduly like the study of morbid cases of the soul." But "I think this *is* the world as it is, and will be—*here* at least," and "in no energetic deed would you attain to a greater general amount of good than you get here."

The words "in no energetic deed" are highly characteristic—for Browning's attack was commonly against the unlit lamp, the ungirded loins, the refusal to act. He liked vehemence, tended himself to act too quickly, to react too vehemently. And probably to see life too much in black and white. He tried to get inside each character for whom he spoke, but at the end the white soul does look whiter, the black blacker than common eyesight sees or common daylight shows the common run of men.

He asks Julia whether the difference in her conception of the world and his would not simply be in the *proportion* of good assigned to each character. The worst she can conceive will fall short of the evil of Guido; will the best achieve the height of Pompilia, Caponsacchi, the Pope?—"your good will want as much of the goodness of these, one with another, as your bad wants of the wickedness of Guido." The good in his picture "comes through—is evolved by—that prodigy of bad": and he will not admit it could come out otherwise. The story was a true one; on her objection that Guido, a cultured nobleman, would not have committed so brutal a crime, he commented that "reaction from the enforced habit of self-denial which is the condition of men's receiving culture" might produce the effect of greater violence. Napoleon "on the large scale" had acted "quite as falsely, as selfishly, as cruelly."

Convinced that throughout the poem he had uttered his own "un-intermitted protest . . . against all the evil and in favor of all the good" he asked: "Where does my *sympathy* seem diverse from yours so long as we watch the same drama? I quite allow you to refuse to watch."

We can, says Browning, indeed some of us should, look at the worst in man without losing faith in good and in God's power still to love and save. The Pope does not despair even of Guido, hence the decision to condemn him:

> So may the truth be flashed out by one blow,
> And Guido see, one instant, and be saved.
> Else I avert my face, nor follow him
> Into that sad obscure sequestered state
> Where God unmakes but to remake the soul
> He else made first in vain; which must not be.

Browning's first letter of this second series: May 17, 1867, was written in reply to a dinner invitation from Julia's mother. He began with the reminder that Julia had spoken three years ago of his offer to show her his poem "before it should be published." He promised the proofs, but would not dine. "I can't resolve to make any banal excuse, nor yet seem fussy and foolish. The truth is best said." A little pompously he explains that the sudden breaking-off of their friendship three years ago might again, he felt, recur as painfully, as inexplicably.

Sending the proofs on November 5, 1868, he asks, "What are the conventionalities and decencies? My sister keeps house here, and people come to see her sometimes,—women people! Is the notion that I might see *you*, so—a birth of this memorable Gunpowder-treason-and-plot-day—fraught with fire and brimstone?" Apparently it was.

Letter after letter follows, concerned with discussion of the poem. These were probably the only proofs sent to a friend before publication. Browning, when he promised them on October 30, had been "awaiting the revises which are to go to America today." He had asked for the frankest criticism—but he may have expected an appreciation beyond Julia's powers. In one letter she describes him as "the most impatient of men," and this is true enough to make his patience with her a little surprising.

"It has been a particularly weary business [he tells her] to write this whole long work by my dear self—I who always used to be helped by an amanuensis . . . all this scribbling, and how much more that you will never see." And now the owner of the first eyes to see, the first mind brought to bear on, the work believed by him the greatest he had done or would ever do, commented, "Yes it is a lovely snowdrop growing out of that dunghill, but I can't forgive you for planting it there."

Browning had scarcely "planted" Pompilia in the dunghill: he had found her growing there. It is arguable that he had too ardently and lengthily analyzed the elements that made it so ill-smelling, but if he lacked proportion Julia lacked it more. Again and again, with varying metaphors, she repeats a criticism which might reasonably have been uttered once.

> You have a photographic impartiality of attention that I cannot understand—you lead us through your picture gallery and your stable yard at exactly the same pace . . . I cannot bear to see your thoughts on loan to deck out a sleek pedantic buffoon. When I bring

out this edition of your works with which I used to threaten you,
I shall only keep enough of Guido and the Lawyers to make an
ebony frame for that pearly image of Pompilia. . . . I cannot endure
to hear your voice in those Advocates' pleadings . . . a wonderful
variety of mud; the defence is even more hateful than the attack.
The impure medium is wonderfully brought out in the contrast between that sullied image seen through it and the picture in all its
native purity. I can not venture to tell you all that Pompilia seems
to me. I felt as if it were only half yours, but indeed I do not divide
the other influence from your own.

Yet even Pompilia she criticized in some degree, as being too un-
educated for the thoughts put in her mind, the words on her tongue.
Browning answered:

It is a shame, that when there is anything you contrive to like in
it, you cry out, "It's not yours, you know—only half yours," and so
on: then comes an ugliness, and "Ah, there you are at home,—there,
I see you at work!" . . . if the good is not mine . . . why may not the
uglinesses be copied too, and so not mine neither? I don't admit
even your objections to my artistry—the undramatic bits of myself
that you see peep thro' the disguised people. In that sense, Shakespeare is always undramatic, for he makes his foolish people all
clever. I don't think I do more than better their thoughts and instruction. . . . Besides it is Italian ignorance, quite compatible with
extraordinary insight and power of expression too.

A primary instance of this among many in his own memory had
been the words of their maid Annunziata after Elizabeth's death—
"She had a certain nobility of mind which, finding in itself nothing
of the base and evil, could not credit their existence in others." The
Italian words he quotes *"una certa nobilità"* sound even more convincing; and there is no difficulty in believing Browning when he asserts
"I hate the lawyers" and describes his own satisfaction in emphasizing
"their buffoonery." But the main question remained—had he made

E

Guido too prominent, *could* Pompilia, Caponsacchi, the Pope be clearly seen, better seen, against a background less dark; was much of the rest too trivial? Above all had Browning too great an "intensity" in his interest in evil, had he lost something essential to himself with the death of his wife—who had, he told Julia, shared her dislike of the subject, not even caring to read the documents.

The best answer to this question is a rereading of the whole poem. Henry James saw *The Ring and the Book* as both great poetry and the material for a splendid novel, in which Caponsacchi at the end stands alone with the Pope: "*There* is a scene if we will: and in the mere mutual confrontation, brief, silent searching, recognizing, consecrating, almost as august on one part as on the other." But in his conception James *almost* falls into the error we have all at one time shared: a playing-down of the minor characters and of the background. We should look again at the comic, tragically prosaic figures of the two lawyers, at the minor clerics; note, sketched in a few lines, the Archbishop, the two evil brothers and the wordly-wise judges; the cynicism in the real or pseudo sympathy of the Roman spectators: the hovering shadows of Molinos and Euripides. Get the "feel" of Rome and Arezzo, the two cities in which the drama is played; sense the immense excitement of the flight and pursuit. In all this, and even in such shadows as the maid who carries the forged letter and the young farm laborers to whom murder seems as commonplace as ploughing—we begin to see why Browning has been compared to Balzac and Dickens as well as to Chaucer and Shakespeare.

Two interesting questions have been asked to which my reply can only be conjectural. Why did Browning offer this plot that so greatly excited him to other writers? Would Elizabeth's distaste for the story have kept him from writing about it had she lived?

The state of her health is a partial answer to both: from the time he found the Book to Elizabeth's death Browning was under great strain: her sister Henrietta's death, Elizabeth's increasingly bad health, her overexcitement about United Italy, *and* about spiritualism; the dependence on morphine, the discovery of dishonesty in her close friend and spiritualist associate, Sophie Eckley—all this must have made concentration difficult for him. And the more he read and reread, the more the hugeness of his conception must overwhelmingly have shown itself. He probably alternated between desire to write it and desire to be rid of it.

As to Elizabeth, my own feeling is that, had her health, and consequently her nervous condition, got back to the point it had reached a few years earlier, her view of the prospective poem would also have changed. She might have wanted a rather different proportion, but she had too much imagination and too good a mind not to have read with interest and seen the possibilities offered by the story.

On the other hand, Elizabeth was so much more subtle than Browning that she may have concealed another reason for discouraging him about *The Old Yellow Book*. With English public opinion in the state it then was he might well have been banging his head against a closed door. His lyrics, which she so loved, *were* probably the best hope at that time of winning over a hostile press and an apathetic public. Had I been she, I would indeed have trembled after the reception of *Men and Women* at the thought of five or six years' work put into this giant effort.

The years in England, *Dramatis Personae*, the turn of a tide that had for so long swept his earlier work into oblivion—all this was literally necessary to pave the way for *The Ring and the Book*.

Browning never used rhetoric of the Carlyle type, but he spoke of "a number of differing points of view, or glimpses in a mirror"; no judgment is passed: the speakers judge themselves. To quote Robert Langbaum in *The Poetry of Experience*: "The moral judgments are definite and extreme, but they depend upon our total apprehension of the characters themselves. What we arrive at in the end is not *the* truth, but truth as the worthiest characters of the poem see it."

On the flyleaf of *The Old Yellow Book* Browning had written: "But for me the Muse in her strength prepares her mightiest arrow," and the poem has been widely accepted as the culmination of his work and the fullest expression (through the Pope especially) of his philosophy of life. Central to this philosophy was love, and only in some of the poems of old age did he appear to weaken in the conception of *Paracelsus* that love and intellect must go hand in hand, growing in brightness and in power against the world's dark forces.

Browning was the poet of married love. In *The Ring and the Book* his general philosophy is expressed through the Pope, but in Pompilia and Caponsacchi he gives us his deepest insight into love since "By The Fireside." And his life now was strangely, sadly, other than he had dreamed it in that exquisite lyric. Chesterton was the first to note that Browning's own experience of the rescue of Elizabeth finds an echo in *The Ring and the Book.* The accepted anguish of his loss is there too—and a firm belief in the richer life, the more total happiness with which infinity will fill the finite, eternity transcend all that time could give.

The opening lines to his dead wife are so hackneyed one hardly dares to quote them, but it is worth noting that while he addresses his "Lyric Love" as "all a wonder and a wild desire," he makes the Pope call Pompilia "one wide glory of desire."

For Caponsacchi marriage would be out of the question. Pompilia says:

> He is a priest;
> He cannot marry therefore, which is right:
> I think he would not marry if he could.
> Marriage on earth seems such a counterfeit.

She has known the bitter experience of a loveless marriage.

> With gold so much,—birth, power, repute so much,
> Or beauty, youth so much, in lack of these!

Sold to Guido as a mere child, she knew nothing of what marriage meant until, two years later, her husband's brother tried to seize her, and then her husband demanded his "rights." She fled to the Archbishop, who told her she must obey Guido, but now Pompilia, dying, has worked out for herself the true meaning of her own powerful instinct:

> I felt there was just one thing Guido claimed
> I had no right to give nor he to take; . . .
> No! There my husband never used deceit.
> He never did by speech nor act imply
> "Because of our souls' yearning that we meet

And mix in soul through flesh, . . ."
He only stipulated for the wealth;
Honest so far. But when he spoke as plain—
Dreadfully honest also—"Since our souls
Stand each from each, a whole world's width between,
Give me the fleshly vesture I can reach
And rend and leave just fit for hell to burn!"—
Why, in God's name, for Guido's soul's own sake
Imperilled by polluting mine,—I say,
I did resist; would I had overcome!

Browning had experienced a love of the body which expressed love
of the soul, but now he was suffering from an often unbearable loneliness. For Caponsacchi there had been nothing of the human experience:

I never touched her with my finger-tip
Except to carry her to the couch, that eve,
Against my heart, beneath my head, bowed low,
As we priests carry the paten . . .

But Browning, looking at his own love and his loss, translates
through Pompilia Christ's words about the souls in heaven not marrying
or given in marriage into a conception that they

Know themselves into one, are found at length
Married . . .
When the true time is: here we have to wait . . .
So, let him wait God's instant men call years.

The love letters of old are echoed as Pompilia feels that in Caponsacchi "God stooping shows sufficient of His light/For us in the dark
to rise by."
But Caponsacchi is awed by the greatness of this child's soul,
shadowed too by the loneliness which as man he must endure until
death.

I do but play with an imagined life
Of who, unfettered by a vow, unblessed
By the higher call,—since you will have it so,—
Leads it companioned by the woman there.
To live, and see her learn, and learn by her,
Out of the low obscure and petty world—
Or only see one purpose and one will
Evolve themselves i' the world, change wrong to right:
To have to do with nothing but the true,
The good, the eternal—and these, not alone
In the main current of the general life,
But small experiences of every day,
Concerns of the particular hearth and home:
To learn not only by a comet's rush
But a rose's birth,—not by the grandeur, God—
But the comfort, Christ. All this, how far away!
Mere delectation, meet for a minute's dream!—
Just as a drudging student trims his lamp,
Opens his Plutarch, puts him in the place
Of Roman, Grecian; draws the patched gown close,
Dreams, "Thus should I fight, save or rule the world!"—
Then smilingly, contentedly, awakes
To the old solitary nothingness,
So I, from such communion, pass content ...

O great, just, good God! Miserable me!

Idealized as all this seems, it does I think express Browning at his best—and at this best he had lived, during the years caring for and loving his wife, during the time since her death: a high pitch of poetic thought, tender consideration for Arabel and for his father, intense preoccupation with his son.

The Ring and the Book marks the end of an important period. Like *Christmas-Eve and Easter-Day*, three of its books—"Caponsacchi," "Pompilia," and "The Pope"—shine with the white light of his supreme moments.

The Pope, as fully as Pompilia or Caponsacchi, sees the flight as inevitable, courageous, innocent "even to its most ambiguous circum-

stance." It is a victory where defeat might well have been, a victory
the world will never recognize:

> Pompilia wife, and Caponsacchi priest,
> Are brought together as nor priest nor wife
> Should stand, and there is passion in the place,
> Power in the air for evil as for good,
> Promptings from heaven and hell, as if the stars
> Fought in their courses for a fate to be.
> Thus stand the wife and priest, a spectacle,
> I doubt not, to unseen assemblage there.
> No lamp will mark that window for a shrine,
> No tablet signalize the terrace, teach
> New generations which succeed the old
> The pavement of the street is holy ground;
> No bard describe in verse how Christ prevailed
> And Satan fell like lightning!

With the character of the Pope history had helped Browning, for
Innocent XII—Antonio Pignatelli—was a remarkable man. He had
been Legate and Nuncio in many countries, Inquisitor, Secretary of
the Congregation of Bishops and Regulars, Maestro di Camera, and
Archbishop of Naples—for a period that became known as the Golden
Age of the diocese. After one of the longest conclaves in history
(February to July 1691) he was made Pope at the age of seventy-six,
and at once began to act on the wide experience that was his, as though
still in his prime. At a time when rulers were surrounded by court and
ceremony, he made himself accessible to all. The poorest could visit
him freely and he appointed the Advocate of the Poor only to advise
him on legal questions.

He started vast building projects to give employment, began the
draining of the Pontine Marshes, had silted-up ports cleared, and tried
to regulate the waters of the Romagna. He established a center for a
large orphanage, a home for indigent women, and other works of
charity. He cut to the bone his household expenses—and he forbade
the sale of offices, insisting that they be filled by merit alone.

It was said of him that he had "stripped money of its power." Yet money was needed for all his schemes and he saved much that other Popes had spent by a total refusal to support his own family—a matter that became the subject of a new law. Henceforth a Pope's relatives were, if poor, to be treated exactly the same as other poor. If a nephew proved worthy of the Cardinalate he was to receive only a strictly limited income, while many other offices that had been the perquisites of relatives were simply abolished. Innocent set his seal to his own law when the merits of another Pignatelli were urged on him as a claim for the Cardinalate: "All quite true," he said in refusing, "but he is my nephew."

He worked for peace in both world and Church, trying to mediate between France and Spain, refusing to condemn the Jesuits for their novel methods of Apostolate in China, bringing about reunion with some of the Orthodox of Rumania. He created cardinals from almost every nation, started reforms among the clergy, and tried to extend them to the religious orders. He was ready always to have the case laid before him of men who were getting into trouble for their ideas— and he seems to have seen how seldom any thought structure is wholly false, to want to avoid those blanket condemnations of which history is full and on which time brings its sure revenge.

For nine years this old man worked on in a period of natural catas-trophe—floods, earthquakes, typhoid—through disabilities that ranged from a broken leg to a lingering illness. He rallied again and again: there must have been enormous strength as well as the will that drove him. Determined that the Holy Year of 1700 be celebrated properly he opened with a Consistory, visited (against doctors' objections) the four chief churches of Rome, and repeatedly blessed the crowds from the balcony of the Quirinal. But by August he knew that he was dying and made a general confession. His last recorded words were "*Ingredimur viam universae carnis* [We enter upon the way of all flesh]."

To me "The Pope" is the greatest of all the books that make up this immense poem. No major work on *The Ring and the Book* has appeared since Vatican II revealed the figure of John XXIII, and the many ways have gone unnoticed in which both historically and in Browning's portrait we are reminded of his predecessor. If the poet is prophetic as a forth-teller in the matter of human love, there is in this book more than a touch of the prophet who *fore*tells. Innocent, a Pope in his eighties, addresses:

> "My ancient self, who wast no Pope so long
> But studiedst God and man, the many years
> I' the school, i' the cloister, in the diocese
> Domestic, legate-rule in foreign lands,—
> Thou other force in those old busy days
> Than this grey ultimate decrepitude,—
> Yet sensible of fires that more and more
> Visit a soul, in passage to the sky."

Browning, so often apparently at enmity with the Church, stands in this poem far more as those Catholic churchmen stand today who unite a total faith with a complete openness of criticism, and to whom the word Christian means more than Catholic. He does not understand Infallibility as Vatican I was soon to define it: it was hardly possible that he should. But in his attack on torture, kept so late in Roman law courts, it is Religion itself and no particular sect he sees, sitting on the old book in which she now claims to have written its condemnation yet in reality only abandoning the practice on the insistence of humanity. He is in no way attacking the Church in this poem but, through the mouth of its ruler on earth, lamenting the failure to fulfill its ideals.

What has gone wrong, when not only the Governor but the Archbishop, not only the Archbishop but the monk, fail to save Pompilia and leave the task of her rescue to one: "In mask and motley, pledged to dance not fight." "Well done!" cries the Pope.

> Be glad thou hast let light into the world
> Through that irregular breach o' the boundary.

But why did it have to be thus? Churchmen as a whole had somehow become

> Unprofitable through the very pains
> We gave to train them well and start them fair,—
> Are found too stiff, with standing ranked and ranged,
> For onset in good earnest, too obtuse
> Of ear, through iteration of command,
> For catching quick the sense of the real cry.

A magnificent passage, too long to quote in full, states again the Christian truth central in Browning's thought:

> O Thou,—as represented here to me
> In such conception as my soul allows,—
> Under Thy measureless, my atom width!—

and yet the choice of *this* earth was made by the Infinite God

> For stage and scene of Thy transcendent act
> Beside which even the creation fades
> Into a puny exercise of power.

Yes Christ had brought salvation, but the Pope cries out

> Well, is the thing we see salvation?
>
>   I
> Put no such dreadful question to myself,
> Within whose circle of experience burns
> The central truth, Power, Wisdom, Goodness,—God:
> I must outlive a thing ere know it dead.

The "deaths of the faith" appear so obvious to the world around, are so unnoted by those within; but there are the resurrections too—Christ, who rose from the tomb in the body He had taken in Mary's womb, rises again in His mystical body. The Pope in Browning sees not death but a *deliquium*, as Newman would later call it: Pliny speaks of the "deliquium solis," called in the dictionary "a fading out." This Innocent saw—and so surely did Pope John. And Browning-Innocent,[2] muses on the great days of faith:

For how could saints and martyrs fail see truth
Streak the night's blackness? Who is faithful now?
Who untwists heaven's white from the yellow flare
O' the world's gross torch, without night's foil that helped
Produce the Christian act so possible
When in the way stood Nero's cross and stake,—
So hard now when the world smiles "Right and wise!
Faith points the politic, the thrifty way."

As Saint Paul had by tradition answered Seneca, Innocent will try to answer the claims of Euripides in an imagined dialogue:

"Pope, dost thou dare pretend to punish me,
For not descrying sunshine at midnight,
Me who crept all-fours, found my way so far—
While thou rewardest teachers of the truth,
Who miss the plain way in the blaze of noon,—
Though just a word from that strong style of mine,
Grasped honestly in hand as guiding-staff,
Had pricked them a sure path across the bog."

It is the cry so often heard to which no Christian should be deaf. The ghastly moral failure of so many believers is highlighted in this story of which Browning ceases not to recall the factual truth. We see the totally wicked Guido ("Not one permissible impulse moves the man"), his four hired assassins, mere farm boys, the weak or cowardly or covetous, parents, nuns, monk, Archbishop—all these relieved only by one brave pure man and one pure brave woman, almost child.

We have seen the failure of Christians through the eyes of those who have not failed in Pompilia, Caponsacchi, the Pope; it is yet more witheringly portrayed as seen by one who has been for years observing and imitating the hypocrisy of churchmen, despising the creed they profess, the values they claim to live by. Guido's scorn for religion is total, his use of it as a means to worldly success, his conviction that even murder will be excused in him as nobleman and churchman, indeed his conviction that it *is* excusable in the cause of an honor smirched by the adultery (even by the imagined adultery) of his wife. Guido is bewildered, he cannot to the last moment really believe that the worldly Church in which he has been living will in the Pope's person betray him, its true fruit.

It is overwhelming to read at this point his second monologue—surely nothing in any literature is as unique as this equal intensity in the presentation of extremes: what Browning had called his "Devil's gospel" following his grand conception of the Gospel of Christ.

Guido speaks:

> Is it not terrible I entreat you, Sirs?—
> With manifold and plenitudinous life, . . .
> Terrible so to be alive yet die? . . .
> Out trundles body, down flops head on floor,
> And where's your soul gone? . . .
>   "I lose my head"
> How euphemistic! Lose what? Lose your ring,
> Your snuffbox, tablets, kerchief!—but, your head? . . .
> "And not much pain i' the process" quoth a sage:
> Who told him? . . .
> Dying in cold blood is the desperate thing; . . .
> I am one huge and sheer mistake,—whose fault?
> Not mine at least, who did not make myself
> Someone declares my wife excused me so! . . .
> There she is, there she stands alive and pale,
> The thirteen-years'-old child with milk for blood, . . .
> Again, how is she at me with those eyes!
> Away with the empty stare! Be holy, still,
> And stupid ever! . . .
> There's God, go tell Him, testify your worst!
> Not she! There was no touch in her of hate:
> And it would prove her hell, if I reached mine!
> To know I suffered would still sadden her. . . .
> All that was is; and must forever be.
> Nor is it in me to unhate my hates. . . .
>   I grow one gorge
> To loathingly reject Pompilia's pale
> Poison my hasty hunger took for food.

> A strong tree wants no wreaths about its trunk, . . .
> I lived and died a man and take man's chance, . . .
> Who are those you have let descend my stair? . . .
> Don't open! Hold me from them! . . .
> Abate,—Cardinal,—Christ,—Maria,—God, . . .
> Pompilia, will you let them murder me?

The final canto entitled, "The Book and the Ring," begins "Here were the end, had anything an end"—and (reluctantly enough) "How will it be, my four-years' intimate/When thou and I part company anon?"

. He hated to finish, arduous though the work had been. For Guido's death, witnesses are called up again who declare that he

> "Finished, as you expect, a penitent,
> Fully confessed his crime and made amends
> And, edifying Rome last Saturday,
> Died like a saint, poor devil!"

This, too, was the official statement. But did Browning want us to believe that Guido repented? Julia Wedgwood had written, before reading his final monologue, "be merciful to us in Guido's last display! Shame and pain and humiliation need the irradiation of hope to be endurable as objects of contemplation."

Browning answered: "Guido hope? do you bid me turn him into that sort of thing? No, indeed!"

Yet commenting to Allingham on the "work underground" in his poem he had listed "Guido's not escaping better, man won't give him post-horses; the Pope as Providence; Guido has time for confession." So it may be that Browning was in fact uncertain in his reading of the living man he had created.

A final reference to Guido's last speech was published in a little-known book, *Frederick James Furnivall, A Record*. Julia Wedgwood and William Allingham both belong to the period of the poem's gestation and birth. It was fifteen years later that Furnivall was busying himself asking Browning endless questions on his works. With *The*

Ring and the Book he was concerned about the relation between historical fact and poetic creation in the outstanding characters of the drama. Browning wrote (February 20, 1883) in reply to his questions:

> There is nothing in any part of the "Ring and the Book" that, properly speaking, is not wholly *mine*,—that is, my imaginary deduction from certain naked *facts* recorded in the original collection of documents. These stop abruptly (the official ones) before any judgment that must have been pronounced on the whole: and but for an expression superscribed on the last paper or two,—to the effect that they relate to the "quondam" Guido,—I should never have known how the sentence really went, did not there follow the M.S. letters mentioning that all the criminals had suffered the same day. I obtained, a long while afterwards, a M.S. account of the story with particulars of the execution. That Caponsacchi and Guido severally were examined is certain from the reports of their evidence and statements: and, guessing at the way each may have spoken, from the facts undoubtedly in the mind of each, I raised the whole structure of the speeches, such as it is. For instance in the last speech to which you refer the fact is that the two ecclesiastics passed the night preceding his execution with Guido: and, knowing as he did the innocence of his wife, what so likely as that, in his last utterance of despair, *her* name, with an appeal to it, should suggest itself?

Returning to the Pope's speech, we find another important element in Browning's thinking. Was the Church's failure a moral failure only? Is not the "iteration of command" matched, created, by a profound intellectual weakness?

In and out of the story run the Molinists (or Quietists), an attack upon whom seemed to be an excuse for any failure to expound and explain what Christianity meant. When Caponsacchi talks of withdrawing from his worldly life to think and pray, he is asked if he intends to turn Molinist, and he answers "What if I turned Christian?" The Pope too feels that there may be in Molinism a necessary challenge to a worldly Church. May they not be "Obedient to some truth/Unrecognised yet, but perceptible?—"

Realizing vividly the possibility that before he can sign the warrant for Guido's execution death may call himself:

> I have worn through this sombre wintry day,
> With winter in my soul beyond the world's.

Yet at the end of the Book, as at the beginning, he is upheld by a burning faith in Christ

> I take His staff with my uncertain hand,
> And stay my six and four score years, my due
> Labour and sorrow, on His judgment-seat,
> And forthwith think, speak, act, in place of Him—
> The Pope for Christ.

And through the gloom pierces the sort of hope Browning always rejoiced in—dragged from the very depths of despair:

> What if it be the mission of that age
> My death will usher into life, to shake
> This torpor of assurance from our creed,
> Re-introduce the doubt discarded, bring
> That formidable danger back, we drove
> Long ago to the distance and the dark? . . .
> And man stand out again, pale, resolute,
> Prepared to die,—which means, alive at last?
> As we broke up that old faith of the world,
> Have we, next age, to break up this the new—
> Faith, in the thing, grown faith in the report. . . .
> Correct the portrait by the living face,
> Man's God, by God's God in the mind of man?

Julia Wedgwood, overwhelmed by the magnificence of this Book, got from it "a sense of everything falling into its place" given her hitherto only by Beethoven's music. "There is a sense of the great schism of life being healed . . . that sense of the wealth and glory of this life, and its insignificance . . . you, in some rare flashes, shew me them together. This miserable incompleteness, this straining of the growing plant against the tiny pot, which in prosaic hours seems hopeless misfit and mistake, by *that* light turns into a promise . . . all the misconception, thwarted plans, broken work, and that sense of incapacity, and poverty within that is harder than all" would be only like "a letter one had tried to read just before sunrise. . . . You do feel that your work is the deliverance of captives, and the opening the eyes of the blind. If those wonderful flashes have ever shewn us a new Heaven and a new Earth, we do not quite go back to the old."

5　St. Martin's Summer

Life's business being just the terrible choice.

THE RING AND THE BOOK

The everlasting No.

CARLYLE

The Ring and the Book appeared in four volumes in November and December 1868, January and February 1869: "the most precious and profound spiritual treasure" proclaimed the *Athenaeum* "that England has produced since the days of Shakespeare." Not all the reviews were so ecstatic—but the most important papers gave the book high praise—the *Quarterly*, the *Edinburgh*, and John Morley in the *Fortnightly*.

Julia Wedgwood had had her proofs well ahead of these reviews—and it must have become irritating for Browning during weeks of nervous strain to receive only her letters. For before he had acknowledged the panegyric on "The Pope" she had done precisely what she had called impossible—gone back to "the old earth" from which "The Pope" had momentarily lifted her. She feels after finishing the entire poem that she cannot look at it "without a squint," making all the old complaints about Guido, about the lawyers. She "cannot sympathise" in Browning's choice of a subject, but she must be wrong: "you cannot have spent all these years on a mistake."

All through this correspondence Browning's patience had been exemplary: he had encouraged criticism, even been grateful for it. But he had not written the delighted reply she expected to her enthusiastic letter of a week earlier. He had "judged it inexpedient to clap my hands ... till I was out of the wood,—and, behold, I was soon ordained to knock my head against a tree!" And a moment of exasperation brought with it a question. "Yes I have given four full years to this 'mistake,' but what did I do with my fourteen years in Italy?"

Great though *The Ring and the Book* is, surely the answer to this rhetorical question might have been "the greatest work of your life"— *Christmas Eve and Easter Day, Men and Women,* much of *Dramatis Personae.*

Julia did not make it; she went on to ensure that the friendship building up again in their letters should again founder. Smiling at the notion that the separation could have been a loss to *him,* she remarks "You know I turned to you almost as a survivor from some elder race."

Declining to "step up on to some pretty sort of pedestal whence I am to observe you somewhere below," Browning affirms: "I lost something peculiar in you, which I shall not see replaced,—is that stated soberly enough? I neither can—ever could, nor would, were I able,—replace anything I have once had: ... Goodbye: I wish I could see you again: last Wednesday I sat at dinner close to an acquaintance of some thirty years. . . . On Saturday he fell dead."

It is almost unbelievable that at this stage Julia told Browning that in asking him to visit her no more she had been motivated by a rumor that *he* had "felt it a gêne." Now he was really angry: the totally different possibility which she had implied earlier certainly excluded this one. He had seldom talked of her, he answered, but had he done so would not "have seen the policy—had I stooped to try—in pretending to ignore a very patent thing, as if it were proper to undervalue a jewel lest one be supposed to meditate stealing it: . . . I enjoyed seeing you much, ... and if you, of your very own self, could, however fantastically, assure me, 'Oh, but it was all done to relieve *you* from a gêne'!—well, I shall say—'you know better.' "

Mrs. Miller in *Robert Browning: A Portrait* sees in Julia's insistent bringing in of Elizabeth the irritant which finally shattered their friendship—and so partly do I, but in a very different way. He had earlier welcomed her into his "sacred places," but it was after this letter that with an unconscious sublime impertinence Julia Wedgwood told him: "you owe us an adequate translation of what your wife was to you."

"But why or how do I owe you—or whomsoever is included in 'us'—any 'adequate translation of what my wife was to me'?—except in saying, as I devoutly do on other occasions than sitting at meals 'For these and all other mercies God be praised.'"

Did she really want to throw away a friendship because nothing beyond it was within her reach? Had she broken it hoping wildly for that something? What part had her mother borne in the whole affair? These are idle questions inevitably suggested by the fascinating picture of a highly intelligent fool.

The summer of 1869 was spent by Browning in Scotland instead of France, son and father both guests of Lady Ashburton at Loch Luichart; Sarianna was there too, the Storys and Lady Marian Alford. Among Browning's later poems can be read a round robin, in no way remarkable except for high spirits and an absurd facility in double rhyming, in which the house party beseech Hatty Hosmer, the young American sculptor whose close friendship with the Brownings is described in Volume I, to join them. "Drowning" and "Browning," "sick heart" and "Loch Luichart," "found with you" and "round with you," "Say not (in Scotch) 'in troth it canna be'— /But, honey, milk and, indeed, manna be!/Forgive a stranger!—Sarianna B."

Lady Ashburton being found absent at the date she had invited them, the Brownings and the Storys had stayed at a rough little country inn, and enjoyed picnic meals in the heather while Browning "loudly read out 'Rob Roy.'" This "baffled" period had ended delightfully: "the delayed visit took place, with compensations abounding, with, in fact, for the consciousness of the present chronicler [Henry James in *William Wetmore Story*] more interesting passages of personal history than may here be touched upon."

Not merely touched upon since but fingered over and worn threadbare! One longs for James at his subtlest to restore the picture, while wondering all the time how much there was to see.

"Lady Ashburton," says James, *"was,* admirably, delightfully, a subject—for irresistible consideration, for, positively, a sort of glow of remembrance, the glow from which artistic projection sometimes eventually springs. This friendly light rests on occasions, incidents, accidents, in which a liberal oddity, a genial incoherence, an *expected* half funny, half happy turn of the affair, for the most part, appears to declare itself as the leading note."

He felt it was so for the party who had awaited her ladyship's pleasure at the little inn. "The Ludovisi goddess in person [Harriet Hosmer describes her] . . . the same square cut and grandiose features, whose classic beauty was humanised by a pair of keen dark eyes . . . a lovely smile . . . a rich musical voice."

Browning too must that autumn have admired this splendid woman. Did she later become the "brisk-marching bold she-shape,/A terror with those black-balled worlds of eyes?" Was it she who had "dared try/ Darker arts that almost struck despair in me"?

The only direct evidence for the theory accepted in the Griffin-Minchin biography and by William DeVane and most of the Browning critics, that Browning proposed to Lady Ashburton at this or possibly some later date, is contained in two letters of his—the first written to Edith Story in 1872, the second to Edith's father in 1886. Both letters describe an attempt by Lady Ashburton to remake a broken friendship, resisted by Browning. In the first he says:

> I suppose that Lady A. did not suppress what she considered the capital point of her quarrel with me when she foamed out into the couple of letters she bespattered me with,—yet the worst she charged me with was,—having said that my heart was buried in Florence, and the attractiveness of a marriage with her lay in its advantage to Pen—two simple facts,—as I told her,—which I had never left her in ignorance about, for a moment, though that I ever paraded this in a gross form to anybody is simply false.

This has been taken by one critic after another as referring to what they (reasonably) call a "clumsy" proposal of marriage from the poet. But given his strange inability, often noted with amusement by Elizabeth, to relate any happening other than backwards or standing on its head, can we be at all certain that this *is* what the letter is saying?

To William Story he wrote of "resisting cajoleries and appeals, for two years together," to renew even an acquaintance, and of the "calumnies which Lady A. exploded in all the madness of her wounded vanity."

In a letter to *Time and Tide*, Dame Myra Curtis asked the question: Who actually proposed to whom? We know from all the records that women were attracted to Browning and that he thoroughly enjoyed the superficial relation of admiration (and affection) known as a flirtation. A successful flirtation engages both parties and the atmosphere was favorable.

Scotland in the autumn: the glory of sun and water and heather, the long idle country-house days, the happiness and well-being of an adored but troublesome son, the flattery of admiration poured by a beautiful woman on a man not unsusceptible either to beauty or to flattery—moreover a woman who wants . . . well what *did* she want?

Throughout the story we must bear in mind the Victorian era, with its curious pattern of social classes. The snobbery of the outsider is often enough described, but what about the far more deep-seated snobbery of the insider? As late as 1922 a titled lady remarked when a poet was courting her daughter: "We ask people like that to our houses, but we don't marry them."

Perhaps not, but when a man had become as frantically popular socially as was Browning, when his hostess had invited besides his attractive son, his middle-aged, middle-class sister, when everything seemed to point to her expectation of a proposal, it is at least possible that Browning suddenly felt entrapped. She may have wanted the proposal while still unclear whether to accept or reject it. It would commit only Browning, leaving her free to keep him on tenterhooks while she thought or talked the matter over. She may have wanted a poet's love or merely the scalp of this renowned warrior to hang at her belt. Without knowing her one cannot tell; but, however she did it, the point was perhaps reached at which Browning felt he must explain why he was *not* proposing and did an awkward thing in an exceedingly awkward fashion.[1]

This would explain the lady's wounded vanity, but would it explain the man's remorse, the feeling of a betrayal of his dead wife, which critics discover in so much of his later poetry?

Here we touch another element in criticism where we should surely walk cautiously: the support of a doubtful interpretation of Browning's prose by bringing in his poetry. Poetry tells us much about the poet's self, but I wonder how much of brute fact goes into it. A poem may as easily be written about action repudiated as about action chosen. Either may kindle the imagination: in fact perhaps the path unfollowed may show itself in stronger colors than the path followed. And critics who accept personal interpretations will almost violently repudiate the conclusions of other critics concerning the same poems.

There is, too, something else: comment appears to sum up the letter of 1872 as the suggestion of a "marriage of convenience"—his genius, fame, and popularity, her wealth and social position. But if the *poetry* is telling any story this is not the story it is telling. I incline to agree with current criticism that we *are*, in the poetry, being told a story: we may get it wrong, but there is only one way in which we can possibly get it right—and that is by examining *all* the poems in which the theme recurs. I do this, however, with profound diffidence: I am not sure it ought to be done, yet one cannot ignore something so possibly important, so much discussed.

Browning was not yet fifty when Elizabeth died, young for his age in mind and body. He could walk twenty miles with ease, could dine out and go on to parties after a hard day's work and be writing again at five the next morning. He was too a man of strong passion, judging from the red-hot lava, deplored by Santayana as barbaric, that poured into his poems from the crater of his being. And he had determined on an eternal fidelity to the wife he had lost. "He is a very Jeptha," Elizabeth had written of her husband in 1854, "for rash vows—and I've stopped him twenty times in such vows as never to take another wife

and the like . . . I've held his lips together with both hands. I won't
have it."

But to himself the vow had been made and was a hard one to keep.
Whether with Lady Ashburton or another he seems in his own eyes at
least to have at some time failed, and if he could not forgive her it may
have been because he could never fully forgive himself.

He was perhaps at Loch Luichart enjoying an agreeable flirtation,
which "St. Martin's Summer" suggests was turning into something else

> You would build a mansion,
>   I would weave a bower
>   —Want the heart for enterprise.
> Walls admit of no expansion:
>   Trellis work may haply flower
>   Twice the size.

But

> Where we plan our dwelling
>   Glooms a graveyard surely!
>   Headstone, footstone moss may drape,—
> Name, date, violets hide from spelling,—
>   But, though corpses rot obscurely,
>   Ghosts escape.

He may be overtimid, over-ready to take fright: but "you if bolder/
Bold— are blind?" Lady Ashburton was a widow and for her too
there would be ghosts:

> Lies nothing buried long ago?
> Are yon—which shimmer mid the shady
>   Where moss and violet run to rankness—
> Tombs or no?

The realization comes suddenly that it is the old love he is seeking
in and through the new. What he seemed to give to the woman of

flesh and blood was in truth given to her whose physical presence he craved as truly as the communion with her spirit which had so often blessed him. Now he has lost both.

> Ay, dead loves are the potent!
>   Like any cloud they used you,
>   Mere semblance you, but substance they!
> Build we no mansion, weave we no tent!
>   Mere flesh—their spirit interfused you!
>   Hence, I say!
>
> All theirs, none yours the glamour!
>   Theirs each low word that won me,
>   Soft look that found me Love's, and left
> What else but you—the tears and clamour
>   That's all your very own! Undone me—
>   Ghost bereft.

Was it in such a moment of sudden revulsion that he spoke as he did to Lady Ashburton—of his dead wife and his living son? If we look at several other poems which precede and follow this one we see something interesting which is hard to express adequately.

"Numpholeptos," Browning said, was a mythological fable, not linked with any human woman, but he uses in the poem the simile he had first used to Elizabeth of prismatic hues and the white light: he sees himself climbing painfully up each ladder of color into the whiteness of the "disempassioned moon," from whom he receives calm unempassioned forgiveness while craving vainly, passionately, a return of love.

Because Browning had called Elizabeth his "moon of poets" and speaks also in this poem of the prismatic hues and the white light, his declaration that the nymph *is* a nymph and no human woman has been set aside. It is *his* passion, says one critic, that meets, "the old statuesque regard,/ The sad petrific smile," his reproaches that are "The true slave's querulous outbreak" which will end in obedience.

Putting aside the question whether a poet's account of his own meaning is to be treated as final, there are several things to be noted about this poem. First, it obviously has, like "Childe Roland," the quality of a dream—passing into a nightmare. He was, perhaps, in that nightmare striving to change the pale moon into the living woman who had of old returned his passionate embrace, living again through the anguish of Elizabeth's first horrified rejection of his proposal, and the period when he had offered to be as one of her brothers rather than lose her wholly. The essence of a nightmare is that we are power-less to throw off the smothering oppression of its monstrous falsity—except by waking. From this nightmare the waking was into an aching void.

It may be after another dream that Browning wrote "Pan and Luna"—in which the moon plunges into a cloud only to find herself

> clasped around and caught
> By rough red Pan, the god of all that tract: . . .
> Ha Virgil? Tell the rest, you! "To the deep
> Of his domain the wildwood, Pan forthwith
> Called her, and so she followed"—in her sleep
> Surely?—"by no means spurning him." The myth
> Explain who may! Let all else go, I keep
> —As of a ruin just a monolith—
> Thus much, one verse of five words, each a boon:
> Arcadia, night, a cloud, Pan and the moon.

In the "vehement sensuousness and frank chastity" of this de-velopment of Virgil's myth, Dowden sees that "with the utmost energy of imagination . . . we are made to feel . . . the transaction of a significant dream or legend." A legend perhaps reflecting Browning's life, a dream of what still lived, lifted into legendary love.

Browning's biographers and critics are all agreed in seeing in *Fifine at the Fair* (published in 1872) a dark mood of Browning's—and W. O. Raymond has linked it convincingly with whatever harrowing experi-ence it was that breaks through so much of his later poetry—from "St. Martin's Summer" to the *Parleyings*. Chesterton more light-heartedly

links it with the entry in the child Browning's journal "married two
wives this morning." For it is a kind of English *Don Juan* in which the
hero, married to Elvire, an ethereal, spiritual woman, is attracted by the
gypsy, Fifine (drawn from a girl observed by Browning at a fair at
Pornic). The hero claims that this attraction can co-exist with the
deeper love. On the way home with Elvire he leaves her—for a moment
only he explains—to clear up a misunderstanding with Fifine. But if
he goes now, on the very threshold of their house, what will await his
return?

> Oh threaten no farewell! five minutes shall suffice
> To clear the matter up. I go, and in a trice
> Return; five minutes past, expect me! If in vain—
> Why, slip from flesh and blood, and play the ghost again!

So the poem ends. The Epilogue begins:

> Savage I was sitting in my house, late, lone.
>   Dreary, weary with the long day's work: . . .
> When, in a moment, just a knock, call, cry,
>   Half a pang and all a rapture, there again were we!—
> "What, and is it really you again?" quoth I:
>   "I again, what else did you expect?" quoth She.

We have moved from the rejecting to the yielding moon. The pale
moon is embodied, the ghost is a living woman, to be told of the daily
worries and the "darker arts that almost struck despair in me."

> "If you knew but how I dwelt down here!" quoth I:
> "And was I so better off up there?" quoth She.

> "Help and get it over! *Re-united to his wife*
>   (How draw up the paper lets the parish-people know?)
> *Lies M., or N., departed from this life,*
>   *Day the this or that, month and year the so and so.*
> What i' the way of final flourish? Prose, verse? Try!

> *Affliction sore long time he bore,* or, what is it to be?
> *Till God did please to grant him ease.* Do end!" quoth I:
>   "I end with—Love is all and Death is nought!" quotn She.

Elvire or Elizabeth? After reading this chapter in manuscript, a very learned Browning scholar dismayed me by asking "Is he really Pan?! And is the chaste Diana really E.B.B.? Pan beguiled Luna, as Virgil says and won her by the treachery of his fleece. How does that fit?"

He said further that in the Epilogue to *Fifine* we should see only Elvire: "Don Juan was expecting the statue of the legend. . . . Browning uses another variation . . . in which the spirit of the dead lover reaches from the tomb, takes Don Juan by the hand, and rescues him from destruction. . . . So much for the biography of the thing!" And again, "Do you identify Browning with Don Juan?"

The answer lies in what Browning says in one of his later poems— "advantage would it be or detriment/If I saw double." Surely it is double vision that is here involved. In each of the poems I have been discussing he is talking of something that exists in its own right, but with overtones of something else.

Before the poet's eyes had been from boyhood a picture of Andromeda chained naked to a rock; he had written of it in *Pauline;* it is a recurrent theme. Perseus is the hero who will rescue her, or alternatively St. George. In the central event of his life Browning "repeated," as Robert Langbaum puts it, "the mythical pattern by rescuing Miss Barrett. And there is no doubt that he recognized the same mythical pattern when he read in *The Old Yellow Book* of Caponsacchi's rescue of Pompilia."

This does not mean that Elizabeth was chained naked to a rock or that Browning was pursued when he carried her off from Wimpole Street by an angry husband and a band of assassins! In every case he is telling a story, valid in itself, yet rich in the echoes given back by life. For every mythical pattern has these overtones. It was, Langbaum goes on, because Browning was able to assimilate the murder case to the myth that *The Ring and the Book* is at once "a very personal and a very impersonal poem."

I have a great deal of sympathy with the literalists driven by the pressing of Browning's poetry into multitudinous psychological molds, but I feel their either-or attitude is also invalid. Nearly everybody does in fact take the Epilogue to *Fifine* as addressed directly to Elizabeth (as most of Browning's epilogues were)—and therefore separates it totally from the rest of the poem. But is this necessary, is it even possible? The return, after all, of Elvire as a ghost is foreshadowed at the end of the poem and takes place in the Epilogue.

With Browning even more than with most poets we should try to discard the mentality that says severely either-or. It is a mythical pattern we are dealing with: the stories stand in their own right, but Browning could not conceivably have written on sexual love without his own story very much present. He *is* seeing double, and it is "advantage," not "detriment."[2]

The mood of "Numpholeptos," the mood of "Pan and Luna," the mood of the Epilogue, the mixed mood of "St. Martin's Summer" come and go with the man, himself also at one moment flesh and blood, at another a diminished half-dead being—to be "Called into life by her who long ago/ Left his soul whiling time in flesh-disguise . . . Waiting the morn-star's reappearance."

These lines come from the "Parleying with Daniel Bartoli" and nothing is more fascinating in so much of the late and very late verse of Browning's than the sudden snatches of this abiding theme song. The moon's self seen years ago in Florence "thrice-transfigured," seen in London "impoverished" and "Hard to greet," is still a guide illuminating from heaven his path on earth.

The life of every creative writer, supremely of every poet must find a reflection in his works but we may fail to read it right. What is certain is that none of these poems suggests the idea of a marriage of convenience, but that in them all Browning seems to be repenting of a sin—at least, of thought against his dead wife, and it is impossible not to speculate as to its nature.

Those were days of discretion—and nobody but a few intimates knew anything very much. The Storys advised Browning to keep carefully some letters of the period, as Lady Ashburton was talking against him. If the "tears and clamour" of "St. Martin's Summer" belong to the story they probably represent her entreaties that he should make up the quarrel—whatever the exact form it had taken. Conscious of a quarrel, friends knew enough from one side or the other to be in two camps and the Storys were "with" Browning, Hatty Hosmer "with" Lady Ashburton.

I am indebted to Douglas Woodruff for a curious letter from Lord Acton to his daughter dated June 15, 1888.

> ... I find I was wrong about R. Browning and Lady Ashburton. He asked her to marry him about ten years ago. She refused, and he went away to Italy. Then she asked him to come back. He came, and they were engaged. Suddenly she broke off, and sent Hamilton Aïde for her letters. Browning returned all but one, which he said he would keep till he died, that he might have a defence against her—a thing scarcely excusable under any imaginable circumstances. This explains the fury of her language about him last night; it was a storm unappeased.

Evidently gossip had been busy and had not died out for twenty years! But this letter shows the great historian wildly at sea as to what are established dates: it was not ten years ago but nineteen (1869) since the party at Loch Luichart, and whatever happened then Browning did not return to Italy until nine years later (1878). Lady Ashburton's demand to have her letters back may or may not be a fact— Story had advised Browning to keep them carefully.

But Lord Acton's own evidence is of real value, for it shows that Lady Ashburton's rage against Browning was as unquenchable after twenty years as his had been at the time.[3]

There is another element in *Fifine*, the expression of a profound urge which had *not* separated Browning from his wife, which had indeed deeply united them. He had seen Fifine at Pornic in 1865 and, even if the poem was not begun before 1871 the subject may well have been growing at the back of his mind. One aspect of it certainly finds expression in his letters to Isa. He is longing once more for Italy or for "Anywhere, anywhere, out of this black, rainy beastly-streeted London world. I get quite sick of dining out—refuse whatever invitations I possibly can." Getting up at five all that winter "even so, I can't get through my work."

And in another letter (March 22, 1870): "If I spend my old age my own way quietly alone,—how odd and dreamlike will all the people come and go in my memory! I suppose it is, on the whole, a gain in some respects to the soul to have seen so many people: I mainly care about human beings, yet I feel weary of the crowd I chose to fancy it would do me good to see."

Fifine at the Fair strikes at the outset the same note, though less clear and less sustained, as Dickens' picture of the circus folk in *Hard Times*. The poem is by no means only a question of whether Don Juan wants a holiday from Donna Elvire—it is the revolt against a rigid society of one at moments "Frenetic to be free" from that "Society, whereof myself am at the beck,/Whose call obey, and stoop to burden stiffest neck!"

Elizabeth and he had been of yore among those "Misguided ones who gave society the slip,"—he above all had felt that nothing so much oppressed his spirit as the atmosphere which today surrounded him. He looked at the gypsies now and asked:

> —why is it, can we guess?
> At somebody's expense, goes up so frank a laugh?
> As though they held the corn, and left us only chaff
> From garners crammed and closed. And we indeed are clever
> If we get grain as good, by thrashing straw forever!...
>
> I say, they sell what we most pique us that we keep!
> How comes it, all we hold so dear they count so cheap?

A shock compounded of many elements had awakened Browning to the realization that he was back in that world of ticky-tacky from which he had so long escaped, back in the world of Podsnappery. Hard to realize it in the aristocratic section of it (so unlike even the world of a Julia Wedgwood) with its large choices in small matters, its binding not at all of the inclinations, fancies, sports and games, but only of the soul. Elizabeth as well as her prince of mystics would have been more at home among the gypsies. I think Elvire, even though a greatly diminished Elizabeth, would have understood Fifine, as Elizabeth showed she could in *Aurora Leigh*. Browning said "Fix into one Elvire a Fair-ful of Fifines." In her one person he had both women of the poem—but she was dead.

6 Mainly About the Greeks

I sat next Mr. Browning at dinner. He described a Greek poem, and suddenly seized my chair and twirled it right round.

ANNE THACKERAY RITCHIE

IT IS a false simplification to see the years after Elizabeth's death as just one undifferentiated period in Browning's life. The divisions of youth and married life are more definitely marked—but a slower yet considerable change took place somewhere around his sixtieth year, 1872. I say somewhere around, because several of his best and worst poems lie on each side of a year that marks a beginning of dullness rather than mere occasional obscurity, a partial loss of vision accompanied by a wearisome ratiocination undermining his own profoundest philosophy of love through knowledge.

Fifine at the Fair, written at the end of the decade which began with his wife's death, and published in 1872, is as he himself felt, boldly metaphysical; is, as Saintsbury saw it, an astonishing triumph in rhythm—skipping with Fifine, tripping with Elvire, through the Fair at Pornic and through the world's vaster fair, passing beyond Pornic, beyond Venice, into regions almost inaccessible: save to the eyes

> Of who kept open house,—to fancies manifold
> From this four-cornered world, the memories new and old,
> The antenatal prime experience—what know I?—
> The initiatory love preparing us to die—

As a whole I would take *Fifine* as marking the divide between greatness and decline, but the poems on each side of it, both in their nature and through the circumstances in which they were written, tell us much about the poet which we cannot afford to miss. The year before *Fifine*, two poems had come, both important though very unequal in poetic quality: *Balaustion's Adventure,* published in August 1871 and ranked by both DeVane and Langbaum as belonging to Browning's best period, and *Prince Hohenstiel-Schwangau* (discussed in my first volume), published in December of the same year.

The Prince was Napoleon III, who had meant so much to Elizabeth. A little more must be said here of what Browning was telling us about him in the light of all that had happened between the Italian episode and the collapse of France in the Franco-Prussian War of 1870. Although the poem came a few months later than *Balaustion* I am putting it first here in order to group together Browning's three long classical poems, so closely related to one another, two of them coming after *Fifine*. Swinburne wrote to Frederick Locker (Lampson): "I did not know Tennyson was about to handle Tristram, nor that Browning's late labours had had for their subject a topic fitter for Swift. If he means to rescue the prey from under Hugo's lion claws, or even mine, he must look to his hunting gear."[1]

Perhaps Swinburne suspected that Browning had shared Elizabeth's near idolatry of Napoleon, but it was more probably on account of Browning's own doubts and questions that his "little hand-breadth of prose,—now yellow with age and Italian ink," had waited so long to be "breathed out into this full-blown bubble." The poem, completed at his friends the Benzons' house in Perthshire on October 7, 1871, makes it clear that Browning had continued to watch Napoleon all these years with a fascinated interest in his development, taking now one and now another view in the changing circumstances. Early that year he had seen a poem on the subject, by the very minor poet, Robert Buchanan, and felt relieved that his "fears that you might treat in your undoubted right the main actor after a fashion repugnant to my feelings were vain enough."

The interesting question—which would never have arisen with

Swift, Hugo, or Swinburne—was what exactly Browning's "feelings" were. One review described the poem as a "eulogium on the Second Empire," another as "a scandalous attack on the old constant friend of England."

Both seem to have missed the point—that Napoleon is in the poem speaking for himself. To Edith Story, Browning wrote (January 1, 1872):

> I don't think, when you have read more, you will find I have "taken the man for any Hero"—I rather made him confess he was the opposite, . . . I suppose there to be a physical and intellectual decline of faculty, brought about by the man's own faults, no doubt—but I think he struggles against these; and when that is the case, depend on it, in a soliloquy, a man makes the most of his good intentions and sees great excuse in them—far beyond what our optics discover!"[2]

Albert Guérard's *Napoleon III* (1963) is a panegyric compared with any contemporary view—but his main argument for Napoleon was already there in Browning. The emperor claimed to—and *did*, says Guérard emphatically—care for the common man.

> He should know, sitting on the throne, how tastes
> Life to who sweeps the doorway. . . .
> Mankind i' the main have little wants, not large:
> I, being of will and power to help, i' the main,
> Mankind, must help the least wants first.

Thus Guérard sees Napoleon setting public works on foot, augmenting trade and immeasurably improving the finances of France, working for peace, though at last driven into war by the machinations of Bismarck, the folly of his own ministers—and the failing health which disabled him in later years. It took some courage in the England of that date, when Napoleon and France had fallen together, to show that this "political adventurer" had anything to "say for himself." Chesterton calls the poem "one of the finest and most picturesque of all Browning's apologetic monologues." And he sees something specially characteristic in Browning's choice of "what would appear the most prosaic kind of villain." We are accustomed to "the generous rake, the kindly drunkard," but Browning "was in a yet more solitary sense the friend of the outcast. He took in the sinners whom even sinners cast out. He went with the hypocrite and had mercy on the Pharisee."

Nothing could be more different from *Hohenstiel-Schwangau* than the poem which immediately preceded it: *Balaustion's Adventure*.

All educated Englishmen at that date, indeed all educated Westerners, had as a matter of course learned Greek and Latin, but Browning was one of that much smaller number at any period for whom love of the classics became a passion.

Years before, he had, it will be remembered, composed "Artemus Prologizes" (published 1862) "much against my endeavor, while in bed with a fever." It was all that remained inside his aching head of a long tragedy, for on his recovery "putting only this much down at once, I forgot the rest." Again he had talked to Rossetti: "In my last good days at Rome, the best in my life," of a projected poem, Helen dedicating a goblet for the temple of Venus. " 'I'll paint it' said he—and there it is, archaically treated indeed."[3]

In 1872, in a single month, he wrote *Balaustion's Adventure, Including a Transcript from Euripides,* and dedicating it to Lady Cowper he described it as "the most delightful of May-month amusements." Delightful though it certainly is, I fancy its instant success came as a surprise to Browning.

Sometimes in the poem he is speaking directly, but chiefly it is Balaustion, telling the Euripides story of Alkestis and describing the play as she had seen it—its scenery even and stage directions. Balaustion herself is a creation of Browning's: the name means "Wild-pomegranate flower"—and one feels his pleasure in its evocations. Euripides was writing about 438 B.C., but Browning, using Plutarch's *Life of Nicias,* set his scene in the second half of the Peloponnesian War when, in 413 B.C., Sparta defeated Athens in the disastrous expedition against Syracuse. Many captives were taken and cruelly used—set half-starved to quarry stone, but Plutarch relates how those who could recite

Euripides or repeat his stories were well treated. This was Browning's setting for the play.

The Fates have decreed the death of Admetos, King of Thessaly, unless he can find somebody willing to take his place. But no one of his subjects, not even his aged father or mother, will sacrifice the years that remain to them.

Alkestis comes forward to save her husband's life, asking of Admetos only that he will give their children no stepmother. She dies, but is brought back from the grave by Herakles.

For three quarters of the poem Balaustion is describing what she had seen and heard, making the best she can of an Admetos who could accept his wife's sacrifice. The aura of sacredness surrounding kingship is an almost impossible thing for the modern world to understand, and with all his efforts to speak through her it is clear that Browning could not accept it. Admetos is depicted as alternately repentant for having accepted his wife's sacrifice and deeply resentful of the failure of his father to have made her sacrifice unnecessary:

> He only now began to taste the truth:
> The thing done lay revealed, which undone thing,
> Rehearsed for fact by fancy, at the best,
> Never can equal.

In the aching void of his loss—" 'Did I mean this should buy my life?' thought he"—a dialogue follows with his aged father in which "Like hates like." Admetos reproaches him for failing to step forward and save Alkestis, revealing

> . . . how weakness strove to hide itself
> In bluster against weakness,—the loud word
> To hide the little whisper, not so low
> Already in that heart beneath those lips!

Shame is beginning to grow in him and he is only saved, in a two-fold sense, by the coming of Herakles, seeking rest between two of his

Robert Browning and "Pen", May 1870

Julia Wedgwood

Lady Ashburton

Browning brings a titled lady to call upon Dante Gabriel Rossetti.
A cartoon by Max Beerbohm

Swinburne and Adah Menken

Disraeli and Gladstone. *Vanity Fair* cartoons

labors. Admetos conceals his own loss, receives his honored guest, and has food and drink set before him in another part of the house while the funeral procession moves away. But a servant, enraged to see the joyous, drinking, flower-crowned guest, reveals the truth, and Herakles, "half God, half man, which made the god-part God the more," throws aside wine-cup and rose-crown:

> So, in a spasm and splendour of resolve,
> All at once did the God surmount the man.

He brings Alkestis back from Hades and offers her to the King, but veiled; and Admetos finds redemption by refusing to accept an unknown woman, even at the hands of a God:

> ... Till Herakles must help:
> Assure him that no spectre mocked at all;
> He was embracing whom he buried once.

It is the best that can be done with the Admetos of Euripides. But it is not good enough to satisfy Balaustion, who wants "to mould a new Admetos, new Alkestis." And in her conception there is a profound change in the character of Admetos. Apollo, having come to live at his court, had transformed him into one who lived only for his subjects' good, and it was Alkestis who had won the god's consent to dying in her husband's place:

> Whereto Admetos, in a passionate cry,
> "Never by that true word Apollon spoke!
> All the unwise wish is unwished, oh wife!
> ... throughout my earthly life,
> Mine should be mingled and made up with thine,—
> And we two prove one force and play one part
> And do one thing. Since death divides the pair,
> 'Tis well that I depart and thou remain
> Who wast to me as spirit is to flesh."

But nowise will Alkestis consent—only she insists that he look steadfastly at her before the last decree goes forth. "Therewith her whole soul entered into his,/He looked the look back, and Alkestis died."

But somehow this death "broke through humanity/Into the orbed omniscience of a God"—and that god, he of Hades, speaks:

> "This is not to die,
> If, by the very death which mocks me now,
> The life, that's left behind and past my power,
> Is formidably doubled. . . .
> Admetos must not be himself and thou!"
>
> And so, before the embrace relaxed a whit,
> The lost eyes opened, still beneath the look;
> And lo, Alkestis was alive again,
> And of Admetos' rapture who shall speak?

But, says Balaustion sadly, of the Golden Age that the two would together bring back on earth, she could not learn "That ever one faint particle came true,/With both alive to bring it to effect:/Such is the envy Gods still bear mankind!"

Despite the interpolations and glosses, the Greek scholar Mahaffy spoke of this poem as "by far the best translation of the Alcestis."[4] And Browning himself, treasuring Balaustion, brought her back again in *Aristophanes' Apology*. He had finished *Balaustion's Adventure* just ten years after Elizabeth's death, and although it was offered to Lady Cowper as a task "imposed" on him by her, it bears as motto, introduced again in the text, a *very* bad verse from Elizabeth's "Wine of Cyprus":

> Our Euripides the human,
>   With his droppings of warm tears,
> And his touchings of things common
>   Till they rose to touch the spheres.

An interesting point about the unanimous conviction that we see Elizabeth in Pompilia and in Balaustion is that to no one except Browning would the wife he had known only as an invalid and middle-aged reappear as a young and beautiful woman. Yet the conviction is well founded—this *was* how Browning had seen her, as noted in Volume I, when Mrs. Kinney aroused his wrath by talking of the beautiful mind and the ravaged face. Balaustion owes her very existence to Elizabeth, and one line in the poem came as an echo to what was now Browning's deepest trouble. Alkestis dying says to Admetos: "Do thou become/ Mother, now, to these children in my place!" And "Child—child!/Just when I needed most to live, below/Am I departing from you both!"

From the first he had known that Pen needed a mother, but like Admetos he had promised himself, if not his wife, to give the boy no stepmother. Now the boy was a man: he had tried to be father and mother both—he had, it appeared, failed.

DeVane has noted that William Morris in *The Earthly Paradise* transforms Admetos even more by sending him into a deep sleep while Alkestis does her dying. Browning may have remembered this. But there was small risk of plagiarism when he handled the same subject as any of the Pre-Raphaelites.

We remember his comment on Rossetti's painting of the goblet— "archaically treated indeed." Browning's men and women were intensely alive—in a Renaissance poem, as Ruskin had noted with amazement, and here in *Balaustion*. The most significant criticism made by Greek scholars was that Browning had made Euripides too much into a man of the nineteenth century; he saw in him a poet who like himself was an innovator, a thinker, and a psychologist.

This applied even more to the next of the Greek-inspired poems, which nobody could have described, as Browning did *Balaustion*, as "A May Day Amusement." Not long before his death, Browning rearranged his whole output for a final complete edition. Immediately after *Balaustion* he placed *Aristophanes' Apology*, published in 1875.

For the amateur, this poem is so difficult as to be in places impossible. Alfred Domett, Browning's boyhood friend now returned from New Zealand, pointed out to him the "large demands" it made "on his reader's knowledge." They would have to refer "over and over again to his Comedies" thus restricting their numbers immensely. But Browning "would not hear of 'explanatory notes.' " This had been his attitude with *Sordello,* but it became even more unreasonable with so densely difficult a poem as this one. It irritated him when a reviewer suggested that the poem was the result of Browning's "Oxford Symposia with the Master of Balliol"—and still more when "half a dozen critics reported the poem to be the 'transcript' of Jowett's talk." He had never, Browning told George Smith, discussed the subject with Jowett, "Knowing as I did his entire difference with me as to every point in dispute."

A notice from John Addington Symonds in *The Academy*—a criticism, yet suggesting the width and depth of Browning's knowledge more than would praise from an ordinary reviewer—blamed him for "special pleading" and for putting into the mouth of Balaustion "the views of the most searching and most sympathetic modern analyst." Symonds considers Browning unrivaled "as a sophist and rhetorician of poetry"—it is the old story of the dramatic monologues, plus the element, now growing in him, which called out Auden's remark that in a less specialized social age he might have been the clearest instead of the obscurest of poets. For this specialization included the sort of intellectual snobbery that would have made him writhe at Saintsbury's suggestion that his curious way of spelling Greek names in English was the product of his term at London University. In his Introduction to *The Agamemnon of Aeschylus* he claimed that he had been getting nearer to the Greek sounds, "with great innocency of intention, some thirty-six years ago," and that others were now following him![5]

Browning could and did soak himself in ancient literature. Few men have worked as he did at the language needed for his subject and the surrounding history, whether Greek or Italian, and he *cared* so much, that just as reading Strauss had stirred him to write about Christ, so did adverse scholarship stir him to write about Euripides. It was the fashion of the moment to exalt both Sophocles and Aeschylus above Euripides. Browning liked to display scholarship, certainly—but the side on which he really laid himself open to attack was that of his loves and hates. Into Balaustion's mouth he puts his own enthusiasm, later defending (in a letter to Swinburne) its extreme nature as that of a woman friend of Euripides who would feel "no such need of magnanimity." Through Balaustion he "had *all but* done with anything like enmity to [Aristophanes]—the reservation being simply due to the circumstances that Euripides was not triumphantly happy like Sophocles."

Browning could not range himself among pure, uncommitted scholars: his classics were part of his own life. With *The Ring and the Book* already shaping in his mind, he had written in 1864 from the Basque country of "having a great read at Euripides—the one book I brought with me."

In 1873 he was absorbed in the *Apology*. As they walked across the Park one afternoon he repeated to Domett the plot of *Hercules Furens,* which he had been translating, collating four different editions: "I think," says Domett, "he made the story . . . more affecting than it is either in the original" or in his own subsequent version. He "was full of the pathos of the scenes in Euripides, particularly of that in which Heracles becomes conscious of what he has done, and his passionate comments upon it to Theseus." This part of the poem even the amateur can understand, but after reading through the whole I feel prepared to accept on faith Browning's immense scholarship rather than struggle to construe it! That Aristophanes did ever apologize to Euripides is a fancy of Browning's; there is no record of it!

After *Aristophanes' Apology,* longest of his poems except *The Ring and the Book* and *Sordello,* Carlyle said to Browning, "Ye won't mind me, though it's the last advice I may give ye; but ye ought to translate the whole of the Greek tragedians—that's your vocation." The "vocation," we note, of a man whose whole university career had consisted of a single term. And it is interesting to realize that Browning had plunged deep, not only into Euripides but into Aristophanes—"literally ransacked," says DeVane, his "eleven extant plays," and also the *Scholia* and parodies thereon, Plutarch's *Lysander* and the *Vitae,* a "repository of idle gossip," which he used with great ingenuity. Browning even created an imaginary play by Aristophanes, *The Grasshoppers,* which some of his commentators have seriously accepted as genuine. He also antedated *The Frogs.*

Balaustion was in this poem married to a man she had come to love in the earlier one, and the sudden burst of loveliness that Browning often brings into even his toughest and least rewarding poetry comes when she talks to her husband of their return to Rhodes and the vision of the grave of Euripides:

> He lies now in the little valley, laughed
> And moaned about by those mysterious streams,
> Boiling and freezing, like the love and hate
> Which helped or harmed him through his earthly course.
> They mix in Arethousa by his grave.
> The warm spring, traveller, dip thine arms into,
> Brighten thy brow with! Life detests black cold.

Browning could be quite furiously perverse—and this was apparent in his final treatment of the Greeks. Carlyle had begged him to translate them, but the world in general had grumbled at the obscurity of *Aristophanes' Apology*. Very well, he would show them! Show them by choosing a play so obscure that a first-class Greek scholar asked him whether he understood it—"for after twenty years of study I do not." *The Agamemnon of Aeschylus* (1877) is perhaps the hardest of all Browning's poems, and to me appears entirely unrewarding, despite a highly enjoyable preface from which we learn that Ben Jonson had called Antoninus Pius Anthony Pie; and that the theologian Salmasius bade those who found obscurity in the books of Scripture to try to read Aeschylus—one of whose plays, the *Agamemnon*, leaves them all behind, "with their Hebraisms, Syriasms, Hellenisms and the whole of such bags and baggage."

To Carlyle, Browning offered the poem in a dedication as "commanded" by him and dignified by the "insertion of his dear and noble name." But Carlyle commented to Allingham, "He's a very foolish fellow. He picks you out the English for the Greek word by word, and now and again sticks two or three words together with hyphens; then again he snips up the sense and jingles it into rhyme!" He *wouldn't*, says Carlyle, do what he so admirably could. And when Domett pointed out to him the need for notes, recognized of old even in the Greek, Browning agreed that notes might well be necessary and he would be perfectly happy if anyone liked to put some in. But, says Domett despairingly, "It should have been done in the first instance."

It seems possible that Browning was just saying "Here is a poet more obscure than I am," but this prime example of his perversity has been seen in various ways. He did not, said Sir Frederick Kenyon, deal thus with Euripides—and was unfairly weighting the scales against Aeschylus. No, says Mrs. Orr, with all his "feeling for the humanities of Greek literature" and love of the language, he never accepted the Greek writers as "models of style." He was getting fun out of challenging the view that they were. Maybe. It is often possible to think up a reason for a perversity baffling alike to the admirer of his poetry and the student of his life and character.

7 A Nest of Singing Birds

Genus irritabile vatum

HORACE

1 POETS AND "POETS"— ROSSETTI, SWINBURNE, HOPKINS, BUCHANAN, GRAY, ALLINGHAM

THE DILEMMA Browning was faced with was not made easier by an element in his own character to which I have more than once referred. Any one of us introspective enough to analyze his own moods would realize how often they change. And in the thoughtful and the sensitive such changes can be bewildering. Wilfrid Ward in his biography quoted letters from Cardinal Newman written within a few hours of one another on the same subject depicting an entire change of feeling. Intellectually as steadfast as the Rock of Gibraltar, Newman's feelings were as variable as the wind. "Sensation is sensation," said Dr. Johnson.

So it was with Browning, who had, like Newman, a deeply intuitive outlook, an intense sensitivity. His wife compared his feelings to the black and white of a chessboard. He could long for Florence yet never return there, could hate London and linger on, could feel that not even an angel's bidding would drag him to a country house yet thoroughly enjoy himself at Belton, Loch Luichart, or Hatfield.

"Frenetic to be free" in one mood, he would in another fasten on himself the bonds of society.

William Allingham had treasured a sad little note from Browning written more than two years after Elizabeth's death. In his profound desolation he was delaying and postponing the things he should be doing: "There seem so many and such long years before one." But, busy diarist that he was, Allingham described a year later a visit to Warwick Crescent after which they walked together to the Underground: "He spoke of his own poems—would rather write music—longs to be a sculptor: 'If we could only live six hundred years, or have two lives even.'"

Thinking of Elizabeth and the past, he felt life ahead infinitely dreary; thinking of his powers and their exercise, he felt life limited in opportunity only by the inexorable limits of time.

His fellow poets were certainly not Society with a big S, but I fancy they sometimes became one of the elements that drove him into it. When Jowett spoke of Browning as the only perfectly sensible poet he knew he was putting his finger on a truth, or at least a valuable half truth. He might perhaps have added Matthew Arnold, but Arnold was of course only a part-time poet: he was a government inspector of schools, he was a brilliant essayist, he was very much a man of the world.

There was a smoothness about Society which made it easier to live in than the world of letters. Politeness was mostly taken for granted, temperament not commonly obtruded. Above all Browning could remain on the surface. The poets, especially the lesser ones, often appear to have had no surface and their exposed depths are remarkably turbulent.

How could Browning have guessed, for instance, that Dante Gabriel Rossetti, with whom he had been on excellent terms, would convince himself that *Fifine at the Fair* was an attack on him? The idea, says William Rossetti, was a sheer delusion born of the chloral and whiskey his brother was taking in vast quantities in a vain struggle against insomnia. That this explanation is correct seems confirmed by the fact that Gabriel saw Lewis Carroll's *Hunting of the Snark* as an attack— as well as by his having broken at the same time with Swinburne, with whom he had had for years a warm friendship. "I shall take every precaution," wrote the puzzled Swinburne to William, "against a meeting. But no man can love his friend more than I love Gabriel."

The friendship with Browning was far less intimate, owing chiefly to the long residence abroad, but hardly less cordial. Of their London visit of 1855 Rossetti had written to William Allingham that Robert and Elizabeth were some time in London, "where I saw them a good many times, and indeed may boast of some intimacy with the glorious Robert." He was reading and rereading the "magnificent series" of *Men and Women*: "they'll bear lots of squeezing yet."

Taking the book with him to be autographed, he "spent some most delightful time with Browning at Paris, both in the evenings and at the Louvre, where (and throughout conversation) I found his knowledge of early Italian art beyond that of anyone I ever met,—*encyclopedically* beyond that of Ruskin himself. What a jolly thing is *Old Pictures at Florence* [sic]!"

He met Milsand, "a miraculous French critic," at the Brownings', and also Sarianna, who "performed the singular female feat of copying *Sordello* for him, to which some of its eccentricities may possibly be referred." Also there was old Mr. Browning, "a complete oddity—with a real genius for drawing . . . fancy the father of Browning!—and as innocent as a child."

Browning holds a large place in *Letters of Dante Gabriel Rossetti to William Allingham*. A year later we read: "The Brownings are long gone back now, and with them one of my delights—an evening resort where I never felt unhappy. How large a part of the real world, I wonder, are those two small people? —Taking meanwhile so little room in any railway carriage, and hardly needing a double bed at the inn." ("Hardly" perhaps—but Elizabeth had written to Arabel of bad nights in those uncomfortable Paris lodgings: "Robert and I have one bed to sleep in—meant to hold one.")

William Rossetti sought Browning out on his return to London, and in August 1863 Gabriel writes of how, Ruskin visiting him, "Browning was here at the same time, very jolly indeed, and stayed and walked many times round the room, and many times stood still, with his hands in his pockets and his eyes wide open."

In a postscript to a letter beginning "Many are Xmas Nuisances," he wrote to Allingham in 1868:

How do you like The Ring and the Book? It is full of wonderful work, but it seems to me that, whereas other poets are the more liable to get incoherent the more fanciful their starting-point happens to be, the thing that makes Browning drunk is to give him a dram of prosaic reality, and unluckily this time the "gum-tickler" is less like pure Cognac than 7 Dials gin. Whether the consequent evolutions will be bearable to their proposed extent without the intervening walls of the station-house to tone down their exuberance may be dubious. This *entre nous.*

Rossetti's view changed as Book after Book was published. In three letters to Browning in January, February, and March, 1869, he grew more and more enthusiastic. Caponsacchi was "the greatest thing you have ever done." But Pompilia is "as noble and lovely as Caponsacchi." And the Pope "must be admitted as the greatest piece of sustained work in the whole cycle of your writing."

Interesting too is his delight in the lawyers "both admirable and astonishingly individual," Hyacinthus recalling especially "the domestic life of my childhood, passed wholly among Italians though in England."

The kinship with Browning felt by Rossetti at this date may well have been compounded of the Italian streak in the feelings and imagination of both and of the aching loss each was experiencing in the death of his wife. For Rossetti concluded:

And highest of all is the fact that it is to the inmost centre of the emotion that the mind reverts in closing the book, and finds itself still gazing with Caponsacchi on the "lady, young, tall, beautiful, strange and sad," and still thrilling to those all-expressive words of his:

> You see, we are
> So very pitiable she and I,
> Who had conceivably been otherwise.

It is understandable after such letters that Browning should have sent him *Fifine at the Fair* on publication with no expectation of the wound it would inflict.

Indeed it is not clear why it should have been wounding. One guess is that Rossetti felt it as an attack upon his own poem "Jenny." Gabriel's brother William and his niece Helen, who wrote her uncle's life, are right, I think, in seeing the root of his trouble in the Epilogue to *Fifine*, not in the poem itself.[1]

Rossetti's wife, Elizabeth Siddall, had died, tragically; he had come home to find her dead, with an empty bottle of laudanum by her side. In a paroxysm of grief the widower had laid his unpublished poems in the grave "between her cheek and her beautiful hair." Friends (and his own desires) later persuaded him to an exhumation after which he "began," says Evelyn Waugh in *Rossetti: His Life and His Works*, "the hideous task of piecing together his work from among the stains and worm-holes of seven and a half years in the grave." Regretting it almost from the first, he came to feel that the act had brought a curse upon his work.

He had taken up spiritualism with the same avidity as Elizabeth Barrett. His niece thinks he might have read one line in the *Fifine* Epilogue—"Darker arts which almost struck despair in me"—as referring to his own attempts to make mediumistic contact with his wife. Most critics see this poem as Browning's cry of longing for reunion with Elizabeth, but there are those who see its He and She as Don Juan and his Elvire. There were phrases in it which fitted Rossetti's case.

And he was in a mood to be especially suspicious. Buchanan's attack on his "Jenny," in an article entitled "The Fleshly School of Poetry— Mr. D. G. Rossetti," had maddened him, causing him to see conspiracy everywhere. It had appeared in the *Contemporary Review* of October 1871 and was answered by Rossetti in the *Athenaeum* of December. Buchanan had concealed himself under the pseudonym of Thomas Maitland, and Rossetti called his own article "The Stealthy School of Criticism."

Robert Buchanan was a Scot whose father had started a successful newspaper in Glasgow. Growing ambitious, he tried to extend into other cities and ended in bankruptcy. Young Robert came to London to seek a fortune, which after many years of writing poetry, novels and plays he found, and in his turn dissipated. David Gray came too, Buchanan's close friend, son of a poor weaver imagining himself another Keats. Gray died of "consumption" after a night spent in Hyde Park, where the only clothes he had got wet through, followed by an ill-heated lodging, with one thin blanket on his bed, and cracks in the walls through which the winds blew. Back in Scotland he wrote his own epitaph:

> Below lies one whose name was traced in sand,
> He died, not knowing what it was to live:
> ... There is life with God
> In other kingdom of a sweeter air;
> In Eden every flower is blown. Amen

Through his friends Gray lived to see in proof one page of his own poetry, and Buchanan later wrote a memoir of a man singularly dear to him. The poems had small success and were referred to by Swinburne as a "poor little book." For that date the phrase was a mild one—Buchanan compared Swinburne in the *Athenaeum* to the Gito of Petronius and William Rossetti retorted that Buchanan was "a poor and pretentious poetaster."

"From that instant," says Buchanan, "I considered myself free to strike at the whole coterie." Later he came to regard his attack on the morality of Rossetti's poems as absurd, but at this date, though he admitted his desire for revenge, the "Fleshly School" article had not, he said, been "conscientiously dishonest."

Tennyson had (according to Buchanan) described Rossetti's sonnet "Nuptial Sleep" as "the filthiest thing he ever read." And, though apparently unable to remember any definite remark of Browning's, Buchanan claimed his agreement "in private conversation." Browning seems, Waugh comments, "to have given both sides reasons to quote him as their supporter," and it may be that his mind was uncertain and his sympathies divided in what was not a simple question. For it was from quite wide-minded people that protests came against what was so wholly out of keeping with the *mores* of the period:

H

> Their bosoms sundered with the opening start
> of married flowers to either side outspread
> From the knit stem. . . .

Not precisely the thing for an annual keepsake or a drawing-room table, though picked out by Swinburne for special praise.

Rossetti had sent the poems to Browning, who remembered vividly, as he returned thanks, "the sympathy" his friend had given him, "beginning at a time when I got few enough gifts of the sort." At that period he had also delighted Rossetti by reading aloud "That 'er Blessed Damozel." He wrote a letter of thanks for the new volume in which he recalled this past, spoke of already knowing well some of the poems, praising, yet mingling criticism with his praise: ". . . here is a book and a delight. Go on and give us another and another. I cannot enjoy the personifications, —Love as a youth, encircling you with his arms and wings, gives me a turn,—and a few archaisms in sentiment and expression please me less than they probably do others."

There should not he felt be "abdication of the critical faculty" even with a friend; but "the main is masterly and conclusive . . . of your right to all the honours in poetry as in painting."

Two months had passed before Browning had occasion to answer Isa Blagden's query as to what he thought of the poems and his reply is quoted with pained astonishment by Rossetti's niece, Helen Rossetti Angeli. But Browning's criticisms were not like Buchanan's. There is not a word about "filthiness": what he dislikes is the "*scented*" quality in Rossetti's poems—"like trifles of various sorts you take out of a cedar or sandal-wood box . . . the effeminacy of his school,—the men that dress up like women,—that use obsolete forms, too, and archaic accentuations."

He goes on to repeat what he had said to Rossetti himself, but with stronger emphasis "I hate 'Love' as a lubberly naked young man putting his arms here and his wings there, about a pair of lovers,—a fellow they would kick away, in the reality. Good-bye [he ends], for I am getting ill-natured."

Apart from "The Fleshly School of Poetry" Buchanan seems hardly worth writing about today, but he is interesting as a laboratory specimen of the difference between memories of the past and letters written when that past was the present. In the memories incorporated by his sister-in-law Harriet Jay in her biography Buchanan relates his first meeting with Browning: "George Eliot took me aside and said smiling, 'Well are you disappointed?' . . . My reply was candour itself."

Not only was he disappointed then at the "commonplace" man lacking the romance he had expected, holding "essentially the opinions of a man in good society," but Browning, he declared, had fawned upon him and made much of his poetry while "I had powerful organs at my command." When his value as a reviewer dropped Browning had dropped him.

The letters, on the other hand, show Buchanan approaching Browning after this meeting (in 1864) first for help over a pension for Gray's parents—("your answer is just what I expected—kind, hearty, generous"), next sending him a volume of his own poetry—"if (after perusal) you find it worth while to say a true word about it I shall be the gainer." Buchanan's books went regularly to Browning and soon he is asking permission to call, and begging for his wife the privilege of shaking hands "with one she adores for my sake." He asks for a copy of Volumes I and II of *The Ring and the Book* "bound up with my name in the front. I want them as an heirloom." He has of course reviewed them. "I hope I have said nothing stupid or false." And in another letter: "Go on I say and do not weary—you grow richer and greater, wealthier and superber of soul. But after all be merciful—what the devil are we pygmies to do?"

Browning invited him and his wife to lunch, went at his request to Buchanan's readings of his own poetry—and praised them. Buchanan borrowed money from him: "Take this affair in your finest spirit—in trust and poetic brotherhood . . . how much would I not do for *you*?" Another letter appeared to show Browning instrumental in helping in a "Pension" matter—"the money is a boon indeed."

Wanting to dedicate to Browning *Napoleon Fallen*, Buchanan writes reassuring him on the line he is taking, "Shall I, who have been howled at for finding brothers and sisters among whores and thieves, hurl epithets as some have done at a tyrant overthrown? I cannot describe with what loathing and horror I have read such verses as those called 'Intercession' by that conscienceless and miserable insanity, little Swinburne."

Browning refused the dedication but praised the poem as "full of power and music." He went on, "I see my fancies or fears that you might treat in your undoubted right the main actor after a fashion repugnant to my feelings were vain enough. I think more savagely *now* of the man, and should say so if needed. I wrote, myself, a monologue in his name twelve years ago, and never could bring the printing to my mind as yet. One day perhaps."

That day came in the following year. But meanwhile Buchanan had begged for another loan, for five of Elizabeth's poems to include in an anthology, for an article from Browning's pen for a new periodical. He was alarmed when "one of these insects" from "The Fleshly School of Poetry . . . stung him" with the suggestion that *he* wanted to wound Browning: "Instead of taking their punishment like men, they are using every effort to blacken their critic. But all I want to know is have they been saying anything to Robert Browning. . . ."[2]

Browning doubtless enjoyed good reviews, but the tedious quality of these letters, the constant mixture of demands and adulation, would surely have bored if not sickened a more patient man than he: One can hardly feel that the desire for reviews would account for his persistent kindness.

Swinburne regarded Buchanan as an "unutterable author," whose verse was "calculated rather to turn the stomach than to move the heart," and he discovered that the pseudonym Maitland under which he had attacked the "Fleshly School" was only one of several protecting him even when he reviewed his own books and "paid pathetic tribute to Buchanan."[3]

"Damn the minor poets," wrote Swinburne, after William Rossetti had told him he must not use a title for a book almost the same as one of William Allingham's. "What right have they to call their titles (or their souls) their own, if *we* condescend to find any use for them?"

William Allingham comes into the same category as Buchanan of minor poet, but there could be no greater contrast in character. There was in this Anglo-Irishman no faintest shadow of conceit or self-seeking. He was a born disciple who felt his natural place was at the feet of the great. As we have seen he began his career in Her Majesty's Customs office but passed thence into the world of letters, where he made many friendships, a close one with Browning, a closer yet with Tennyson. Like Froude, he gave himself to the service of Carlyle, walking with him, and listening to him.

He jots down notes on them all and on their friends and relatives. Miss Helen Shelley had said to him, "After Shelley, Byron and Scott you know, one cannot care about other poets."

"Somebody had once read to her a poem of Tennyson's," notes Allingham, "which she liked, but she could not remember what it was. It seemed doubtful that she had ever heard of Browning. . . . When I mentioned Tennyson's poetry, Sir Percy said fellows had bored him a good deal with it at one time."

Tennyson had told Browning that "Sludge" was too long. "I hope," replied Browning, " 'he thought it too long!'—that is, Sludge when the confession was forced from him."

The journal goes on from year to year, recording how "B. and I chatted till near one"; "Cab to Browning's, invited to luncheon, R.B. (grayer)." He is "the great Robert." But: "too often a want of solid basis for R.B.'s brilliant and astounding cleverness. . . . He has been and still is very dear to me. But I can no longer commit myself to his hands in faith and trust." The greatest poets—Dante, Shakespeare— are not "enigmatic in the same sense. . . . If you suspect and sometimes find out, that riddles presented to you with sphinxian solemnity have *no* answers that really fit them, your curiosity is apt to fall towards freezing point."

The ambivalence in Allingham's view of Browning noted in Vol. I suggests something that Edmund Gosse would later attack—a tendency "to treat this vehement and honest poet as if he were a sort of Marcus Aurelius and John the Baptist rolled into one. . . . Well, I did not know that holy monster."

But to disciples of this kind, Browning's careless speech, his occasional self-contradiction, above all his real inability to translate his poems into prose, became serious stumbling blocks.

Swinburne was twenty-five years Browning's junior and a late-comer into the Pre-Raphaelite group. He had been at Balliol and was a special protégé of Monckton Milnes, to whom Browning wrote anxiously in 1863 about a report that on *his* judgment Chapman had rejected a volume of Swinburne's poetry. He had heard Swinburne read aloud a few: "I thought them moral mistakes redeemed by much intellectual ability." But these were all he knew. He liked Swinburne personally and it was, he felt, unfair "to quote my blame of two or three little pieces given on a demand for unqualified praise which was impossible—as the reason for rejecting a whole bookful of what may be real poetry, for aught I am aware . . . he only uses my witnessing when he wants to cover his own conviction."

Many years later, in 1883, Browning wrote to an unknown correspondent: "There are many English poets well worthy of your study —it is difficult, indeed, would be presumptuous in me to seem, by naming a few, to exclude the rest. Tennyson, Matthew Arnold, Swinburne, William Morris,—nobody is wronged by the mention of their pre-eminence."[4]

This letter is interesting for its inclusion of William Morris and Swinburne. Was the second put in from a sense of justice toward one already classed among the great, or did Browning's feelings go up and down in his judgment of poetry as in more personal matters? There seems hardly a poet who does not thus waver in judging his contemporaries; they all have to go back to Shakespeare, Dante, or Chaucer to be fixed in their faith or their unfaith.

To Isa Blagden he wrote in March 1870 of Swinburne's "*minimum* of thought and idea in the *maximum* of words and phraseology." But he continued to like him and wrote with pleasure "Swinburne came and paid me a call of four hours about last week." And Swinburne, confined to bed after a slight accident, received "with great cordiality" says William Rossetti, "Browning's attention in calling."

A few years earlier Swinburne had written to Milnes of "the Brownings and other blatant creatures begotten on the slime of the modern chaos"—but indeed of all the changing moods expressed by eminent Victorians in their letters his were among the most changeable—and the most violent in either direction.

With Jowett in Scotland he reported Browning coming over "in high feather. I have just read his new poem—it has very fine things in it, especially in the part about Hercules—much finer than anything said about him by Euripides.—But the pathos of the subject is too simple and downright for Browning's analytic method."

The conversation among the three men was, said another visitor, "animated and interesting. . . . Who shall tell of Swinburne's paradoxes and hyperboles . . . and how he and the Master capped quotations from Boswell." (But Jowett, Swinburne says, objected "and that very strongly and regretfully, to the tone of personal and general reverence for the character and genius of Carlyle which disfigures my said pamphlet.")

There was much to draw the two poets together as well as much to drive them apart, but they seem, though meeting occasionally, not to have known each other well when in 1875 Swinburne, in a book on George Chapman, paid a tribute to Browning so important that it must be discussed at length in a postscript to this chapter.

Reminding his readers that "To do justice to any book which deserves any other sort of justice than that of the fire or the waste-paper basket, it is necessary to read it in the fit frame of mind," Swinburne begged them to do such justice to this difficult but important poet. "The proper mood in which to study for the first time a book of Mr. Browning's is the freshest, clearest, most active mood of the mind in its brightest and keenest hours of work."

When Browning answered with warm thanks Swinburne further endeared himself by the confession that many years earlier he had failed an examination at Oxford because "the hard hearts of examiners would not have accepted a declamation of Salinguerra's soliloquy as compensation for a sum in rule-of-three."

He continued to read Browning and usually to send in return his own latest book. He hoped his friend John Nicoll admired "'A Confession,' which I think is in his very finest and subtlest tragic style, and the hideously-named, but wonderfully suggestive little poem 'Bifurcation.' "

Two letters followed the appearance of *Agamemnon*. To Browning, Swinburne wrote on October 24, 1877: "Of course the fine scholarship and subtle dexterity of the version is far beyond my poor praise; but (e.g.) I was especially amazed at such wonderful instances of triumphant success in the all-but impossible as the 'transcript' of the brief choral strain beginning 'What evil O woman. . . .' " (Swinburne quoted in Greek.)

But in January he was writing to John Nicoll: "A presentation copy of Browning's *Agamemnon* was the last straw that broke this camel's back. I wrote a line of thanks, and went straight to bed. It is beyond belief—or caricature. Some devil possesses him whenever he touches on anything Hellenic."

One cannot entirely account for such a change of tone by the difference between speaking to or of an author, and it is not surprising that Swinburne became afraid that he had offended Browning. Perhaps, he wrote to Lord Houghton (Milnes), his letter of thanks for the *Agamemnon* had gone astray, or Browning had not received his own latest volume. This regular exchanging of gift copies was perhaps a mistake in its forcing of a favorable opinion.

It may have been some outside influence acting upon Swinburne— Jowett's perhaps—or the feeling that only an Oxford man could be a first-rate Greek scholar; it may have been merely the difference between writing before and after dinner that sent their temperatures up and down about each other's poetry. There were besides changes in their social relations.

"Oh! if we were not now unhappily on friendly terms," wrote Swinburne at one point, "*what* a Thesmophoriazusae I might, could, and should, and *would* write on *him!* . . . the new Socrates-Euripides of London Society!"

The ups and down between them are far more entertaining than the real friendships between Browning and Rossetti, Browning and Tennyson, partly because Swinburne was more amusing than either.

He parodied everyone—including himself. His "Nephelidia" must be the highest point self-parody ever reached. But unluckily one needs more initiation than ever came my way into four-letter words to understand the parodies he made of both Brownings. (The editor of his letters has substituted polite asterisks throughout!)

It is curious to compare these parodies with Swinburne's attitude toward Browning's own use of coarse words, in the *Agamemnon* especially, and in other of his later poems. "I have been wanting," he writes, "for some time to have a cut at the new cult of the 'Chaunoprokt'—as Browning alone has the audacity to say." To be sure, he notes, so had Chapman and Shakespeare, and one cannot be certain from this letter whether he admires or blames this audacity. But protesting strongly to John Morley at finding the word "copulation" changed into "union" in an article of his own in *The Fortnightly Review* he says: "Where I cannot use the right word, I will use none. I do not ask for the license of Shakespeare and of Browning. . . . I do not want like them to talk of 'open—xxxxxs,' à Dieu ne plaise."

A letter to Lord Houghton, after a *Times* article which stated that there were no living poets in England, asks whether "Mr. Tennyson and Mr. Browning" had in consequence

> "Shaken hands in death" by shutting themselves up in a hermetically sealed room with a pan of ignited charcoal between them? and that Mr. Thomas Carlyle, regardless alike of his years, of the weather, and of the law of the land prohibiting indecent exposure, has been seen dancing a Highland fling, in a state of total nudity and partial intoxication, down and up the whole length of Cheyne Row, Chelsea, with a Scotch cutty-pipe in his mouth and the Scotch fiddle on his back, by way of expressing as in a Phyrrhic war-dance the triumph of an "inarticulate poet" over the downfall of the last articulate individual of that ilk?

Funny too, though not consciously so, are Swinburne's terribly dignified letters to Browning when he and Frederick Furnivall became engaged in mortal combat concerning one Halliwell-Phillips, with whom Furnivall was fighting one of the everlasting wars of experts about Shakespeare. The point to which academic disagreements among distinguished men can develop is always amazing—and in Victorian days the sky was the limit.

Swinburne having written a skit about the "New Shakspere Society" founded by Furnivall with Browning as president, Furnivall in return referred to him and another of the group, Halliwell-Phillips, as Pigsbrook and Co., the word Pigsbrook being derived from the Anglo-Saxon words *swin* and *burn*. Swinburne in return called Furnivall Brothels-Dyke (from the Latin *fornix* and *vallum*); or alternatively Brothelsbank Flunkivall. Of all the letters that followed, Browning's alone (to Halliwell-Phillips) is both brief and dignified. He had not seen Swinburne's attack, his own position was

> purely honorary, as I stipulated before accepting it, nor have I been able hitherto to attend any one of its meetings; and should I ever do so, my first impulse will be to invoke the spirit of "gentle Shakespeare" that no wrong be done in his name to a member of the brotherhood of students combining to do him suit and service.

This letter satisfied nobody. Halliwell-Phillips published it in a pamphlet that attacked impartially Browning and Swinburne, while Swinburne wrote to A. B. Grosart describing Furnivall as a "brothel-lacky" and "bastard of Thersites." Browning by remaining in any kind of association with him "proves (in my opinion and I presume in yours) that he has not the feelings of a gentleman."

This was a common exit line of those "better born" than he when Browning annoyed them, but Swinburne was carrying on the quarrel in spirited fashion. To Browning he wrote two days later that Furnivall, "Founder and Director of a Society of which you are, actually or nominally, the President," had called him "a person of damaged character. . . . If this imputation is true, it follows of course that I am unfit to hold any intercourse or keep up any acquaintance with you. If it is a lie, it follows equally of course that no person who remains in any way or in any degree associated with the writer of that pamphlet is fit to hold any intercourse or keep up any acquaintance with me."

Browning's answer was sent by return of post—to be answered again by return. Evidently he had tried once more with singular unsuccess to throw oil on very turbid water. Swinburne was highly indignant. He had *not* called on Browning

"to take my part." I have never in any case called upon any man to do anything of the kind. Having been publicly and personally insulted in a manner too infamous and blackguardly for description, I did call upon you—as any man with any sense of honour or self-respect would in my place be bound to call upon you, or upon any other acquaintance—to let me know whether or not, after this, your name is to remain in any way publicly associated with one which in my humble opinion it is degrading if necessary, and disgraceful if unnecessary, for a gentleman to pronounce, to transcribe, or to remember. . . .

I have no such impertinent and preposterous pretension—need I say so?—as would be that of prescribing or suggesting to you any course of conduct. But it is obvious that in addressing the President of the "New Shakspere" Society, I could no longer without degradation subscribe myself as yours very sincerely, A. C. Swinburne.

Swinburne was given to strong language. Rossetti, on whom he had "lavished . . . deep, devoted and unselfish affection," had become, after his unhappy alienation, "the meanest, poorest, most abject and unmanly nature." Yet a reasonable number of months—in the case of Browning from February 1881 to December 1882—could bring about a partial revulsion. Browning did not give up either Furnivall or the society founded by him, yet on December 5 Swinburne was telling Nicoll that though he thought of Browning "but a little more favourably than you, . . . in short conversation tête a tête I have found him a very delightful companion, and not too overpoweringly talkative considering the really marvellous variety of really interesting knowledge he has to display—and to display with real mother-wit and natural eloquence."

Furnivall was dangerous both as friend and foe—and so was the presidency of a literary society. Thurman Hood, editing his letters, believes that this quarrel was one of Browning's reasons for refusing in

1885 the presidency of the Shelley Society. Clearly it was not one he could express to its founder—and there were other reasons too. He wrote to Furnivall:

> You are, as always, very good in wishing to invest me with new honors, but the acceptance of this last is impossible; it would be tantamount to a profession of belief that what the Browning Society has done so helpfully in my case—mine, who stood in need of it— should now be repeated in the case of Shelley who, for years, has tasked the ingenuity of his admirers to leave no scrap of his writing nor incident of his life without its illustration by every kind of direct or cross light—not, I very much suspect, to the advantage of either. For myself I painfully contrast my notions of Shelley the *man* and Shelley, well, even the *poet,* with what they were sixty years ago, when I only had his works, for a certainty, and took his character on trust.[5]

I discussed in my first volume the curious idea of Browning's "be-trayal" of Shelley, but it is perhaps worth adding here that it was some forty years *after* the "betrayal" that his feelings showed any real change. He had still been a wholehearted admirer when, as I relate in my first volume, he wrote the Introduction to the spurious letters and tran-scribed and restored "The Indian Serenade" at the baths of Sisted.

After discussing with him in 1869 the tangled story of the deser-tion of Harriet, Swinburne wrote to Rossetti: "Now of course Browning loves Shelley even as much as you and I do."

Reaching his seventies Browning would confess himself (to Mrs. FitzGerald) sick and tired of the subject, feeling "an increasing irrita-tion at the poor silly boy." No guilt sense here—but a sign (perhaps) of what Herford calls a slackening of the poetic nerve noticeable in Browning's old age.

Yet the word "boy" is significant. For the last recorded utterance of Browning on the subject was to a friend in Venice, D. S. Curtis, stress-ing the tragedy that the dead Shelley was still in early youth.

"He was coming out of it when he died. And had he lived he might have been—Anything!"

It was left to Francis Thompson and Lytton Strachey to amplify this, but each only in an essay. None of Shelley's biographers, says Strachey, has recognized that Shelley was still an adolescent, nineteen when he married Harriet, twenty-one when he deserted her for Mary. Strachey hates alike the "distressed self-righteousness of Matthew Arnold" and the "solemn adoration of Professor Dowden. . . . Shelley's fire and air . . . transmuted into Professor Dowden's cotton-wool and rose-water is a subtler revenge of the world's upon the most radiant of its enemies."

The nature of Shelley's world enmity was very different from that of another poet whose time relation to Browning was much that of Browning's to Shelley.

It was tragic indeed that Gerard Manley Hopkins should have joined a religious order in one of its narrowest periods. He had already in boyhood and youth distressed his mother by his tendency to asceticism. In his journal of 1866 he wrote Lent resolutions which included "Meat only once a day. *No verses in Passion week or on Friday* [Italics mine] . . . Ash Wednesday and Good Friday bread and water." As a Jesuit, Hopkins was not content simply to live by the strict enough rule of the order, but made his own additions to its severity. The cramping of immense possibilities by such deplorable "mortifications" as a closing of his eyes to the beauties of nature on one of the rare walks breaking the monotony of his daily life, and his destruction of a poetry, so often the highest prayer, make one weep. Temperament and training alike set up also an attitude blocking communication with the other poets of his era. For Swinburne he had simply abhorrence and scorn. His feeling about Browning was more mixed. So few people, he said, "have style, except individual style or manner—not Tennyson, nor Swinburne nor Morris, not to name the scarecrow misbegotten Browning crew." He then partly relents, remarking "The Brownings are very fine too in their ghastly way."

W. H. Gardner in his *Gerard Manley Hopkins (1844–1889) A*

Study of Poetic Idiosyncrasy in Relation to Poetic Tradition who quotes
these remarks from his letters sees Hopkins among the many modern
poets who later developed what "were bold innovations in Browning.
. . . He had forced a new diction into the old metres, and thereby
brought the everyday moods within the scope of poetry." There was in
Browning what he calls a "Hopkinsian" streak, and Gardner notes with
surprise that in his list of earlier poets who sometimes used sprung
rhythm Hopkins omits Browning (also Donne, Blake, Shelley, Meredith, Arnold, and Christina Rossetti). But Gardner sees a quite special
influence in Browning's compound words and epithets: fawn-skin-
dappled, green-flesh, many-tinkling.

> By the many hundred years *red-rusted,*
> Rough *iron-spiked,* ripe *fruit-o'er-crusted.*

Hopkins may have been half unconscious of the influence, deeming
Browning "not really a poet," having "the pearls without the string;
rather one should say raw nuggets and rough diamonds." He admires
"the touches, the details but the general effect, the whole, offends, I
think it repulsive."

The climax comes with *The Ring and the Book:* "As the tale was
not edifying and one of our people who had been reviewing it said that
further on it was coarser, I did not see, without a particular object,
sufficient reason for going on with it."

It may seem strange to introduce in a biography of Browning a man
he never met and whose poetry was printed only after both were dead.
Yet the immense originality of these two men and their affinity is of
great interest—above all perhaps in the light of their overwhelmingly
different experience. Browning had every human advantage: fulfillment in marriage, friendships, knowledge of other lands. Hopkins had
condemned himself to the narrowest and most monotonous of lives in
his experiences of men, places, daily labor. "Not edifying," said the
pious Jesuit teacher of a book that should have thrilled the poet through
every nerve.

And yet here was no minor but a major poet. And so was John of the
Cross.

2 ARNOLD AND TENNYSON

"What a brute you were," wrote Matthew Arnold to Clough in 1848 or 1849, "to tell me to read Keats' Letters. However it is over now: and reflexion resumes her power over agitation.

"What harm he has done in English Poetry. As Browning is a man with a moderate gift passionately desiring movement and fulness, and obtaining nothing but a confused multitudinousness, so Keats with a very high gift, is yet also consumed by this desire: and cannot produce the truly living and moving, as his conscience keeps telling him."

Ten years later, sending his own tragedy *Merope* to a friend, he wrote: "Make Browning look at it, if he is at Florence; one of the very best antique fragments I know is a fragment of a Hippolytus by him."

This was of course "Artemus Prologizes," and perhaps *Men and Women* had changed Arnold's view of Browning since he was increasingly realizing his intellect. Criticizing Tennyson's *Idylls*, he wrote to his sister:

> The real truth is that Tennyson, with all his temperament and artistic skill, is deficient in intellectual power; and no modern poet can make very much of this business unless he is pre-eminently strong in this. . . . However, it would not do for me to say this about Tennyson, though gradually I mean to say boldly the truth about a great many English celebrities. . . .

And assessing his own position in what has been christened the "Big Three of Victorian Poetry," he wrote to his mother in 1869: "It might be fairly urged that I have less poetical sentiment than Tennyson, and less intellectual vigour and abundance than Browning; yet, because I have perhaps more of a fusion of the two than either of them, and have more regularly applied that fusion to the main line of modern development, I am likely enough to have my turn."

His "turn" has been a fairly long one, though perhaps passing away today, but the interesting thing about these letters is how different they sound from the general "sweetness and light" that Arnold appears to have shed in the world which was both his and Browning's. The two men were already friends, and in an article in the *Cornhill* John Drinkwater collected letters from Arnold to Browning and inscriptions in gift books from one to the other.[6] Arnold begs for the name of Pen's music master "for my little boy"; he supplies an introduction to an eminent lawyer when Browning is writing *The Ring and the Book*. He sends repeated invitations to dinner. He describes how one invitation grew from small beginnings. He had invited Milsand and one other friend "then I found [he tells his mother] Milsand was staying with Browning, and I added Browning." Meeting him at a lecture he found Lord Houghton was a friend of Milsand's and asked him too. Finally the party sat down ten in number. "This is how," comments Arnold, "one's resolution of having no more dinner parties gets set aside."

Browning's letters to Isa Blagden contain a great many allusions to Arnold, but they are almost all allusions to one poem, "Empedocles on Etna," and most of them to one verse of that poem. The verse belonged to the friendship between Isa and Browning, and to a dream he cherished of an old age near her in Italy.

> And there, they say, two bright and aged snakes,
> Who once were Cadmus and Harmonia,
> Bask in the glens or on the warm sea-shore,
> In breathless quiet, after all their ills.

There are fifteen mentions of this poem in *Dearest Isa*, Browning writing twice of his delight in the fact that Arnold had restored it to his collected poetry because of his brother poet's admiration for it. And both the admiration and its effect on Arnold are the more interesting because of the note it strikes, so different from Browning's own "dominant's persistence." The despair in "Empedocles" was indeed alien to his philosophy, but its power and beauty would appeal not to his poet's ear only but to his intense realization of the dark side of life which faith could—but might not—conquer. Guido may have despaired, but the Pope still prayed and hoped for him.

Browning and Arnold belonged to the same club, the Athenaeum, and to the same college, Balliol. They moved in the same intellectual world, although Arnold with his family ties went less into general society. They met frequently enough to explain the shortness of Arnold's letters. But with his tendency to destruction it seems interesting that Browning should have kept them at all. And whenever he mentioned Arnold it was with affection as well as admiration. He was always "dear Mat. Arnold. . . . I like the man," he wrote, "as much as his poems." In Glanville's *Vanity of Dogmatising,* inscribed to him by Arnold, he wrote: "It contains the story which suggested to M. Arnold his exquisite poem 'The Gipsey-Scholar' [sic]." And, criticizing Trollope for working too hard, he quotes: "Then God said 'Thou fool this night shall thy soul be required of thee: and then whose will be those things thou hast laid up!' " He goes on: "I was pleased to hear Mat. Arnold say much the same thing some time ago. 'Build a house? No, I am a traveller in this world,—only need a tent.' "

Both Arnold and Browning were, to use a word more common today than in the nineteenth century, totally "committed," though not in precisely the same way.

Arnold's poetical power diminished in middle life. But there was, I think, another reason for this besides time. He wrote in "Dover Beach":

> And we are here as on a darkling plain
> Swept with confused alarms of struggle and fight
> Where ignorant armies clash by night.

Arnold saw more clearly than most of the sociologists one problem to be discussed in the chapter I have called "The Two Nations." How much could the individual achieve in face of the selfishness, blindness, and cruelty which governed the relations between master and man? Must not the State be invoked not to destroy, but to preserve what liberty was left to the wage slave, above all in face of a philosophy leading to the idea that poverty, once called "holy," was on the contrary

I

blameworthy? Industriousness had become enthroned as the first of virtues—and through their industry men became capitalists; if a man succeeded he did so through virtue—the thriftless and unsuccessful were not merely financial but human failures. Dickens brilliantly shows the effect of this attitude in *The Chimes:* Trotty Veck is made by the pompous alderman to believe that he and his fellows suffer because they are fundamentally bad. "Riches," says Lionel Trilling in his deeply interesting *Matthew Arnold,* "once regarded as the enemy of religious life, now became its instrument."

Arnold gave much thought to the possible effects of unbridled liberty (and consequent class warfare) which issued in his book, *Culture and Anarchy,* originally a series of articles in the *Cornhill.*

With all the charm, and even power, in his writing there is in Arnold's prose as in his poetry a sense that he is leading up to a climax which he never quite reaches: "Murmurs and scents of the infinite sea" is one of his loveliest lines but leaves us in the same indeterminate state as the suggestion in *Culture and Anarchy* that the discovery of our best selves will solve all the problems of society.

So now, dreaming of a culture that should include Christianity but become somehow wider and deeper, he did little to overcome the dilemma except to coin phrases that have passed into the language: "Barbarians, Philistines, Populace," "Something not ourselves which makes for righteousness," "Hebraism and Hellenism," trains which only carry men "from an illiberal dismal life at Islington to an illiberal dismal life at Camberwell." But the best-known of his phrases Arnold borrowed from Swift: "Sweetness and light."

The ideal liberal-Christian, deeply cultural attitude could permeate society only if education reached the masses, so it was logical enough in Arnold, as well as a means of acquiring income enough to keep a family, that he should have accepted the position of Inspector of Schools. He took this seriously enough to explore the Continent in search of the best methods of establishing at least universal primary education in England. He had become Professor of Poetry at Oxford in 1857, and been re-elected in 1862. His term ended in 1867 and the last of his lectures formed the first chapter of *Culture and Anarchy.* After this came the abortive attempt to put forward Browning's name for the office. And I fancy Browning's lectures on literature would have been rather different from Arnold's—if we are to judge from his magnificent discussion of Shelley described in my first volume.

After Arnold lost his eldest son in 1868 he wrote to Browning of his gift of *The Ring and the Book* "with its kind—too kind—inscription. . . . It will rouse me and bring me back to life as few other things could. I shall busy myself with it all this next week while I have to sit presiding at a long, weary examination."

The state system was in its infancy and letters from Arnold to his mother show him working for long hours. "A great British school 250 boys, 150 girls, and 150 infants, and the pupil teachers of these schools to examine. . . . I had a perpetual stream of visitors from the town—people interested in the schools." He would work all day, going on to another school on the next. "Biscuits and wine were brought to me where I was," or "getting a biscuit at the station."

No wonder that it helped him to live through this draining commitment of his to read poems giving him the "impression" which he now (erroneously) believed, "your writings from the first have given me, and which the writings of so few other living people give me, that the author is what the French well call a 'grand esprit.'"

But Browning's "commitment" was to poetry: he could not conceive of any other. I half wonder that John Holloway did not choose him among the Victorian sages in his interesting book. But he chose no poets: Arnold was the "sage" of his prose writings. Perhaps also the second Browning would have kept the poet out—that social figure who appeared to brush off altogether the commitment proclaimed by his poetry.

Yet here, as so often, theorizing is challenged by a fact: in Arnold as well as in Browning we see a sharp contrast between the man of his prose writings, his friendships, his profession—and his poetry. The urbane phrases tinged with irony, and then

Empedocles!
Nothing but a devouring flame of thought—
But a naked, eternally restless mind! . . .

In Arnold indeed:

> Somewhat of worldling mingled still
> With bard and sage.

Returning from Arnold's Memorial Service, Browning said to a visitor, "He once told me when I asked why he had not recently written any poetry, that he could not afford to, but that, when he had saved enough, he intended to give up all other work and devote himself to poetry. . . . I wonder if he has turned to it now?" Browning added musingly. No doubt he thought of Arnold, and of himself, as pouring out in the courts of heaven better poetry than they had ever written here below.

The poetic friendship which I think meant most to Browning, which certainly extended over the longest period, was with Alfred Tennyson. Charles Tennyson's biography of his grandfather brings out Browning's affection for this "fine, large-featured, dim-eyed, bronze-coloured, shaggy-headed man" (so Carlyle described him). "I never see enough of Tennyson," Browning wrote to Woolner, "nor get to talk with him about subjects we either of us value at three straws, I suppose, but I always enjoy smelling (even) his tobacco smoke."

Carlyle too enjoyed both Alfred and his smoke. He describes how Tennyson: "Swims outwardly and inwardly, with great composure in an articulate element as of tranquil chaos and tobacco smoke . . . a most restful, brotherly, solid-hearted man."

It is curious that Carlyle, always attacking poetry, seemed so singularly drawn toward poets: and there were indeed elements of likeness between these two favorites of his as well as great differences. Like Browning, Tennyson had determined to be a poet and refused to be deflected from his course. Both were poor men though Tennyson came from a rich family, his grandfather having disinherited his father in favor of a younger brother. The resultant resentment had seriously damaged Alfred's youth, for a father, as capable as Browning's own of instructing and amusing his large family, had brooded on his wrongs and sought consolation in the bottle. Alfred Tennyson had had, however, the inestimable advantage of a university education. He met at Cambridge men who both stimulated his mental development and were able later to forward his career. Yet he suffered, as Browning did, from years of public neglect and abuse. For a long time he shrank altogether from publicity. The attacks were curiously similar—on "obscurity, wilful archaism and affectation." "The Rhapsodies of Insanity," said one reviewer. Fox alone in *The Monthly Repository* gave an enthusiastic reception to *Poems, Chiefly Lyrical,* just three months earlier than his review of *Pauline.*

Tennyson's period of trial was far shorter than Browning's. He was three years older; but by 1839 admiration for him had begun in the United States—and he probably had only himself to blame when it lagged in London, for he had refused to publish new poems or republish the old from fear of a fresh onslaught from the press. In 1842 came two volumes, still, says Charles Tennyson, received "tepidly" by the critics, but winning a circle of warm admirers. His very small fortune Tennyson lost through investing in the unsuccessful invention of a friend; but two of his admirers, Arthur Hallam and Monckton Milnes, supported by Gladstone, persuaded Sir Robert Peel to give him a pension from the Civil List. Carlyle suggested the idea to Milnes, who asked what would his constitutents say—"that he is a poor relation of my own—that the whole affair is a job?"

"Richard Milnes," said Carlyle solemnly, "on the Day of Judgment when the Lord asks you why you didn't get that pension for Alfred Tennyson, it will not do to lay the blame on your constituents. It is you who will be damned."

Browning, seeing Tennyson in these earlier years, felt he needed the care of their common publisher Moxon: it was "the charmingest thing possible." It was at a public dinner, and "he seems to need it all being in truth but a LONG, hazy, kind of man, at least after dinner—yet there is something naive about him—the genius you see too!"

With no *Sordello* to set him back, Tennyson's success became meteoric, culminating in the publication of *In Memoriam,* the immense réclame of which, and its effect on the Prince Consort, brought him the Laureateship in 1850. It was a vast wave of popularity; sales such as poetry has rarely brought, an income rising to a yearly £5,000, £10,000 and more. Critics often remained cold: "Obscurity taken for profoundity," "rampant and rabid bloodthirstiness of soul," said they about *Maud*. This mattered little by the sixties, but the Brownings, in the fifties, after listening to his reading had thought it worthwhile to write to Mrs. Tennyson—"You do not mind [said Elizabeth] the foolish remarks on *Maud* do you? These things are but signs of an advance made, of the tide rising." And Robert added: "God bless you, dear and admirable friends. My wife feels what she says and so do I."

The happiest result of his improved fortunes had been that Alfred Tennyson could marry the remarkable woman with whom Elizabeth had struck up an instant friendship. Arabel, teasing her sister on her penchant for kissing, was told to "observe" that Emily Tennyson's had been the first move. "The two women," says Charles Tennyson, "met like sisters."

Browning must have felt his own loneliness the more keenly as he witnessed the Tennyson union, as perfect as his own, of heart and mind, though there was one difference that perhaps struck neither of them. Tennyson, though not I think a selfish man, was like Carlyle served by his wife while Browning had served Elizabeth. Tennyson's circumstances became easy fairly early: there were servants in plenty, but Emily as well as being his housekeeper was his secretary and waited on him devotedly. When she could not carry on, their son Hallam gave up all career of his own to take her place at his father's side, while Browning was expending all the energy Pen lacked first on his education and then on promoting his career.

When Elizabeth died, Browning had lost something that Tennyson kept to the end—a critic and moderator. It is probably true that Elizabeth did not commonly show him her poems while they were in the making: but he certainly showed her his. Consider how ably she had criticized his work during his courtship and how out of seventy suggestions on one poem, he had accepted all except two. And although she told him his self-criticism was bad and he had better instantly restore any word he struck out he did not, during the time of their marriage, fall into the opposite pit of a morass of verbiage as he later too often did. Elizabeth would naturally, with her fame so far higher than his, have done all in her power to prevent the world from knowing that she had any influence on the man whom she not only loved but rightly recognized as immeasurably greater than herself. And never in Elizabeth's lifetime did Browning *publish* anything like *Pachiarrotto*. Yet compared with Tennyson's attack on a reviewer, James Haines Friswell, who had been, says Charles Tennyson, "peculiarly offensive," *Pacchiarotto* is almost mild. This "would-be poet" the Laureate described as

> Friswell, Pisswell—a liar and a twaddler—
> Pisswell, Friswell—a clown beyond redemption,
> Brutal, personal, infinitely blackguard.

Charles Tennyson surmises that even Emily saw only an "expurgated version" (*how* expurgated?) and that Tennyson's increasing wisdom saved him from publishing it. But of course any wife would have saved him—above all a wise woman like Emily or Elizabeth.

Tennyson's grandson, quoting Sir Harry Taylor, tells us that he alternately desired and detested the publicity brought by his fame. He would complain of a "syncope" in the public when for two days he received no letters. Yet he envied in another mood Shakespeare and Jane Austen, of whom we know only the words: they had never been "ripped open like pigs."

What would he have felt could he have read the article in *The Twentieth Century* for October 1955 in which Mrs. Miller applies to him the same type of criticism with which she had filled a whole book about Browning. Tennyson, she tells us, had learned as a twelve-year-old boy that a woman was "a major source of ill to the man she marries"; what fascinated him was the medieval idealization of men friendships "lover-like in their intensity." This phrase was quoted from C. S. Lewis. "The poet," Mrs. Miller goes on, "was to find in his love for Arthur Hallam the most profound emotional experience of his whole life."[7]

This scarcely fits with Charles Tennyson's more factual account: that for nearly eleven years Alfred and Emily had exchanged intensely loving letters, that it was almost certainly she who had persuaded him to publish *In Memoriam,* and that she had suggested a visit to Arthur Hallam's grave "as a kind of consecration of their marriage." Tennyson said, "The peace of God entered into my life when I married her." And in old age after walking over the downs, when the heather was faded and the ferns bright, he wrote the dedication to his last volume of poetry, offering:

> This and my love together,
> To you that are seventy-seven,
> With a faith as clear as the heights of the June-blue heaven,
> And a fancy as summer-new
> As the green of the bracken mid the gloom of the heather.

Both Browning and Tennyson have been described as lauding one another's poetry to one another and condemning it to their friends— but insofar as this is true it would appear to have been only a condemnation of certain individual poems. And I would like to enter a caveat against criticism which treats the expression of a mood as a considered opinion. Is it really fair to assume that, when—if—Tennyson growled that he could not read the fellow, it was more than a mood? Or that Browning was insincere because at one moment he told Tennyson that his "Grail" idyll was the best of his poems and at another told Isa Blagden that "the old 'Galahad' is to me incomparably better than a dozen centuries of the 'Grail'?" As with William Morris's later poetry the newer Tennyson had, he felt, "the old flavour but not *body.*" A new poem may thus take one back to the old with an astonished recognition of how much better it was. (Of Morris, he writes, "sweet, pictorial, clever always—but a weariness to me by this time. The lyrics were the 'first sprightly runnings.'")

The friendship between these two men was a warm and a lasting one. Charles Tennyson says of his grandfather that by 1864 Browning and Gladstone were "in his inner circle of friendship." When a little later Tennyson "shared" a house in Seamore Place with a relative and

Browning often visited them, he delighted Emily by declaring at the end of their stay that he had not for a long while had so happy a time. Sir Algernon West talks in his *Recollections* of meeting at Watts' old studio, become the Cosmopolitan Club, "Browning and Tennyson between whom no spark of jealousy existed, and Thackeray who never took in the spirit of the place."

The frontispiece of Sir Charles Tennyson's delightful book is a photograph taken by the rather eccentric Mrs. Cameron, who was one of the first to see the possibilities of photography as an art. (My father used to relate the rather painful experience of having his hair grasped by one of her minions to place and keep him in the right position.) And she once draped Browning in a toga—and left him thus enveloped while she sped on some other quest. Tennyson she would soothe by a constant stream of admiration which some of his friends thought enervating and damaging to his work—for she was a close neighbor in the Isle of Wight and saw him almost daily. There was a story that she once took a visitor into Tennyson's bedroom exclaiming "Behold the most beautiful old man on earth."

When someone suggested to Browning that all this adulation was damaging to the poet and his work he disagreed. "After all what harm does she do Alfred? . . . There will always be a buzzing of sillinesses about such a person. Depend on it, nobody has done him the least harm at any time: nobody has more fully found at the beginning what he was born to do,—nor done it more perfectly."[8]

But Jowett, with the professional teacher's instinct which he never lost, was less indulgent. One day Tennyson was inveighing against flatterers and declaring "no flatterer is a friend of mine." My father, who was present, described how Jowett's silence called out from Tennyson the question "Don't you agree with me, Master?" And Jowett answered, "Well Tennyson while you have been talking I have been reflecting that in this house, and in this room, I have seen a good deal of incense offered, and it was not unacceptable."

The good-natured answer "You're always chaffing me" fitted Browning's view of a man essentially unspoiled though of an almost childlike simplicity.

Browning's *Selections* of 1865 were dedicated "To Alfred Tennyson, in poetry consummate and sublime, in friendship noble and sincere."

"Very welcome is the nosegay," wrote Tennyson, "not only for the love in the gift—which makes me, who am physically the most unbumptious of men and authors, proud—but also for its own very peculiar flowerage and fructification, for which I think I have as high a respect as any man in Britain. . . . My wife always remembers you—and another."

Both felt they met too seldom. Browning wrote when Tennyson had been severely ill regretting that "the circumstances of life" never seemed to permit the close neighborhood he would so deeply have valued. And Tennyson was a bad correspondent. After one of Browning's tributes came an undated letter relaying a talk between himself and Emily (whom Browning once said "I love singularly"). She said:

> . . . he has given you a crown of violets.
> H[usband]:   He is the greatest-brained poet in England. Violets
> fade; he has given me a crown of gold.
> W.:   Well, I meant the Troubadour crown of golden violets. . . .
> H.:   Then I'll go up and smoke my pipe and write to him.
> W.:   You'll go up and concoct an imaginary letter over your pipe,
> which you'll never send.
> H.:   Yes, I will. I'll report our talk. . . .

And so he did.

POSTSCRIPT
SWINBURNE ON CHAPMAN
AND BROWNING

We meet frequently with a quotation about Browning from Swinburne's study of George Chapman, Elizabethan poet and playwright, whose identification Swinburne accepts with "the rival poet referred to in Shakespeare's sonnets with a grave note of passionate satire."

But no one quotation can at all convey the fascination of the four-teen pages in which he elaborates a comparison between Chapman and Browning. (Chapman is best known to the modern reader by Keats's sonnet "On First Looking into Chapman's Homer.")

The holograph in the Berg collection shows Swinburne getting slowly off the mark, making many alterations, and then swinging into his subject with smooth and probably swift writing. The small book was reprinted by Edmund Gosse as a long chapter in *Contemporaries of Shakespeare*. Swinburne's poetry and his reputation do not at all prepare one for the critical acumen and the knowledge of Elizabethan literature revealed in this book. He was an amazing phenomenon and surprising as a Browning critic. For many who were Browning's friends —Carlyle especially—put nothing of their praise into print, as did this rather critical acquaintance.

We know much today about Swinburne that Gosse was prevented from revealing in his rather Victorian biography. He did his best, but there were too many living relatives to threaten legal proceedings, the family was too high-placed in the country's aristocracy, too rich and too determined, for him to tell even the story of Swinburne's frequent state of drunkenness. Apparently a glass or two went to his head; but after a bottle he was still convinced of his own sobriety. Stories were current in Society, such as of his trying on after a party many silk hats in search of his own exceptionally large one—and finally throwing them all on the floor and destroying them in a wild war dance.

But the drink was a comparatively slight matter; one can hardly blame the relatives for objecting to a further revelation which Swin-burne himself had spent much money to hide. For he had been black-mailed by the possessor of drawings he had made of boys in different positions being flogged. This, unattractive as it sounds, seems hardly matter for blackmail, but Gosse left in the British Museum an ex-planatory supplement to his biography, to be opened after his own death. In it he says that he believes the consequence of suppression will be a later exaggeration of an aberration of Swinburne's dating from boyhood. In his letters there are frequent allusions to flogging, stories such as that of a boy whose blood leaked through a pair of white trousers to the amusement of his school fellows, and the acknowledgment of his own pleasure in being flogged. While this is a well-known aberration connected with sex, several of Swinburne's friends, believing he had never had sexual experience and that it would be beneficial for him, introduced him to a noted American courtesan, Adah Menken, who had already had affairs with Dumas, Hugo, and Gautier. She has been taken to be the "sanguine and subtle Dolores" to whom he addressed his best-known poem: Chesterton was to write some stanzas in which Dolores replies. Actually the poem was written before he knew her well, but Dolores *was* one of her names. Swinburne wrote of her at the time of her death as having been his mistress. But she spoke of Swinburne as her solitary failure! Chesterton may have been close to the mark when Dolores says to her lover

> O pagan Priapean poet
> You give me a pain.

Anyhow, Swinburne resorted at times to a brothel where women whipped the client at a high rate of pay. Gosse believed apparently that Swinburne felt the power to bear pain offered a challenge and that it did also by itself sufficiently stimulate his nervous system. But the impossibility is clear enough, even when Victorian had passed into Edwardian days, of putting into print such a picture of the dear departed, even when depicting with equal truth the classicist trained under Jowett, the Elizabethan scholar with so sure a touch.

The early part of the essay laments Chapman's obscurity: "There are beauties enough lost in this thick and thorny jungle of scholastic sensuality to furnish forth a dozen or so of pilfering poeticules with abundance of purple passages to be sewn in at intervals to the common texture of their style." Yet the fogginess seems almost deliberate, with a scorn of those who do not understand: "the profane multitude I hate." "It is not usually," comments Swinburne, "till he has failed to please that a man discovers how despicable and undesirable a thing it would have been to succeed." Chapman, like Demosthenes, filled his mouth with pebbles, but neglected to remove them before an oration: "the jaws are stretched wellnigh to bursting with the largest, roughest and most angular of polygonal flintstones that can be hewn or dug out of the mine of human language; and as fast as one voluminous sentence or unwieldy paragraph has emptied his mouth of the first batch of barbarisms, he is no less careful to refill it before proceeding to a fresh delivery." Chapman has

> thought hard and felt deeply; we apprehend that he is charged as it were to the muzzle with some ardent matter of spiritual interest, of which he would fain deliver himself in explosive eloquence; . . . no pretender but a genuine seer or Pythian bemused and stifled by the oracular fumes which choke in its very utterance the message they inspire, and for ever preclude the seer from becoming properly the prophet of their mysteries.

One can imagine many a man who had thrown down *Sordello* in despair, or groaned over *Fifine at the Fair*, rubbing his hands in anticipation of one contemporary poet attacking another as he began the next page with its statement of the charge of obscurity—"the likeliest to impair the fame or to imperil the success of a rising or an established poet." Here was Swinburne saying all our imaginary reader had ever thought about a poet obviously the twin brother of Browning. And, indeed, the idea that he *had* impaired his message is one we meet often enough, whether the reason is held to be merely impatient stammering or an impediment of speech arising from a soul at odds with itself.

But Swinburne will have none of it; it is a contrast not a comparison that he is drawing out: it is

> hasty or ignorant criticism . . . never misapplied more persistently and perversely than to an eminent writer of our own time. The difficulty found by many in certain of Mr. Browning's works arises from a quality the very reverse of that which produces obscurity properly so called. Obscurity is the natural product of turbid forces

and confused ideas; of a feeble and clouded or of a vigorous but
unfixed and chaotic intellect. . . .

Now if there is any great quality more perceptible than another
in Mr. Browning's intellect it is his decisive and incisive faculty of
thought, his sureness and intensity of perception, his rapid and
trenchant resolution of aim. To charge him with obscurity is about
as accurate as to call Lynceus purblind or complain of the sluggish
action of the telegraphic wire. He is something too much the reverse
of obscure; he is too brilliant and subtle for the ready reader of a
ready writer to follow with any certainty the track of an intelligence
which moves with such incessant rapidity, or even to realize with
what spider-like swiftness and sagacity his building spirit leaps and
lightens to and fro and backward and forward as it lives along the
animated line of its labour, springs from thread to thread and darts
from centre to circumference of the glittering and quivering web of
living thought woven from the inexhaustible stores of his perception
and kindled from the inexhaustible fire of his imagination. He never
thinks but at full speed; and the rate of his thought is to that of
another man's as the speed of a railway to that of a wagon or the
speed of a telegraph to that of a railway. . . .

Only random thinking and random writing produce obscurity;
and these are the radical faults of Chapman's style of poetry. We
find no obscurity in the lightning, whether it play about the heights
of metaphysical speculation or the depths of character and motive;
the mind derives as much of vigorous enjoyment from the study
by such light of the one as of the other. The action of so bright
and swift a spirit gives insight as it were to the eyes and wings to
the feet of our own; the reader's apprehension takes fire from the
writer's, and he catches from a subtler and more active mind the
infection of spiritual interest; so that any candid and clear-headed
student finds himself able to follow for the time in fancy the lead
of such a thinker with equal satisfaction on any course of thought
or argument; when he sets himself to refute Renan through the
dying lips of St. John or to try conclusions with Strauss in his own
person, and when he flashes at once the whole force of his illumina-

tion full upon the inmost thought and mind of the most infamous criminal, a Guido Franceschini or a Louis Bonaparte, compelling the black and obscene abyss of such a spirit to yield up at last the secret of its profoundest sophistries, and let forth the serpent of a soul that lies coiled under all the most intricate and supple reasonings of self-justified and self-conscious crime. And thanks to this very quality of vivid spiritual illumination we are able to see by the light of the author's mind without being compelled to see with his eyes, or with the eyes of the living mask which he assumes for his momentary impersonation of saint or sophist, philosopher or male-factor; without accepting one conclusion, conceding one point, or condoning one crime.

It is remarkable that the man who wrote "Thou hast conquered, O pale Galilean; the world has grown grey from Thy breath," should thus select "A Death in the Desert" as an example of Browning's mastery. No poem could differ more totally from his own outlook: he even left word that *no* religious ceremony was to mark his own funeral. But he sees in Browning "in the supreme degree the qualities of a great debater or an eminent leading counsel . . . the ardour of personal energy and active interest . . . we feel, without the reverse regret of Pope, how many a first-rate barrister or parliamentary tactician has been lost in this poet."

Dwelling with great admiration on Hohenstiel-Schwangau, Swin-burne hesitates as to whether with him, with Guido and others, the "counsel" has not given them thoughts as well as a tongue beyond their own power. He feels too that Browning's "incomparable genius of analysis," with "the apology and the anatomy of such motives" as Napoleon's could never "be touched with the fire which turns to a sword." Denying the "lyric rapture" discovered by some of Browning's admirers, Swinburne returns to the question of obscurity in an analysis of *Sordello,* which, as Coleridge said of Persius, is "hard—not obscure," —"only," says Swinburne, "the hard metal is of a different quality and temper, as the intellect of the English thinker is far wider in its reach, far subtler in its action and its aim, than that of the Roman Stoic."

It is deeply interesting that without knowing the story of its writing, which DeVane has so ably worked out, Swinburne saw that there was in *Sordello* "an amalgam of irreconcilable materials that naturally refuse to coalesce; and, like a few of the author's minor poems, it is written at least partially in shorthand, which a casual reader is likely to mistake for cipher, and to complain accordingly that the key should be withheld from him."

If, says Swinburne, the poem is a historical narrative enshrining and developing a story there is not enough "frame of circumstance," if the concentration is on "the inner study of an individual mind" there is too much.

> The poem, in short, is like a picture in which the background runs into the foreground, the figures and the landscape confound each other for want of space and keeping, and there is no middle distance discernible at all. It is but a natural corollary to this general error that the body like the spirit of the poem, its form not less than its thought, should halt between two or three diverse ways, and that the style should too often come to the ground between two stools or more; being as it is neither a dramatic nor a narrative style, neither personal nor impersonal, neither lyric nor historic, but at once too much of all these and not enough of any.

Swinburne goes on to show that what he calls a "monodrama" is Browning's greatest strength, dramatic speech between two or many his chief weakness. But he had hit, I think, on one of the most important comments ever made on Browning himself when he says of *Sordello* "there is no middle distance discernible."

8 Two Nations

> *Whene'er I take my walks abroad,*
> *How many poor I see!*
> *What shall I render to my God*
> *For all his gifts to me?*

> DIVINE SONGS FOR CHILDREN, (iv.)
> "PRAISE FOR MERCIES"
> ISAAC WATTS

THE STRANGEST gap in all the accounts of Browning's conversation, in all the mass of letters that have been published or are still to be found in libraries, is the absence of reference to English politics or English social conditions.[1] Yet the "sad dishevelled state" in which Sordello found mankind was in this century as deeply true of England as of any country at any date. Millais and Holman Hunt had marched with the Chartists in the forties. Ruskin was overwhelmingly alive to it—and spent the latter part of his life studying how best to give away the large fortune he had inherited, and to get other wealthy men to pledge at least some proportion of their yearly income to the relief of misery. Dickens was aware of it as he paced the streets of London at night and poured out in his novels what he had seen. Both men had a measure of success, Dickens dealing a death blow to the Yorkshire schools and a body blow to the workhouse and its parent, the Poor Law; Ruskin helping Octavia Hill over housing, educating one class and lecturing the other, persuading a group of young Oxonians to turn a rough track into a road. Morris and Tolstoy were his disciples.

K

Gladstone declared that Ruskin had changed his life, while post-humously he became the chief inspiration of the majority of Labour men in the 1906 Parliament. Carlyle was intensely conscious of the country's social sores, and in *Past and Present* he chooses some few horrifying things on which with iteration he strikes home his blows against an inhuman society: "two million industrial soldiers already sitting in Bastilles [the workhouses], and five million pining on potatoes."

All the Chartists had asked was, he said, "in return for their work such modicum of food, clothes and fuel as will enable them to continue their work itself." And he mocks at an "overproduction" which, with men going naked, had turned out superfluous shirts in vast quantities. "Liberty, I am told, is a divine thing. Liberty when it becomes the 'Liberty to die by starvation' is not so divine."

Browning was intimate with Carlyle and Ruskin. Daily he visited his sister-in-law Arabel, whose chief interest lay in her "Ragged School" —yet this too goes unmentioned in his letters.

There is nothing much more difficult than to travel imaginatively into a past age. The nineteenth century presents a very special problem because it is at once so close in time, so remote in atmosphere, from the world of today, which repudiates furiously relations then considered admirable. Take any Dickens novel. The brothers Cheeryble, the re-pentant Scrooge, Mr. Pickwick himself, were all wholeheartedly paternalistic—and Dickens and his readers wholeheartedly admired their paternalism—as did the grateful objects of it, from the childish Kit Nubbles to the intellectually independent Sam Weller.

Paternalism at its best assumed a basis of justice, the absence of which many of the best Victorians failed to realize. Even Carlyle, writing of model prisons in his *Latter Day Pamphlets*, forgot that of the "criminals" in a Victorian prison a huge proportion were there, not because they had broken God's law, but because the wicked laws of their country condemned them—for "stealing" for instance, the food without which they and their children would have starved, for gathering in a group of eight or nine to press for wages of ten instead of eight shillings a week, for snaring a rabbit on the common lands taken away from them by enclosure. "The method of love," said Carlyle, "had failed. These abject, ape, wolf, imp and other diabolical specimens of humanity" should be ruled by "a collar round the neck, and a cartwhip flourished over the back [in] a just and steady human hand."

Each man's world in that era was a smaller place and his duties in it more clearly defined. First came the family, parents and children and remoter relatives (lonely aunts and cousins who gathered at Dingley Dell as well as the country seat of "Sir Leicester Dedlock Baronet"). The servants in the houses of even the moderately well-placed added up to an immense number, as did the tradesmen with whom they dealt, employees not of vast enterprises but of an immense quantity of small shops. It was a structured society, with all the education as well as all the wealth at the top; even while depicting its dark underside, few Victorians dreamed of changing the structure. When, late in the century, William Morris, discovering Karl Marx and Engels, proclaimed himself a socialist, Tennyson exclaimed that he was crazy.

In that structured society the behavior of each individual in the upper echelons was of tremendous significance to those beneath him. Mrs. Gaskell noted as a weakness in Florence Nightingale that after her stupendous social work began she lost interest in the individuals of her home village. She had declared, too, that no mother should bring up her own child: "If she had twenty children she would send them all to a crèche. . . . That exactly tells what seems to me THE want—but then that want of love for individuals becomes a gift and a very rare one, if one takes it in conjunction with her intense love for the RACE; her utter unselfishness in serving and ministering."[2]

Of course it is possible to have both the public and the private virtues, but it seems rare: Byron ready to die for Greece, Shelley passionately engaged in the fight for human rights, Ruskin pledging his life and his fortune all made a pretty unattractive mess of their private lives.

Florence Nightingale was as great a genius in her own field as were the poets in theirs, and it may be that in the deepest sense the fulfillment of one's genius may make perfect balance impossible: Manning saw and combatted social evils ignored by Newman, but he could no more have written *The Grammar of Assent* than could Carlyle or Ruskin have written *The Ring and the Book.*

We see Browning as immensely responsible in his intimate world; devoted to son, father, and sister, winning the love and gratitude of his own household, paying punctually every bill from tradesmen who often suffered much from dilatory gentry and aristocracy. But one feels that, while Elizabeth had dragged him into enthusiasm for the cause of Italy, no one succeeded—if indeed they even attempted—in enlisting him among the crusaders for a better England.

He was making a home for himself and Pen, he was transcending grief and accepting success, above all he was for long in travail with the great conception of *The Ring and the Book.* Yet his silence on evils so great and so close poses a question. I do not claim that I can answer it, but we should at least see the question. For that, the background must be sketched of this England in which Tennyson could cry to Lady Clara Vere de Vere "Are there no beggars at your door,/Nor any poor about your lands?"

When Disraeli returned to power in 1874, his first act was—"in a letter," according to Froude, "as modest as it was dignified"—to offer Carlyle the Grand Cross of the Bath, an honor never before given to an author, with a life income befitting the honor. Carlyle of course refused to take it. "Very proper of the Queen to offer it," said a bus conductor to Froude, "and more proper of he to say that he would have nothing to do with it. 'Tisn't they that can do honour to the likes of he." Carlyle had never said a good word of "Dizzy"—had on the contrary frequently abused him,—and two years later referred to him as "a cursed old Jew, not worth his weight in cold bacon."

Yet the fact remains that without having the genius of Ruskin, of Dickens, or Carlyle, Disraeli had pictured in *Sybil* conditions for which he found a single phrase more valuable than anything said by his great contemporaries. "Our Queen," claims Egremont, in *Sybil,* "reigns over the greatest nation that ever existed."

"Which nation?" asked the younger stranger, "for she rules over two. . . . Two nations between which there is no sympathy, who are as ignorant of each other's habits, thoughts and feelings as . . . inhabitants of different planets . . . are fed by different food, are ordered by different manners, and are not governed by the same laws."

"You speak of . . ." said Egremont hesitatingly,

"The Rich and the Poor."

The same language was used by Disraeli defending the Chartists as by Carlyle, the same picture drawn of Mammon enthroned by landowners, of which Ruskin wrote: "Even the cruelest man living could not sit at his feast unless he sat blindfold."

Disraeli depicts one landlord who claimed that his employees could well keep a family on seven shillings a week, who gloried in having pulled down so many cottages—and then shows us a laborer trudging miles to his work and returning home to a hovel with mud floor, leaking roof, no sanitation, and filthy smells of the human and animal garbage piled up in heaps outside for its leisurely collection to be used as manure. He shows us a poor weaver earning one penny an hour for skilled work that the machine had rendered superfluous, his wife and children trying to keep warm in bed for lack of fuel or clothing. George Eliot's Silas Marner, we remember, would be paid as much as five guineas for a fine piece of work, and like Silas this man had once had a comfortable cottage and spare time to cultivate a garden.

The machine was eating men—and again we are taken to a mine where children of five are coming out who have charge of opening and shutting a door on which men's lives depend—and have been doing this for twelve hours or more. Women are coming out naked to the waist with the chains hanging between their trousered legs with which they have been dragging carts in the depths of the earth. The miners, paid usually in scrip, would, they say, be sacked if they demanded their legal right—"the Queen's picture," i.e., coin of the realm. The scrip must be spent at shops called "tommies" kept by "butties" or middlemen between the pit owner and his workers. At these shops Disraeli's hero has seen intolerable delays in opening and in serving, even bodily violence offered by the shopman's son, has noted prices half as high again as elsewhere, for inferior goods. He has seen fever, ague, consumption, and malaria as guests around the empty hearths of "this unhappy race."

What was to be the remedy? Here I fancy Disraeli began much closer to Carlyle than he later became. For Carlyle's emphasis was on the duty to work on the one side and to pay properly on the other, to abandon Mammon for God. Carlyle, like Ruskin, knew "no previous instance of a nation establishing a systematic disobedience to the first principles of its professed religion." And both men repudiated Mill, who by his political economy was "aiding and abetting [wrote Ruskin] the commission of the cruelest possible form of murder on many thousands of people yearly, for the sake of simply putting money into the pockets of the landlords." "A right gallant thrust," cried Carlyle.

That the Law of Supply and Demand, with its policy of "laissez-faire," was no law but a specious defense of oppression was agreed on by these men—and that government must interfere. Almost twenty years had passed since the great Chartist procession when a coroner wanted the death of a woman in a rat-ridden cellar reported to the authorities and a juror objected on the ground that half the houses in London would have to be closed; when Bright in the House of Commons opposed inspection of food for adulteration; when the ten-hour act caused manufacturers to multiply machines, while fainting men were carried away and replaced by others; when in a land where starvation was frequent, fish were being thrown back into the sea to keep prices up. It had been in an almost empty House of Commons that (in 1842) an immense petition with more than a million signatures had been presented; Disraeli's had been the one speech in its favor and the embittered Chartists had felt the futility of an appeal to an assembly that refused even to attend at the reading of it.[3]

Party government in England was called by Froude "a disguised civil war" and in the nineteenth century it was a very bitter one, but the "other nation" felt that whichever side won they remained the losers. To quote Froude again, the country was "committed" to laissez-faire. And because of the "civil war"—to which the very constitution also committed them—the best men on the two sides *could* not act together. The two who increasingly stood out as leaders, who became the only two in their later years, Gladstone and Disraeli, were both concerned with social reform,. yet how little either of them effected. Dropping the Corn Laws was, as Froude points out, an inevitable measure, but in essence only a minor expedient. The cheapest bread might never reach the multitudes whose wages depended on tyrannical and uncontrolled employers. Yet it was unthinkable that either party would propose a minimum wage. With a general election always in view, does any party government dare to govern?

Disraeli was openly cynical; he would not have minded, it was said, "Gladstone playing with three aces up his sleeve had he not tried to persuade you that God almighty put them there." Had the aces been up Dizzy's sleeve, he would certainly have boasted of them when the game was won. The two are a fascinating study and it is a thousand pities that Browning, so much more interested in men than in parties, should not have drawn them both in their strengths and their weaknesses. But, for him, as for most of the liberals I have ever known, Gladstone was the Grand Old Man of politics. Disraeli's admirers enjoyed his cynicism, laughed at the jokes against him; Gladstone's admirers revered the man, in whom there was indeed much that was admirable, and tended to be sensitive about jokes on so sacred a topic.

What Browning as a good liberal eventually did is interesting. In *Parleyings With Certain People of Importance in their Day* he depicted George Bubb Dodington, a figure from political history, and showed how he failed, and why *he could have succeeded had he had the qualities of Benjamin Disraeli.* Disraeli's name is never mentioned: Browning begins with a bird feathering his nest—rough outside but "A snug interior, warm and soft and sleek." It would not however suffice the more ambitious of the feathered tribe.

> Birds born to strut prepare a platform-stage
> With sparkling stones and speckled shells, all sorts
> Of slimy rubbish, odds and ends and orts,
> Whereon to pose and posture.

There must be a skill in self-display, other qualities, too.

> An imperturbability that's—well,
> Or innocence or impudence—how tell
> One from the other?

Not too loud a profession

> that your sole intent
> Strives for their service. Sneer at them? Yourself
> 'Tis you disparage,—tricksy as an elf,
> Scorning what most you strain to bring to pass,
> Laughingly careless,—triply cased in brass.

All this for the masses, with for the elite "a touch of subintelligential nod and wink." Disraeli had been foolish enough to try this on Browning at an opening of the Royal Academy. In his speech he had praised "the *imagination* of the British School of art," but when Browning later asked for his opinion, he said, "What strikes me is the utter and hopeless want of imagination." "As much as to say," commented Browning, " 'you didn't think me such a fool as I seemed in my speech.' " Relating the incident to Gladstone, he evoked a minor explosion: "It's hellish," said Gladstone. "He is like that in the House too—it's hellish."

"And so it is," Browning commented—and most seriously thought. He told Allingham, who has recorded the incident in his diary, that he intended to attack Disraeli. "What a humbug he is! Won't I give it to him one of these days." It took him a good many years to get around to it, for this poem belongs to his last volume but one.

George Bubb Dodington, who became Lord Melcombe, was a politician of the reign of George II, patronized by the King and by Walpole. His wealth was immense and he controlled six pocket boroughs. This makes it curious that he was finally beaten for another borough, Bridgewater, after representing it for some years. He describes the voters as "low and venal," as if, said the editor of his diary, "a bribe taken by a miserable voter, and possibly for the support of a numerous and indigent family, was more dishonourable than a place or pension, enjoyed or coveted by the opulent."

His fall was celebrated in a popular song:

> How he lost his good place,
> And is in disgrace,

And does not know where to show his flat face;
For the Tories will never receive such a scrub,
And no Whig at court will be civil to Bub.[4]

Dodington had been a trickster but an unsuccessful one. Disraeli not only had a sort of inspired and light-hearted impudence—he had another quality which had always fascinated Browning.

One of the Liberal trump cards against Disraeli was his origin, and with many people this meant his Jewish background. Browning loved the Jews but Disraeli was not an English Jew—his paternal grandfather had been a merchant in Venice, his maternal ancestors came (he claimed) from a famous Portuguese family, ennobled in that country at the time of the Saracen kingdom.[5] It may be, the poem suggests, that Dizzy's power over men was won through the display if not the reality of magical power, an "influence such as we/Are strangers to." And what was that?

Man's despot, just the Supernatural
Which, George, was wholly out of—far beyond
Your theory and practice.

Was Disraeli really another Sludge—in a field where he could do infinitely more harm? Amazed to see how this strange man in his outlandish dress, with curls like Byron's, could "induce/The puppets now to dance, now stand stock still,/Now knock their heads together, at your will." Browning asks whether it is not

through terror at the heart:
"Can it be—this bold man, whose hand we saw
Openly pull the wires, obeys some law
Quite above man's—nay God's?"

Disbelieving alike in the magical and sinister role assigned to Disraeli, and the scarlet-faced conservatives' denunciation of Gladstone's hypocrisy, one could still see dark angels at work on this political scene, frightening good men from acting with even elementary humanity.

The only political issues much talked of in Browning's letters are not English ones, but Italian unity and liberty, the American Civil War, and the Franco-Prussian War.

His letters to Story show that at first he did not realize how strongly most of the English governing class were in sympathy with the South: he attributed "our neutrality, poor cold, hard thing indeed" to a lack of realization that "The *spirit* of all Mr. Lincoln's acts is altogether against slavery in the end." In fear "of losing the uncertain states," Lincoln had "declared his intention to be quite otherwise"—and England had not understood this diplomacy.

But, for English aristocrats especially, an aura of sentiment hung about the South, while the quite unaristocratic Carlyle was crying out that the white slaves should be freed before the black. Browning gradually realized that what he had called "the malice of the 'Times,'" (at that date *the* Tory paper) represented a wide feeling, and he worked to get some letter-articles by Story printed and widely circulated. They appeared in three successive numbers of the *Daily News*—and Browning wrote of the opposing paper: "Don't mind the mean, vindictive 'Times.'"

Another factor in English opinion was the cotton supply for the Lancashire mills. The white slave owners needed the southern cotton to keep their machines at work, but, with wonderful gallantry the white slaves, despite the horrors of starvation attendant on unemployment, heartily supported their black brethren.

Browning was beginning to see less of that world of literature and art, of the Carlyles and Ruskins, the Rossettis and Holman Hunts than of yore. Both would have hated the bracketing, but Browning, like Disraeli, was being wooed with some success by a "great society" much narrower and much less great than that of his youthful dream.

He was, I think, not so much blindfolded as blinkered. It was an hour of world optimism: evolution, discovery, invention all pointed in the direction of a steady inevitable improvement which the political economy of the hour reinforced. Even while describing the miseries of factory workers, Mrs. Gaskell, through one of her characters, gives a wage-slave a lucid explanation of how his lot must inevitably improve if the laws of supply and demand are not interfered with. Carlyle thought many of the aristocracy "noble"and fiercely criticized an extension of the franchise.

The Industrial Revolution with its vast and too rapid changes had caught good men unprepared, while bad men were grasping its unholy advantages. That most wicked of all thefts—the enclosure of the common lands—had been presented and widely believed in as an essential expedient to increase the food supply during the French wars; an intelligent man like Arthur Young did not realize until after the laboring class had lost them that common rights were vital. He had thought them "perfectly contemptible." Firewood, rabbits, rushes for thatching, food for the communal flocks of geese, even supplementary pasturage for the cow kept on garden stuff. Two nations indeed—when one knew so little of the other.

Staying at country houses in his later English years Browning would often meet the good landlord of Disraeli's novels—Mrs. Fitz-Gerald, for instance, recipient of the letters collected under the title *Learned Lady,* built cottages, brought water to their doors, even went farther afield and, with the warm cooperation of her cottagers, worked to feed and clothe the Manchester Operatives during the American Civil War.

Mrs. Orr tells us that, at Llangollen in 1886, Browning was so impressed by another landlord's provisions for the comfort of the "men and animals" under his care that he exclaimed, "Talk of abolishing that class of men! They are the salt of the earth!" She thought this a surprising remark for a liberal—which clearly she herself was not.

As late as the beginning of this century I remember men on one estate who would remark cheerfully as they grew older, "Time for me to come and work for you, Squire," for this happened always as they became useless to the farmers. And another such landlord, with vast domains, instituted a system of old-age pensions long before government had dreamed of it. Browning did not care for novels; but there were plenty about the good landlord and the grateful tenant; and if he ever visited a factory it would be a model one—what town shows off its eyesores?

The voice of Macaulay, too, was loud in the Liberal camp, offering to prove by statistics the steady improvement in social conditions wrought by simply leaving things alone. The death rate was falling, especially in the manufacturing cities, where the poor rate was also falling. Machinery was so great a boon that it had "brought within the reach of the poorest some conveniences which Sir Thomas More or his master could not have obtained at any price." As to food (he declared), while in More's time many of the students at Cambridge "dined on pottage" and a laborer's bread was often compounded of beans, oats, and even acorns, "Our parish poor now eat wheaten bread." And again: "The advice and medicine which the poorest labourer can now obtain, in disease or after an accident, is far superior to what Henry the Eighth could have commanded."

In short, setting aside the new commonwealths with their vast lands and rich uncultivated soils "we must confess ourselves unable to find any satisfactory record of any great nation, past or present, in which the working classes have been in a more comfortable situation than in England during the last thirty years."

Pouring scorn on Southey, the poet laureate of that date (1829), Macaulay described his creed as "Rose-bushes and poor rates, rather than steam engines and independence." And after a perfunctory bow to that reliance on God which Southey felt could alone remedy England's woes he went on, "We rely on the natural tendency of the human intellect to truth, and on *the natural tendency of society to improvement.*"

The italics are mine, for this intense belief in a natural law of progress was *the* great support of the doctrine of laissez-faire. "Railroads and steam boats," chanted Macaulay, increase in the population, diminution in the death-rate, higher revenues and lower taxation. "On what principle is it that, when we see nothing but improvement behind us, we are to expect nothing but deterioration before us?"

"He seemed sometimes," says Chesterton, "to talk as if clocks produced clocks, or guns had families of little pistols, or a penknife littered like a pig." Macaulay spoke against the Chartists but splendidly in favor of the Reform Bill. We were, he had admitted in passing, at a moment "of great distress." But it was only a moment. "A single breaker may recede; but the tide is evidently coming in!" Let rulers confine themselves "to their own legitimate duties, by leaving capital to find its most lucrative course, commodities their fair price, industry and intelligence their natural rewards, idleness and folly their natural punishment, by maintaining peace, by defending property. . . . Let the Government do this; the People will assuredly do the rest."

When the theories of Bentham were thus put forward in the ringing prose of Macaulay, it needed real experiences such as those of Dickens, Engels, or Marx to see through his sophistries. It was in fact thanks to government interference that social conditions *were* less bad when Browning returned to England in the sixties than when he had left it in the forties, but the gulf between the two "nations" remained basically the same. The "nation" Browning was living in communicated with the other through intermediaries—the good squire knew his farmers intimately and commonly viewed the laborers through their eyes or those of his agent. A good landlord was essentially one who was patient when farm rents were paid late, who did all the repairs requested even if himself pressed for money, who cared to know his tenant farmers' problems. I knew one with a legal training whose tenants would expect him not merely to draw their wills for them but to guide them in an equitable division among their children. The laborers on such a man's home farm might be envied by the farmer's employees, but even of these he might have only such information as his middleman thought desirable.

Above all it was the pride of the period that so many men could pass from one of the nations into the other. The opportunities were exaggerated, and it would often be the least worthy who grasped them. But, in the manufacturing world especially, the "self-made" man was taken as a proof that all the rest had but to be laborious, as resourceful as he. It was an hour of opportunity—there was presumably room at the top for everyone.

One sees the enormous problem presented to men of good will, evaded by putting their consciences in the keeping of *some* leader, when we look at the two men whose survey of the suffering masses had been so similar—Dizzy and Carlyle—and see what opposite conclusions they finally reached as to what reform should mean. In the Bill of 1867, Disraeli extended the franchise to all householders and cried in triumph, "We have dished the Whigs." Carlyle replied with *Shooting Niagara.* The bill was a Whig measure passed by a Tory government. Was it not delightful, Carlyle asked, that "other jugglers of an unconscious and deeper type, having sold their poor mother's body for a mess of official pottage, this clever, unconscious juggler steps in? Soft you, my honourable friends: *I* will weigh out the corpse of your mother—mother of mine she never was, but only step-mother and milch-cow—and you shan't have the pottage."

Unlike Browning, Carlyle disliked Jews and readily suspected a Jew of the last thing for which it was fair to suspect Disraeli, for indeed his profound fault was that he destroyed the dream he had cherished of the "great society" by a crazy ambition to consolidate and extend the British Empire. He filled Queen Victoria's heart with joy by acquiring the Khedive's shares in the Suez Canal, borrowing (though at immense cost) the four million pounds required from Rothschild's bank; and by the act that conferred on her the title "Empress of India." With brilliant diplomacy he saved England from a war with Russia, brought on by the old parrot cry "The Russians shall not have Constantinople" —and England emerged from the negotiations in possession of Cyprus. But the fighting in Southern Africa and the annexation of the Transvaal led to the terrible battle of Majuba Hill, after which, says Froude, "jingoism came to its miserable end. The grand chance had been given to English Conservatism, and had been lost in a too ambitious dream."

Disraeli's dream had been a splendid one[6]: the pacification of Ireland with its absorption in the "great society" to be brought to birth in England, and an Imperial Parliament, in which each colony, become self-governing, should bear its part. Yet neither of these things did he really attempt to achieve.

Gladstone, with a greater realism, saw that the first country to get back its own government should be Ireland—and to this Dizzy and most Englishmen were bitterly opposed. "Geographical position," says Froude crudely, "compels us to keep Ireland subject to the British Crown. That is the first fact of the situation."

And one is tempted by the nineteenth-century record, as by earlier history, to echo the famous "Holland House parson" Sydney Smith who like all great wits could sometimes be fiercely serious: "The moment the very name of Ireland is mentioned, the English seem to bid adieu to common feeling, common prudence and commonsense, and to act with the barbarity of tyrants and the fatuity of idiots."

The Brownings had been in Italy during the whole period of the first great famine. It goes unmentioned in his few and her many surviving letters. More astonishingly one finds hardly a mention of it in Blake's excellent biography of Disraeli, who, despite the ideals of his early books seems to have totally failed in humanity where Ireland was concerned.

The two years of the famine were at their worst when in 1847 Daniel O'Connell the Liberator in a debate on the Soup Kitchen Act made his last appearance in the House of Commons. Already Ireland had lost hundreds of thousands by starvation or an emigration often ending in death—the scene is described by Cecil Woodham-Smith in *The Great Hunger*.

> The once-splendid physical presence had gone, and with it the magnificent voice; he spoke with difficulty, and his words were audible only to those nearest him; "Ireland is in your hands, in your power," he whispered. "If you do not save her, she cannot save herself. I solemnly call on you to recollect that I predict with the sincerest conviction that a quarter of her population will perish unless you come to her relief." The dying Liberator, broken in health and spirits, was listened to "in almost reverential silence . . . rancour and party spirit were forgotten at the spectacle of so great sorrow." Disraeli, however, who was present, saw only "a feeble old man muttering before a table," and O'Connell's last appeal for Ireland had no result.

The remoteness of Ireland, the terrible doctrine of "laissez-faire" which had in effect destroyed also the British army in the Crimea had been, Gladstone realized, in operation all too long. For Ireland Home Rule was the only answer.

Browning was among those Liberals (as the party was increasingly called) who parted company with Gladstone on this issue. As of custom we get no account from him of the why and wherefore of his views and only rub our eyes to see a man who had supported the Risorgimento taking such an attitude. Nervous at the prospect of meeting Gladstone, he was relieved at finding the Prime Minister still perfectly friendly. One could bet that Home Rule was not discussed, but if it was, we hear nothing of the discussion. And this indeed is the point at which any attempt breaks down at comprehending Browning's attitude. He had left England when things were at their worst for his dispossessed countrymen, now become factory hands. The Reform Bill of 1867, even if passed by the "wrong" party, following as it did a series of Factory Acts, did seem to point in the direction of steady improvement. To one long out of the country it might appear credible that improvement would continue if the "law of supply and demand" was left to operate in an England ahead of every European country in her inventions and discoveries. But now the "right" party, under the leader he revered, was attempting to offer liberty, spelling merely elementary justice, to a country far longer oppressed than Italy; and Browning the liberal was joining the side of the oppressors. Nor was this, as with some Englishmen, for religious reasons. We do learn from Gavan Duffy (*Life in Two Hemispheres*) that when Forster defended the imposition on the country of the religion of a tiny minority, Browning called this "altogether indefensible. The Catholic Church was the Church of the Irish people and this was a fact of which legislation might properly take cognisance."

Liberty was the cry of the nineteenth century—liberty for the enslaved nation, liberty for the individual. Browning must have forgotten Ireland when he wrote, in 1885, "Why I am a Liberal."

> "Why?" Because all I haply can and do,
> All that I am now, all I hope to be—

Whence comes it save from fortune setting free
Body and soul the purpose to pursue,
God traced for both? . . .
Who, then, dares hold—emancipated thus—
His fellow shall continue bound? Not I
Who live, love, labour freely, nor discuss
A brother's right to freedom. That is "Why."

The adjective appalling is not too strong for the difficulty of gathering and evaluating all the material that exists concerning a long and full life. Which of a mass of incidents is significant in its revelation of character, which is almost irrelevant? Sometimes the answer comes through what a man's contemporaries felt—and it is certainly interesting that not even the most socially minded of Browning's friends seems to have resented his absentmindedness about what was most present in their own thinking.

And this brings in another question. It has been deduced from Browning's account book in the British Museum, and from his irritable refusal to contribute to one or two people for causes which he disapproved, that Browning was stingy, or at least "Scotch," in money matters. He was certainly careful, he had to be especially with so extravagant a son as Pen became. But there is no trace in the account book of the large payments of Pen's debts, or of such smaller ones as the loans to Buchanan, the contest in generosity between himself and his publisher George Smith (discussed in the next chapter), of his passing over to the Browning Society the profit made when Mrs. Hickey staged one of his plays—or the fact that he was the first to contribute when his friend, F. J. Furnivall, appealed for funds to buy two sculling boats for his Working Men's College team.

These things may mean little—or much. But when Kenyon defends the poem so often deplored—the Epilogue to *Asolando*, he does so largely by describing a roomful of soldiers who after hearing it recited begged for pencils to record it for themselves. The gift of his poetry is a poet's best gift even if this Epilogue was not the best sample of this particular poet's wares.

After Browning's death, the Congregational Chapel where he had gone Sunday by Sunday with his parents, where his weariness had shown itself in so open a manifestation as to bring him a rebuke from the pulpit, was transformed into the Robert Browning Settlement.

Settlements of this sort were perhaps the final effort of Victorian philanthropy. The idea was that the rich should go down to live for a period among the destitute, bringing culture *and* material assistance. School dinners for children for instance were started by some of these settlements and carried on until the government took them over. In my own youth I helped with dinners for children whose mothers were reduced to feeding them on soup made from such offal as fish-heads cut off and tossed aside in the market.

Punch produced a parody of "Love Among the Ruins," its final line being a straight quotation. *Punch* announces "Shade of the Author of 'Sordello' sings":

> Can the poet, memory-warmed, do ought but smile
>   On that mile
> Of poverty's scant pastures, where toil's sheep
>   Herd and creep,
> That square mile of clustering tenement, coster-crop
>   And small shop? . . .
>
> Where the Congregational Chapel which I knew
>   Well-to-do,
> Stood, they now have got a building which they call
>   Browning Hall!
> Whence at eve you hear the husky coster squalls
>   From their stalls. . . .
>
> Well! it does me truer honour, I protest,
>   Than the quest
> Of my minor mystic meanings, cryptic, crude,
>   By the brood
> Of "disciples" who at meetings Browning-Clubbish
>   Talk such rubbish! . . .

Well, a Walworth chap may not quite grasp Sordello
    Poor, good fellow!
But the author of Sordello hath the whim
    To grasp *him*.
But for Hall and Settlement to bear his name,
    He holds fame.

With this Robert Browning Social Settlement
    I'm content;
Over poverty, pain, folly, noise and sin,
    May they win.
As I sang, despite wit, wealth, fame, and the rest,
    "Love is best!"

9 *From* Red Cotton Night-Cap Country *to* La Saisiaz

> *"That bard's a Browning; he neglects the form!"* one
> of the characters exclaims with irresponsible frankness.
>
> HENRY JAMES ON THE INN ALBUM

AMONG Browning's Greek poems came, in 1873 and 1875 respectively, *Red Cotton Night-Cap Country* and *The Inn Album*, which show an increase in what he had described to Julia Wedgwood as an undue liking for the "study of morbid cases of the soul." Among his famous Fifty twenty years earlier there is hardly a man or a woman we would wish away; among the speakers in *The Ring and the Book* there are monsters indeed, but even Guido is an interesting monster, the lawyers are redeemed by the sheer fun of them, the three great characters stand out in splendor as much against a variety of colorful mediocrity as against the sheer blackness of shattering evil. In *Red Cotton Night-Cap Country* there is no single really interesting character, though there are two rather touching ones—the central half-crazed man trusting in a miraculous intervention and his pathetic mistress whose feelings for him seem fundamentally those of a mother.

The story was in outline as true as it was strange—and Browning was advised by Lord Chief Justice Coleridge to alter the names of people and places just on the possibility of a libel action—unlikely, the lawyers admitted, since the French newspapers had reported it in full.[1]

Léonce Miranda, to use Browning's name for him, had lived with his mistress in his old Breton home, building fresh additions, spending freely, till his dying mother reproached him bitterly for his neglect of her and her interests. In a violent mood of repentance he thrust his hands into the fire and burned them off. But he returned later to his mistress, Clara, had false hands fitted, and learned to use them with extraordinary skill. A jeweler by trade, he had allowed his cousins to take over the business in Paris while he continued to make love, to build, and to give alms on a big scale, sharing his devotion between Clara and an allegedly miraculous shrine in the neighborhood.

The end of the story, believed by many to be plain suicide, was accepted by others, including Browning, as a fantastic but perfectly sincere act of faith. Miranda flung himself from the belvedere of his house trusting in a divine rescue—and was taken up dead. He had left his property to Clara for life and then to the Church. The cousins brought suit that he was of unsound mind, but were defeated.

There are flashes in the poem of the old Browning, who could discover under perversity some reality of truth. Not only in the description so often quoted of his friend Milsand, who would have been a far safer guide for Miranda than the money-blinded clerics, but also in his near-approval of the strange wild plunge, his conviction that faith, not despair, was its motive. The gardener speaks:

> "This must be what he meant by those strange words
> While I was weeding larkspurs yesterday,
> 'Angels would take him!' Mad!"

Browning would have it otherwise:

> No! sane, I say.
> Such being the conditions of his life,
> Such end of life was not irrational.
> Hold a belief, you only half-believe,
> With all-momentous issues either way,—
> And I advise you imitate this leap,
> Put faith to proof, be cured or killed **at** once!

Strangely enough for a man who knew his Bible so well, Browning does not mention the devil's urging—"Cast thyself down. . . . He has given His angels charge over thee"—and Christ's answer—"Thou shalt not tempt the Lord thy God."

The title *Red Cotton Night-Cap Country* was the result in Browning's mind of so painful a story being played out in this peaceful countryside, dubbed by Anne Thackeray, when they were spending a summer there, "White Cotton Night-Cap Country." Browning dedicated the poem to her and she appears to have been embarrassed by some of the hostile reviews.

With all its grimness this story pales in horror beside that of *The Inn Album*, which it seems Browning had thought of turning into a play. It has in fact many of the defects of his youthful dramas although cast in narrative form.

Again the story was largely founded on fact—it was the last of Browning's studies drawn from criminal records. And he was very happy about his performance, writing to George Smith (April 22, 1875):

> the said poem is quite finished—is on so very modern a subject that it concerns last Whitsuntide—and English country life,—and moreover means to be abundantly passionate and pathetic:—I did it with a will in two months exactly: it is some 3,500 lines in length, and, in fact, is a tragedy in a new style. What do you say to this?

It was not in fact quite so long—but even 3,078 lines in "two months exactly" suggests something that may account, as much as overmany social engagements and his advancing years, for a deterioration in Browning's poetic power. Think of the seven years that had gone into *Men and Women,* of the gradually growing intensity with which *The Ring and the Book* had possessed him from its first inception to its completion eight years later. However much "will" had gone into *The Inn Album,* the likelihood of a great poem was small—with over 3,000 lines of blank verse written in two months, for the most part "smoothly and easily" says DeVane, who had examined the manuscript.

There is much to be said later of Henry James's insights about Browning, but I think nothing shows better than his review of *The Inn Album* how rent he was between admiration and exasperation over the man's "great genius," yet "his wantonness, his wilfulness, his crudity." This was no poem, James felt, but "a series of notes for a poem," with "that hiss and splutter and evil aroma which characterise the proceedings of the laboratory."

And what maddened him most was that "a great poem might perhaps have been made of it, but assuredly it is not a great poem, nor any poem whatsoever." And for several pages James descants on Browning's determination to create for his admirers an increasing difficulty in defending him.[2]

Swinburne, however, was enthusiastic. "A fine study," he said, "in the later manner of Balzac." The utterly unpredictable *Athenaeum* was disposed to place it above *The Ring and the Book*—and set it beside *Pippa Passes*, but most reviewers liked it no better than they had liked *Red Cotton Night-Cap Country*.

There are four characters: a young man; an older man who has educated him in the world's ways and partly corrupted him; a girl the young man hopes to marry; a slightly older woman friend of hers, whom the young man, not knowing of this friendship, had earlier seen and loved, and whom the older man had seduced and abandoned. Each bit of this past history is known only to those who have taken part in it; each meeting is a surprise as they enter the inn, with its album lying on the table, opening at the words "Hail, calm acclivity, salubrious spot!"

The woman friend after her horrible experience had married an oldish clergyman with whom her life was utterly dreary. She has not seen a tree for four years, has no joy in her work, abides in despair. The girl, believing her the happiest of women, had begged her to come out of hiding and counsel her whether to marry the youth. In this friend the young man recognizes the woman he had loved; the older recognizes the woman he had betrayed.

Not even Shakespeare could have brought drama into the most dramatic of situations when the leading characters were so lifeless. The slaying of the older man by the younger (to whom he tried to offer his cast-off mistress in return for the canceling of an immense gaming debt) and the suicide of the woman leave one indifferent. The girl is a mere shadow and the younger man the only living and, mildly, though not very interestingly, amiable character.

They are what James called the poem as a whole, "notes," but notes which in his great days could have been developed into four splendid dramatic monologues. After several readings it is possible to see glimpses of how he could have done it. The seeds are there, when the older woman describes her misery with her pseudo-religious husband, when the young man talks to the older of his initiation into "life"—but they remain seeds.

The most depressing thing in both these poems is Browning's view of the religious and human surroundings. The French priests and nuns are without exception "on the make," the English clergyman has lost all sense of reality in religion apart from a fanatical belief in hell, and the woman who has married him, still suffering from her own traumatic experience, seems no more than he to see anything of the goodness, the immense *human* values, in ordinary men and women.

>   Being brutalized
> Their true need is brute-language . . .
>   Selfishness
> In us met selfishness in them, deserved
> Such answer as it gained. My husband, bent
> On saving his own soul by saving theirs,—
> They, bent on being saved if saving soul
> Including body's getting bread and cheese . . .
>   Talk at end of the tired day
> Of the more tiresome morrow! . . .

Worst of all was the long copying of her husband's sermons:

> Heaven he let pass, left wisely undescribed: . . .
> But Hell he made explicit.

The unfinished quality in this poem brings it to the verge (but no further) of the social studies which Browning so sedulously avoided.

It may well be that in his shadowy heroine he was reading rightly a woman shattered by one great disillusionment and drained of all that remained in her by the second, perhaps greater one, of marriage to her "pious" husband. For the picture is that which John Stuart Mill powerfully drew when he described how Christians had in nineteenth-century England lost the primary idea of their own religion—that "of being spiritually-minded—of loving and practicing good from a pure love simply because it is good," exchanging this motive for the horrible notion that "God is stronger than we are and is able to damn us if we do not." Virtue is changed into self-interest, a self-interest far more abject than that of the hungry needing bread and cheese for themselves and their children.

But in his speed Browning rushed on, leaving his heroine oblivious both of the evils of a system that made men so dependent and of the agonies, the brief joys, the humor and kindliness so brilliantly depicted by Dickens—which even a superficial experience of naked humanity reveals to every one of us.

The older woman can look only at her own misery—and perhaps today's fashion for dark pictures might find more to admire in *The Inn Album* than did Browning's contemporaries. Both husband and wife might have benefited from a psychiatrist—had they been living beings instead of melancholy shadows.

To a man unskilled in self-criticism the world of periodicals was disconcerting. Browning wrote to George Smith after a review of another poem: "There is a complaint, I see, that I no longer write 'those matchless men and women.' As if, when I did write them, the 'Times' said a single good word for them!"

Browning had changed publishers between *Dramatis Personae* and *The Ring and the Book*. His relations with Chapman and Hall had never been really satisfactory: many letters during Elizabeth's lifetime show that George Chapman was dilatory in rendering his accounts and lazy about writing the letters on which authors living out of England so greatly depended.

Until after Browning's return in 1861 his wife's poetry had been Chapman's chief motive for publishing Browning, and for many years yet Elizabeth's sales remained well ahead of his. But the situation was beginning to improve, and it has been thought a little hard that the change of publishers should have been made after his first publication to reach a second edition—*Dramatis Personae*. Yet Browning felt, with justice, that even this was a "comparative failure." Nor had business matters improved when, after George Chapman died, his brother Frederick succeeded him as head of the firm.

To Isa Blagden, Browning wrote in August 1866 that he hated "quarrelling with the poor fellow," and in February 1867: "I can't help it, but distrust the man, without dislike of the poor good-natured fellow otherwise."

Muddling may be as great a curse as dishonesty, and there appear to have been two other reasons causing Browning to give up the firm he had put up with for so many years. Isa Blagden, probably taken on as an author to please him, was convinced and was convincing Browning that she was being badly treated. It seems again to have been a muddle—this time between the printers, Bradbury & Evans, and the publishers—which had delayed payment of her account. Browning wrote to Chapman in June 1866: "You see, poor Miss Blagden has been too well justified in her complaints; and it is a worse case apparently than I or she supposed."[3]

While engaged in the quarrel over Isa's interests, Browning was receiving good offers from "many booksellers," but with none of these was he concerned, for another element in his decision to leave Chapman was a friendship which had begun between him and George Smith of Smith, Elder & Co. The correspondence between them is mostly unpublished and belongs now to John Murray, whose publishing house absorbed that of Smith, Elder in 1917.

As one who has been both I can testify that a cordial and lasting relationship between author and publisher is not an easy but can be a very delightful one. Between Browning and George Smith it existed to a rare degree for over twenty years. It was in 1867 that Browning wrote: "You need no telling·that your offer is a most liberal one which absolutely contents me,—but I need some reflecting on the possibility that you understand business, and will not harm yourself by your generosity." It was in 1887 that he wrote:

I supposed that there *was* an agreement between you and myself, and one of long standing, that you should give me for my books exactly what you saw fit,—seeing that I have always been sure that you would deal far more generously by me than I should ask or hope for by any arrangement of my own. As for your "new and improved plan" of rendering accounts—all I can say is, it may be "new" but "improved"—in my case—it certainly will not be: and if I might decide, the old bottles should be retained for the old wine—'20 Port of its kind as drunk gratefully by

Yours ever
Robert Browning

The sixties had brought Browning his first serious recognition since *Paracelsus*. The sales of the collected edition, the welcome given to the various volumes of selections, above all the enthusiasm of so many over *The Ring and the Book*, meant a new climate in which he was basking. But the poems of the seventies did not add to his reputation. And in his rapidly changing moods he passes from high-spirited good humor over criticism to a crude mockery scarcely concealing exasperation. The treatment of the three long poems *Prince Hohenstiel-Schwangau Saviour of Society*, *Red Cotton Night-Cap Country*, and *The Inn Album*—critical on the part of friendly reviewers, and sufficiently savage on the part of the unfriendly—must have made him feel that he was back where he had been for so many weary years and in this mood he wrote *Pacchiarotto and How He Worked in Distemper* (1876).

Crude the title poem certainly is—to a point that shocked Browning's admirers. He had told Elizabeth during his courtship how little he cared, he had addressed in *The Ring and the Book* the British Public "Ye who like me not, (God love you!)" with most tolerant good-humor. Yet "such love of a lie have the verminous tribe" he now writes concerning reviewers. As time went on the situation had worn him down. He appeared to resent with special intensity this return to their early bad manner. Besides disagreeable reviews there was what might be called a constant rearguard sniping—especially from one very unsuccessful poet, Alfred Austin (ironically later made Poet Laureate as a reward for his able articles in the Conservative interest!).

Alfred Austin I remember vividly: he used to stay at our house and we collected some pleasing stories, including the remarks of a hatter when my father observed in his shop an unusually high hat of the type denominated stove-pipe. "Yes, Sir, that's Mr. Alfred Austin's. 'E's a very small gentleman, but what with 'is 'at and what with 'is 'eels 'e do make up wonderful."

When Browning sent Tennyson some word of praise saying "I beg to stick the bunch in your buttonhole" and Tennyson declared he felt ——'s "cork heels added to my boots," surely the dash meant Austin.

We young ones enjoyed his efforts to add inches if not a cubit to his stature. We particularly relished it when, balancing precariously on his 'igh 'eels, he fell into the fireplace. He was terribly soulful and had written a poem called "Madonna's Child," which he used to read to my mother. I imagine I annoyed him when in all innocence I proclaimed my enthusiasm for Browning—and I still remember my rage when he described Elizabeth as "his lyric love half governess half bore." Browning had long been dead when I knew Alfred Austin—but could this remark or something like it have been made earlier and got back to him?

Anyhow, Alfred Austin did attack him often, not only his poetry but his alleged social ambitions, in which Browning discerned the voice of envy. He enjoyed, he told Isa Blagden, when questioning the wisdom of his own immersion in the world of fashion, the thought of how it annoyed "that filthy little snob." (Perhaps it is worth noting that the only writer, wooed as Browning was by the world of fashion and steadily resisting absorption in it, seems to have been Dickens.)

Why did not Browning ignore Austin's sniping—why bring into "Pacchiarotto" an allusion to the tiny stature of which Austin was so painfully conscious? Apart from this the May dance of the chimney sweeps (bringing in more dirt than they removed) is simply riotous fun, and he might have gone down to posterity as a fundamentally good-natured man.

He was obviously having tremendous fun with his chimney sweeps—and if, as DeVane suggests, Austin's articles in the Conservative interest were also stirring his wrath, there must have been a special relish in depicting Austin among the sweeps. Political passions ran high, as we see in Browning's references to Disraeli and the remarks exchanged with Gladstone about his insincerity. Austin was tarred with Disraeli's brush before he began journalistically to collect Browning's soot. Pacchiarotto had been as unsuccessful a painter-politician as Austin a poet-politician. Disraeli, after meeting Browning, the friend and supporter of Gladstone, wrote: "a noisy conceited poet; all the talk about pictures and art, and Raffaelle, and what Sterne calls 'the correggiosity of Correggio.' "[4]

The chimney sweeps clad in "drab blues and yellows" represent, DeVane has noted, the colors of the leading periodicals in which Browning's critics wrote. But besides the magazines a book published in 1870 by Alfred Austin, *The Poetry of the Period*, had attacked both Browning ("muddy and unmusical to the last degree") and Tennyson, asking where we were to look for the next poet. In "At the Mermaid" Browning transfers this question to an earlier age, quoting Ben Jonson and speaking as Shakespeare: "I—'Next Poet?' No my hearties, / I nor am nor fain would be!" This poem, with "House," "Shop," and the Epilogue, gives Browning's answer to the critics and his general view of privacy and publicity. He often did himself an injustice by the violence of his more one-sided statements, and one sees at a first reading a real contradiction between the opening of his heart in so many poems and his insistence in "At the Mermaid":

> Which of you did I enable
> Once to slip inside my breast,
> There to catalogue and label
> What I like least, what love best.

In these four poems he solves the contradiction almost exactly as Chesterton did with the Love Letters, of which Browning would have abhorred the publication. But in the controversy that followed Chesterton pointed out that the wrong reason was given against it. How could it be shocking to reveal a love which both poets had shouted from the housetops in their poetry? Chesterton held (I think wrongly) that these letters obscured rather than revealed, with their private language, little intimate jokes, and allusions to whose point we have no clue.

Turn to "House," which for some will bring Blitz-time memories of fancies and surmises when a dwelling was thrown open, as it is in this poem by an earthquake:

vi

The owner? Oh, he had been crushed, no doubt!
   "Odd tables and chairs for a man of wealth!
What a parcel of musty old books about!
   He smoked,—no wonder he lost his health!

vii

"I doubt if he bathed before he dressed.
   A brasier?—the pagan, he burned perfumes!
You see it is proved, what the neighbours guessed:
   His wife and himself had separate rooms."

To such impertinences the poet's calling perpetually throws him open, and this was what Browning hated: unknown people writing for information about his wife, unending questions about personal meanings in his poetry, newspaper paragraphs:

viii

Friends, the goodman of the house at least
   Kept house to himself till an earthquake came:
'Tis the fall of its frontage permits you feast
   On the inside arrangements you praise or blame.

ix

Outside should suffice for evidence:
   And whoso desires to penetrate
Deeper, must dive by the spirit-sense—
   No optics like yours, at any rate!

"The poets pour us wine," quotes Browning from Elizabeth in his Epilogue—and he questions whether that wine can be at once sweet and strong. Not, he concludes, while it is new. And he doubts whether the best of brews is drunk as abundantly as readers claim. "There are forty barrels with Shakespeare's brand. / Some five or six are abroach: the rest / Stand spigoted, fauceted. . . ." The same is true of Milton. As for himself " 'Tis said I brew stiff drink, / But the deuce a flavour of grape is there." Shall he today strip his meadows bare of cowslips to make wine, sweet at the moment or "help to concoct what makes you wink / And goes to your head till you think you think!" Or shall he resort, for "a tongue that's fur and a palate—paste?!" to something stronger than cowslips but not sweet at all. "I'll posset and cosset them, nothing loth, / Henceforward with nettle-broth."

Strong wine needs keeping, sweet can be drunk at once. His own is

> Sweet for the future,—strong for the nonce!
> Stuff you should stow away, ensconce.
> In the deep and dark, to be found fast-fixed
> At the century's close: such time strength spends
> A-sweetening for my friends!

This volume is too often judged by its title poem which is the longest but very far from the most important. Besides "Numpholeptos" and "St. Martin's Summer," both discussed earlier, Browning makes two important contributions to his own philosophy in "Bifurcation" and "Fears and Scruples." Swinburne, as we have seen, thought highly of "Bifurcation," and it is important in making clear something left vague in "The Statue and the Bust." "Bifurcation" is a straight piece of casuistry—in the correct meaning of the word, not in the sense often attached to it of its *mis*use. For casuistry means that conscience must be followed even where it is ill-instructed, even where its demands conflict with law not merely human but divine. The outsider, however well he knows that law, *can* only be left with a question mark about each individual case, for he cannot read any conscience but his own.

In "The Statue and the Bust" it is argued that Browning did not condone the sin of wife and lover but only attacked their weakness over the constantly postponed, finally abandoned, flight. In "Bifurcation" man and woman love unlawfully: he wants to carry that love to its conclusion; she from conscience refuses: "We were two lovers; let me lie by her, / My tomb beside her tomb. . . ."

Each tomb should be inscribed with the fact of their choice between duty and love, she confident "That heaven repairs what wrong earth's journey did, / When love from life-long exile comes at call."

But hers had been the easy journey through "a smiling country"; he, tripped by stones, pierced by flint, looks to a heaven

> *"Where love from duty ne'er disparts, I trust,*
> *And two halves make that whole, whereof—since here*
> *One must suffice a man—why, this one must!"*

> Inscribe each tomb thus: then, some sage acquaint
> The simple—which holds sinner, which holds saint!

The special occasion for Browning's protest against intrusion may have been the attempt to publish a biography of Elizabeth during his lifetime. Against this he always fought tooth and nail. A couple of interesting letters from Christina Rossetti,[5] who had been asked to write one, express her strong feeling that it should not be undertaken unless with Browning's entire good will. It might have been an exquisite interpretation of one poet by another, which one feels sad to have lost: but how fantastically difficult of accomplishment in the husband's lifetime.

Whatever the immediate cause, we see in these very various poems something of a perpetual strife in Browning between two conflicting desires: a longing for the white light—for a revelation at once clear and profound of his deepest thoughts—and a shrinking from this revelation, a dissolution of it into prismatic hues brilliantly painted, yet so apt to be falsely interpreted. He must speak out *himself*; but poetwise he was never satisfied that he had so spoken—and the constant accusation of obscurity confirmed this feeling.

Publication year of the *Agamemnon* brought a summer holiday spent with perhaps the closest friend Browning and Sarianna shared— Anne Egerton Smith. The great link between her and Browning was music; they seldom missed an important concert, seldom left London before the musical part of the season ended. But Miss Smith was not a social person in the seasonal sense and all three enjoyed long walks in the Swiss countryside, the beauty of mountains and sunsets. In "La Saisiaz" (1878) Browning gives a vivid picture of the high-perched villa where he and Sarianna spent so many months—and of the tragedy when their friend so suddenly died.

The last day they had walked together and had planned a longer expedition for the morrow. They had talked much too of the soul and immortality, on which a symposium was appearing in *The Nineteenth Century*, started by Frederick Harrison. It was almost an extension of the Metaphysical Society. "Ideal" Ward, R. H. Hutton of *The Spectator*, Huxley, and others were writing, the debate continued, and the friends were following it eagerly.

In the morning Browning, after an early swim, waited awhile for their hostess on the terrace, then seeing her shutters open but no sign of her through the window he called his sister.[6] They entered the room and found her lying on the floor—still warm but dead. It came as an appalling shock as well as an immense grief—and called forth the poem which has been praised as one of the most moving of his later works. Yet to me it seems strangely arid. True there are lovely touches, but the *discussion* rather than any vision of immortality most unpoetically dominates.

"La Saisiaz" has been considered Browning's contribution to the symposium. He had foredoomed it to dreariness—and possibly to ineffectiveness—by leaving aside the Christian revelation. For Browning once told Churton Collins how profoundly he believed alike in God and in immortality, but that he *did not* believe we could reach the absolute certainty of survival by reason alone: we need God's revelation. Such being his view it is not surprising to find a dryness in his exposition of arguments which he himself found inadequate (or unconvincing).

M

Meeting him at this time, Buchanan was, he says, shocked. Here was a man who had written so beautifully on death and immortality "completely agitated and unstrung," at the suddenness, the "piteous circumstances. He was like a child, startled amid its play, by a lightning flash which strikes down one of its companions."[7]

In the volume entitled *La Saisiaz* we find also "The Two Poets of Croisic," which has stanzas lifting it in importance far above its average pedestrian level. Some of these appear at first a flat contradiction of two of the most discussed lines in "La Saisiaz," where we read:

> I must say—or choke in silence—"Howsoever came my fate,
> Sorrow did and joy did nowise,—life well weighed,—
> > preponderate"

Yet in "The Two Poets" Browning makes happiness the test of success.

> "What quality preponderating may
> Turn the scale as it trembles?" End the strife
> By asking "Which one led a happy life?"

The lament in "La Saisiaz" is surely the expression of a universal experience. A sorrow brings with it the memory of all sorrows, a loss renews each earlier sense of loss. This fresh loss at La Saisiaz had widened the gap left by father, mother, above all, wife. Once more made aware of mortality he could not instantly react with the joy remaining in this life, the clear vision of the life to come.

But there is another element in the later poem: no real contradiction, Browning is saying, exists between a happy life and the sorrows it contains. The man weakly unhappy "shrieked or sobbed, or wept or wailed / Or simply had the dumps." The other, overcoming,

> . . . prevailed
> A strong since joyful man who stood distinct
> Above slave-sorrows to his chariot linked.

Was not his lot to feel more?

"When the knife cuts," Elizabeth had written long ago, "one cries: that is certain. A special pang from a special wound is different from habitual depression. . . . I struggle against habitual sadness as against corruption or ignorance, and against ingratitude besides." And life's comforts, said Browning to the young daughter of a friend, are greater than its sorrows "because their sources deeper are!"

We are aware in these two poems of a struggle and a reconciliation between the two moods in which this alleged optimist faced life, seeing deeper than most pessimists into its darkest places. Of his own life in the years he most treasured he had written to Isa in 1867:

The general impression of the past is as if it had been pain. I would not live it over again, not one day of it. Yet all that seems my *real* life—and before and after, nothing at all; I look back on all my life when I look *there:* and life is painful. I always think of this when I read the Odyssey—Homer makes the surviving Greeks, whenever they refer to Troy, just say of it, "At Troy, where the Greeks suffered so." Yet all their life was in that ten years at Troy.

Returning to the Croisic poem one becomes aware of vision striving for expression. Browning tells of the "orgasm" which effects the conception of poetry. "I remember," wrote Edmund Gosse, "Browning telling me that old as he was, he never ceased to suffer from 'puerperal fever' immediately after having published a book." The poet's life, absorbed in creativeness, passes only too swiftly

> On earth's break-up, amid the falling rocks,
> He might be penning in a wild dismay,
> Caught with his work half-done on Judgment Day.

Yet the incomplete poet even if held in by "earth's dim and dense," reminds us of earth's values:

. . . stars abound
O'erhead, but then—what flowers make glad the ground!

And the volume ends with the cricket of the Epilogue, whose song
supplied the note when the poet's instrument failed him

> With its little heart on fire,
> Lighted on the crippled lyre.

10 The Public Face

*She died alone in the room with Browning. . . . He,
closing the door of that room behind him, closed a
door in himself, and none ever saw Browning upon
earth again, but only a splendid surface.*

G. K. CHESTERTON

"THE WALL that built out the idyll," says Henry James, "of which memory and imagination were virtually composed for him stood there behind him solidly enough. . . . It contained an invisible door . . . of which he kept the golden key—carrying the same about with him even in the pocket of his dinner-waistcoat, yet even in his most splendid expansions showing it, happy man, to none."

But was this really to be happy? The genius like all men needs interchange, revealing more than a surface however splendid, and Browning had had it—to a great extent in youth with his intimate friends, especially Alfred Domett, then far more fully from 1845 to 1861 with Elizabeth. Since her death the letters to Isa, to Story, to his sister, and the intense devotion to Pen partly fill the gap on the emotional side; nothing fills it on that of the intellect, up to the friendship with Julia Wedgwood, the breaking of which was a minor tragedy. He needed for his genius an outpouring and a response, which included a critical admiration for his work.

Henriette Corkran once remarked to the American novelist Gertrude Atherton that Browning was longing to marry one of the pretty young women who worshiped him, but would not abandon his public image of eternal constancy to the memory of his dead love.

Henriette, the novelist says, was a highly malicious gossip—and Julia Wedgwood was neither very young nor very pretty. Yet I cannot but feel that had she patiently accepted suspense for a few more years of friendship she might have won more—not all that Robert had to give Elizabeth twenty years earlier, but enough for a happy marriage. As things were, the recurring mood "frenetic to be free," was not enough to save an immensely popular man lacking a wife's protection from a tremendous pressure brought by the surrounding society.

There is nothing in Browning's life of the enormous public acclaim won by Tennyson—nothing to match the strangers who would sneak into the garden at Farringford or mob the poet at a railway station; nothing like the world publicity of Dickens or the public readings when young women would lie prone on the platform in an overcrowded hall and each petal of the rose he wore be seized as a precious relic.

Browning's steady refusal to speak even a few words in public, his almost savage insistence on the separation between public and private life, plus the widespread belief that he belonged only to the intellectuals and would be found unintelligible by the masses, put this kind of popularity out of the question. But he got another kind from which both Tennyson and Dickens escaped, Tennyson by living in the country, Dickens by electing to be host rather than guest, king of his company and not merely a companion, valued indeed, but one among many.

Browning's qualities and defects alike narrowed his fame in a wider world, but increased it among just those who most readily put pen to paper. Literary characters, men and women whose social life left time for diaries and letter writing, journalists, fellow poets, aspirants to fame, American visitors: all these had their word to say about the man who by the middle seventies had become an "inveterate diner out."

If, in estimating the man, his poetry comes first, his actions and his letters next, a place must still be given to the impressions which, over the next twenty years, would pour forth from every kind of person and record every aspect—from the outer side of the "wall" where Henry James stood with a keen eye more intelligently observant than most of his contemporaries.

"I have often heard people say," writes William Sharp, "that a handshake from Browning was like an electric shock." Pleasurably exciting to some, it was to others disturbing: one woman asked not to be seated next to him as she felt his mere proximity like an attack of pins and needles.

This is typical of all the memories of Browning: his was a strong, sometimes overwhelming, personality; he was loved, he was detested. Mrs. Orr speaks of the "hysterical sensibilities which for some years past he had unconsciously but not unfrequently aroused in the minds of women, and even of men." Elizabeth had written with pleased amusement that many women loved him too much for decency—"perhaps, a little, I also."

Yet it was chiefly women who were repelled or irritated. Miss Mitford had annoyed Elizabeth by her carping criticisms, Joseph Arnould's sister complained of his pomaded hair and "Jewish" appearance, Mrs. Carlyle, as we have seen, grew to dislike him more and more, describing him rather oddly as "a fluff of feathers." Mrs. Drew (Mary Gladstone) in her diary complained of being constantly sent in to dinner with "old Browning." He sat too close, she complained, he puffed and blew and even spat into her face; she saw him wipe Lady Marian Alford's eyes with a dirty handkerchief. She tried in vain to think of "Abt Vogler"—but no "he *could* not have written it."

Later on, as the Browning craze increasingly swept the country, above all the social and intellectual group to which she belonged, Mrs. Drew changed her mind. Her eyes, she said, had been "holden." They still met often, and she claimed in her diary to have gone "Browning mad."

W. H. Mallock, author of a best-selling social and philosophical novel, *The New Republic*, had sent his own poems to Browning and received "a message of a flattering kind in regard to them." He described in his *Memoirs of Life and Literature* the meeting that followed:

he held out both his hands to me with an almost boisterous cordiality. His eyes sparkled with laughter, his beard was carefully trimmed, and an air of fashion was exhaled from his dazzling white waistcoat. He did not, so far as I remember, make any approach to the subject of literature at all, but reduced both Jowett and myself to something like complete silence by a constant flow of anecdotes and social allusions, which, although not deficient in point, had more in them of jocularity than wit.

It is a little comic to see the Barrett objection to his marrying Elizabeth—that he was not a "gentleman"—revived at the moment when Browning was being, in Henry James' words, "crowned and recrowned" by so many "importunate hands." There was, said John Churton Collins, a "marked vulgarity in Browning. A certain indescribable savour of sycophancy of a man eager to be of a grade to which he did not belong." And Julian Hawthorne (son of Nathaniel), remembering Italian days, wrote: "Browning had become another Browning": the barbered beard, the silk hat "all below it of Piccadilly and Pall Mall . . . staid, grave, urbane, polished; he was a rich banker, he was a perfected butler, no one would have suspected him of poetry." Sir Sidney Colvin thought all this ridiculous. On Browning's "loudness of voice" and "vigorous geniality of bearing" he comments: "the veriest oaf could not have taken them for vulgarity . . . an inborn vital energy surpassing by fivefold those of other men."[1]

One can see the debate continuing in that ridiculous Victorian society, the more intelligent recognizing with Colvin that the exuberance and the loud voice (resulting, said his sister, from the deafness of two of Browning's intimate friends) were very different from vulgarity. "Cordiality," Colvin went on, was his chief quality, and his "admirable constancy to old friends." At a wedding party "Orion" Horne, with whom before their marriage both Brownings had worked, began without invitation and with singular inappropriateness to sing Spanish songs accompanying himself on a guitar. The guests grew impatient, the host increasingly embarrassed. Browning, "throwing a protecting arm around him," brought the songs to an end, saying, "That was charming, Horne. It quite took us back to the warm south." But George Russell, another inveterate diner out, describes how, when intensely bored by a man asking questions about his poetry, Browning "laid his hand on the questioner's shoulder saying 'But, my dear fellow, this is too bad. I am monopolising you,' and skipped out of the corner."[2]

Russell was no devotee of his poetry—"very ugly and unmusical and quite unintelligible . . . attempts to turn the thirty-nine articles into verse." But he found Browning "socially delightful . . . bright, cheerful and quite unaffected. No slouch hats or conspirators' cloaks for Browning."

Even newspapers entered into this particular debate. "Imagine their surprise," wrote *The World* of the poet's addicts, "on discovering that the crabbed and mystical poet is identical with the possessor of the compact little figure," with his "urbane and genial bearing, the well made clothes," yet as "far from a dandy as a sensible man can be."

His tailor, Browning commented, "seemed a little more careful in his measurements than normal—so can fame impose."[3]

Acknowledging Browning's identity with Vaudrey in "The Private Life," James writes: "I have never ceased to ask myself, in this particular sound, normal, hearty presence, all so assertive and so whole, all bristling with prompt responses and expected opinions and usual views . . . what lodgment on such premises, the rich proud genius one adored could ever have contrived a lodging." But in his *Reminiscences of Lord Bath*, M. McCall writes of Browning as "the best talker of the evening. . . . From poetry he passed on to printing, then to the doctrine of evolution, and then to Plato's *Phaedo* as an argument for immortality; to his *Republic* as a study in politics, and to his Dialogues in general as superb exhibitions of literary style. Browning's enthusiasm seemed to inspire Lord Bath." At past two in the morning, one of the guests made a move to depart, but Browning suggested "that we should make a real Greek symposium of it, and continue the dialogue until breakfast."

Even the "public" man, as distinct from the seer and poet, offered, it would seem, astonishing contradictions. "Who is that too exuberant financier?" someone asked, but other guests tell of hostesses sending the butler several times to get the men to leave the dining room for the drawing room when Browning was of the company. When the famous actor Henry Irving was there, they would talk of Shakespeare until the whole party gathered around them. When Justin McCarthy, an

Irish member of the House of Commons, made a casual remark about Edmund Kean, Browning gave him "a perfect picture of the great tragedian's style and manner." "There was not," McCarthy continues, "the faintest suggestion of the clever talker talking to show his cleverness; it was simply the outpouring of a man filled with his subject," a subject "started by the merest chance." Amazed by the judgment of some "English authoress" of the date that Browning was "a mere chatterer in society and a devotee of rank and fashion," he goes on, "then let chatter thrive, and the more we have of it the more happy and the better cultured shall we be." And he and others note that Browning took as much trouble and talked as readily to the least important as to the most important of the company.

In his *Memories of Half a Century* R. C. Lehmann tells of an inherited friendship with Browning, who wanted to give him Pen's pony when Pen had outgrown it; and he remembered well the "extraordinary cordiality" which made a boy feel that Browning had a real interest in talking with him and hearing of his own small concerns. "No man," he felt, "was ever more free from bardic pose"—but he was the more aware of the poet through the absence of the "bard."

Lehmann remembered an occasional flare-up of anger and he sets down a story by his father of one bad quarrel. For Forster, Browning had a sincere gratitude and affection, but he had let himself get into a difficult situation in which he *had* to dine with him every Sunday. "Anyone wanting Browning to dinner on Sundays could only secure him after some diplomatic negotiations, of which one of the fundamental conditions was that Mr. and Mrs. Forster were to be invited." Browning, Lehmann surmises, had got a little tired of this "literary bear leading," but the occasion of the quarrel was a story he told which Forster ridiculed as a foolish invention. The Princess Royal being taken ill at Marlborough House, no carriage could be found to fetch a doctor. To Forster's disbelief Browning replied that some titled lady (the name is discreetly omitted) vouched for its truth. Forster continuing contemptuous, Browning became furious at the aspersion on his informant's truthfulness and, seizing a decanter, threatened to throw it at Forster's head. The host got everyone else out of the room and tried in vain to reconcile them. Lehmann declares that "a kind of peace" was patched up only shortly before Forster's death; but in *New Letters* is one of gratitude to Forster for a good review and an assurance that the break in their friendship has not destroyed Browning's warm memories of all Forster had done for him.

There was in Browning a curious streak, always latent, but much accentuated since his wife's death. An early critic C. H. Herford talks of moods of "savage isolation"—but actually he needed the isolation to calm the moods. "Be gentle in your thoughts of poor Robert," Elizabeth once wrote to an intimate friend, "who means more affectionately than appears sometimes." He had enormous trouble, I think, in handling his own moods. Lady Ritchie (Anne Thackeray) tells an odd story of a period when he suddenly would not speak to her—turning to his other neighbor throughout a dinner, avoiding her at parties. Browning had heard a rumor that she had started one of the endless stories of his remarrying. Milsand telling him that he was acting childishly, Browning repented with equal suddenness. He rushed across the fields (they were all in Brittany for the summer) to her cottage. Seeing him "running violently towards my lodging, I rushed downstairs, leapt into his arms, we both cried together and had a lovely time."

The anonymous writer of *Leaves from a Life* records the kindness with which Browning not only gave him an autograph for an invalid friend but added a sentence in four or five languages: Italian, Greek, Latin, Hebrew, and, he thinks, German. They would meet often at dinner parties and on Sunday afternoons at Mrs. Procter's, "whose gatherings were famous because she never admitted a bore twice, or anyone who had not in some way or other contributed to the mental wealth of nations." As she grew older, Mrs. Procter would speak of Browning as always faithful in his visits, while twice a week he would read aloud to an even closer friend, Alexandra Orr, whose eyes were failing her.

Certainly these two never made the complaint which Stephen Coleridge (in *Memories*) tells us he had heard—that Browning "almost always talked down to ladies and discoursed to them about bonnets and clothes: this not seldom filled clever women with annoyance." I find it hard to believe in this as habitual, given the recorded memories of Browning's many women friends. But a man who dines out every night probably makes a good many rather silly mistakes. And one has to remember that no memoir of the period, American or English, was complete without a Browning story.

Visitors to the Casa Guidi had commonly ended by finding their best expectations fulfilled—but of course most of them were seeking the "poetess," whose dark hair, tragic eyes, sofa and obvious ill health filled the part so completely. Now it was Browning's turn—the American visitor—like the one approaching Boston, heard sounds "which turn out to be its people reciting Browning" or he embarked for London as, even more than Boston, the shrine "where Deity deigns to touch the earth."

Thus wrote half-mockingly the Quaker singer David Bispham. But Mrs. Bailey Aldrich recounts how Browning's "immortal books" had "come a' wooing with my lover, and had we not weighed and pondered ... seeking to pluck out the heart of the mystery." Arriving in London she was "thrilled" to be meeting him at dinner.

But with the first glance the knees that had involuntarily bent stiffened and my idol fell shattered to the floor. Rising from its place stood a man of medium height, rather robust, full beard and the perfect air of *savoir-faire* that comes only to the man of society, the man of the world ... the white waistcoat, the galloon on his trowsers, all were of the *dernier cri*. The diamond studs at his breast ... seeming to say "Ah simple one, where is your lost leader now?"

Above all was she disturbed by a crush hat carried under the arm and sat upon through dinner—and we leave this pathetic worshiper almost weeping into her soup.

The great actress Mary Anderson felt that Browning "resembled one of our old-school Southern country gentlemen more than my ideal of England's mystic poet." His "friendly chattiness" was "more agreeable than distinguished." But a merely society acquaintance "least of all reveals the deep, earnest and best side of any character," and it was in friends' studios that she saw Browning at his best, more especially in his "fearlessly enthusiastic appreciation" of young and struggling artists. To one of them he said, "Sir you are a genius and I am proud to shake you by the hand." Leslie Stephen was critical of those who

> accept the commonplace doctrine that the poet and the man may be wholly different persons. Browning, that is, could talk like a brilliant man of the world, and the commonplace person could infer that he did not possess the feelings which he did not care to exhibit at a dinner party.

And in a footnote Stephen adds:

> I happened to meet Browning at a moment of great interest to me. I knew little of him then, and had rather taken him at the valuation indicated above. He spoke a few words, showing such tenderness, insight and sympathy that I have never forgotten his kindness; and from that time I knew him for what he was. . . .[4]

Leslie Stephen had made a fusion which a yet abler man was still seeking. Henry James, whose complete confrontation of what may be called the Browning riddle would come only after the poet's death, differed from the observer who thought he "talked down" to women, and differed also from the suggestion of Browning's snobbery. He wrote (in 1888) to their mutual Venetian-American friends the Daniel Curtises:

> I am a little vexed with Browning for not humoring a little more our so honorable countess—but he has nothing of that in him, and has never had, and it is partly what I have always liked him for, that he is exactly the same with everyone and has only one sturdy manner and attitude. But he isn't soothing enough with women—though apparently your remoter neighbor thinks so. How pleased she must have been at the failure of the Pisani's encounter with him— though doubtless *he* was too unconscious of it to inform her of it. I am glad he has given you some glimpse of his diviner part—I have never seized the link between the two—it is a solution of continuity. But I have lately been reading him over a good deal and it

seems to me that he is on the whole the writer of our time of whom, in the face of the rest of the world, the English tongue may be most proud—for he has touched *every*thing, and with a breadth! I put him very high—higher than anyone.[5]

Young people enjoyed Browning and he enjoyed them. Sitting next to the seventeen-year-old daughter of Boyd Carpenter he told her of the famous hair-brushing of his childhood and how the teacher, oiling the hair after brushing, would chant "while countless blessing on me shed/Like holy oil upon my head." He told her how Leigh Hunt had recognized himself in the Skimpole of *Bleak House* and felt "as if I was dining among friends and received a slap in the face." He expatiated on the goodness of Charles Lamb, thought by Barry Cornwall the best man he had known. And of course he spoke of Pen.[6]

Frankness in criticism he and Elizabeth had always recognized as a prime duty—to Alice Corkran sending him poems he questioned whether even the brightest moonlight would show flowers in their vivid colors; he also entreated her not to use "he" or "she" for animals or inanimate things.

To a godson, christened Alfred Stanley Browning (Tennyson), he wrote: "You have three names, one glorious, the other good, and the last that of an old friend, who feels a great interest in you." To which the boy replied, "But are not you too rather glorious?"

Lady Troubridge related in *Memories and Reflections* how at the age of twelve she was standing in an art gallery staring at a very un-draped picture, the Judgment of Paris. "Presently an elderly gentleman, with a short grey beard and a pink flower in his buttonhole asked her what she thought of it—and then said gaily 'Well, let us make a funny rhyme about it.' 'You begin,' I said to my new found friend: ... Listeners came a little nearer.

" 'Well now,' he said, 'I think this is what we might say:

> He gazed and gazed and gazed and gazed
> Amazed Amazed Amazed Amazed!'

"That was all, but the way he said it was indescribably humorous. So many people laughed that I felt shy."

No one, it seems, young or old, could dare return home after dining in Browning's company without a good story. One is told by the novelist W. B. Maxwell in *Time Gathered*. Browning who, in Italy, had gone from light wines to no wine at all, drank in his later dinings-out neither sherry, claret, nor champagne, but hostesses who were at all intimate would see that a bottle of port was put beside him. Among these was a Mrs. Skirrow, known, says Maxwell, as a lion hunter whose prize specimen was the poet. There was a real affection between him and both Skirrows as many letters bear witness; and when (as was so often the case) his hostess was obliged to place in her own neighborhood men of rank, she would by affectionate glances and "little swift noddings" indicate to Browning that he held the first place in her thoughts. One evening these signals met with no response. "He sat there very solemn. If he nodded his head it was gloomily, and never a smile came back from him." After dinner the dire truth broke upon her. "You had your port of course?" she asked, and he replied, "No, I had no port." "Oh how dreadful, will you have some now?"

But it was too late. "Oh pray," said Mr. Browning, "it does not matter in the least."

"But," comments Maxwell, "of course it mattered most frightfully."

How much more frightful to have the eyes of journalists, diarists, all those who live by the pen, fastened upon one with merciless, unremitting observation. I wonder if in those later days the prize lion looked back longingly, not only to the happiness of his married life, but to the more tranquil atmosphere of being "le mari de Madame."

Did Browning have a sense of humor? His friend Story said "great vivacity but not the least humour—some sarcasm." It is a question almost impossible to answer with a century's gap scarcely bridgeable by the printed word. In Browning's favor is his power to laugh at a joke against himself. Take the incident of the group of young women who crowned him, slightly buttery from their crumpets, with a wreath of roses, while he, instead of feeling the fool he may have looked, enjoyed their enjoyment and suggested that the poem he should recite was "It was roses, roses all the way." Or in *The Inn Album:* "I myself could find a better rhyme!/That bard's a Browning; he neglects the form:/But ah, the sense, ye gods, the weighty sense." Take his answer when asked if he minded "all this adulation" from the Edinburgh undergraduates: "I have waited forty years for it—and now I enjoy it." Take above all his attitude to the Browning Society, the story of which will be told in Chapter 12. Only a man with a good sense of humor could have received without embarrassment the slightly comic adulation of many of its members and the mockery it produced among most of his friends.

Henriette Corkran, visiting Sarianna, found Browning with a sick goose in his arms, one of the two pets he had christened Quarterly and Edinburgh. Fond of him herself and having especially loved his father, she observed quite unemotionally Browning's rather gushing manner as he linked her arm in his. It meant, she said, "nothing but hearty genial goodwill." But this explanation was not relished by some, and Henriette was much amused by one wealthy American widow who claimed to have just discovered that Browning's affection for her was *not* merely platonic. Henriette herself, watching "his behaviour to each and all," thought him "a bit of a snob, but that is a small and common fault, especially in England," and in this case it went with attention to young or old, plain or beautiful from "a strong poet-thinker." It was pleasant to be with him in his home, against the background of the tapestry and furniture of the old Casa Guidi, with the bust of Elizabeth and her pervading presence—and above all to see his touching pride in Pen's work. On a central easel was a landscape: "Dear Millais came here yesterday, and praised the picture enthusiastically, . . . always encourages Pen. . . . He has found his vocation at last."

Felix Moscheles, an artist of the period, felt that Browning himself was an artist *manqué*. Browning told him that he had never learned to paint, "form had more attraction for him than colour." He sat for Moscheles, who, surprisingly with such an impatient man, found him an excellent model. But it was a chance of watching the painter at work "always enjoying as I do the sight of creation by another process than that of the head with only pen and paper to help. How expeditiously the brush works." And in another letter: "the old aspirations come thickly back to memory when I see you at work as who knows but I myself might have worked once."

Perhaps he did some sketches in the studio, for Moscheles relates how he would tip the model; he also waxes eloquent over Browning's determination to take trouble for others, to prevent them from taking trouble for him: "That was Browning all over." And after his friends had had pictures rejected "Browning had his visits of condolence to pay . . . telling me how for years not a poem of his was read." Now a large new edition sold in a month—"To be sure one must live long enough," he added—for late in his fifties he had still described himself to Millais' wife as the most unpopular poet that ever was.

The enormous number of his dinner invitations was due no doubt in part to the lion-hunting instinct, but far more to the fun of listening to Browning's talk.

> I can now see your father [wrote Heywood Sumner to the son of Sir James Paget] with Browning on one side and Romanes on the other, telling stories about the stigmata (there had been a girl in Belgium who had been attracting much attention by her claim to this manifestation)—then about blushing—then about electrical fishes—and last, a story of Browning's, of a girl in their lodgings somewhere in Italy, who they found regularly stole their tea, which they bore with, but rebelled when they found that she likewise stole their candles, yet were mollified when they found out that she stole their candles in order to burn them before a little shrine in expiation of her sin in stealing their tea.

Paget remembered too how Browning remarked that he and George Eliot were not at one about the giving of autographs, which she refused. He usually gave them "but he drew the line at the request for an old necktie, from somebody who was constructing a quilt of great men's neckties."[7]

N

11 Daily Life in London

Browning was not only a very indulgent father, but an indulgent father of a very conventional type: he had rather the chuckling pride of the city gentleman than the educational gravity of the intellectual.

G. K. CHESTERTON

BROWNING'S favorite pose was that of man-of-the-world, but his home life had always come first. He had remade it now with son and sister, pale shadow though it must at times have seemed. Not that Sarianna was shadowy: we hear from Elizabeth of her clear good sense, from Henriette Corkran of her humor, power of telling a story, and immense vitality. Probably she was only occasionally included in dinner and country-house invitations. But Henry James wrote to Mrs. Curtis, wife of their mutual friend in Venice, in Browning's last year: "I took Miss Browning down, the other day, at a long, dull dinner and Sordello was opposite to us—and he dozed. But Miss Browning didn't!"[1] Sarianna was, one realizes, a good deal excited about the new world in which she found herself as sister of a famous brother. Devoted to him and to Pen, Sarianna seems to have echoed his ideas a little more than was good for him. He had lost with Elizabeth the healthy criticism which a wife his equal in intelligence would be more ready and able to give than a younger sister. Still, it was much to have her companionship, and she was a willing hostess to the more intimate friends who came to tea or lunch at Warwick Crescent.

The dinner party of Victorian days was an awesome affair with its many courses (soup, fish, main dish, pudding, savory, cheese, fruit, with all the appropriate wines, coffee, liqueurs, and port). Browning seems seldom if ever to have attempted to give one. Tea may still have been an evening event for those, like Carlyle, who dined early, but Browning was not one of them: anyhow he was out so often as greatly to prize a solitary evening. References to tea mean probably the afternoon cup.

Two friendships, one renewed after twenty-one years or more and one recently made, were with Alfred Domett on his return to England in the early seventies (already mentioned in Chapter 6), and with George Smith, of whom something has been said as Browning's publisher.

The correspondence between Browning and Domett seems to have lapsed during the Italian years. Domett, beginning a letter in 1864 "My dear friend of old days," laments the ill success of his efforts to get to England, tells of his delight when he realized that there was in Browning's "Guardian Angel" an unmistakable "apostrophe" to himself. "It was like a flash of light, piercing from the upper world down into the God-abandoned glooms of our infernal 'bolge' where one lay lost for ever in a life-in-death or a death-in-life worse than death itself." He had not written then—nor, it would appear, at the time of Elizabeth's death, but "What a loss has the breaking of our acquaintance and communion been to me!"[2]

This letter is in the Alexander Turnbull Library, Wellington, but not Browning's reply to it, which Domett probably brought with him to England. The next information we get about the renewal of their friendship comes eight years later in a letter to a New Zealander called by Domett "Arcturus." He was suffering now from a common reaction of returned expatriates, disillusion. His feelings on returning to England from New Zealand are interesting in their similarity to Browning's on returning from Italy. Both felt acutely the absence of sunshine and the pressure of fog, the lack of light and color. And both felt, too, what Browning later did not, the snobbish outlook, which, as he then described it, made "getting aristocratic connexions and friendships" man's "chief end" in Victorian England. The weather, Domett declares, only

Hamlet's words will fit: "O *horrible, horrible,* most *horrible.*" Worse still is the social order: the inhabitants smile at his criticisms "with a *fatuousness* of perfect content with their lot which is truly irritating if not disgusting. . . . The higher classes *seem* to have less freedom of thought, more regard for conventions of all kinds and as thick-skinned and fashion-driven or nose-led as ever. . . ."

The climax of reaction is reached when at the end of the letter he sighs over "the want of our fine little *Library* at Wellington, one seems in a cloud of physical and intellectual darkness. One never sees a *book* and hardly a periodical even."

The rest of the letter is filled with Browning and with the fate of Domett's own Maori poem in which Browning took a great interest.

Yes—I *have* seen Browning many times. . . . We had to pass near Warwick Crescent Paddington—where the Directory set down R. B. as Resident. So, though I somehow had got it into my head that *he lived* in Italy—we stopped at the house indicated. I rang and asked if Mr. B. *used not* to live there! Whereupon the *liveried* youth answered with a *look of surprise*—"Yes, he does live here: but is not at home!" but that *Miss* B. and Mr. *B.* junior were. So I sent up a card and was asked up—and there found the "Sarianna" (Miss B. R. B.'s sister) I had known in old days—unmarried still—and just as lively and friendly as ever. . . . The next day came a note from R. B. urging me to come and see him. Well—I went and found him just as of old—put his arms on my shoulders—expressed greatest delight etc. Of course we had all kinds of chat on all kinds of things. He looks as you see in the photographs—pale—grey—stouter than of old—but hard and vigorous—never had had, he said, a day's illness in his life. He lives in a modest sized house in a *stucco-row,* overlooking the Regents Canal, all the furniture brought from their Florentine house—*all* old—(medieval a good deal) black *ebony*— old tapestry on the upper walls—marble busts of Mrs. B. self and son. . . . There was a little desk at wh. Mrs. B. wrote all her poems (you know she has been dead 11 years)—he showed me her classi- cal books with her own *annotations* in *Greek* etc. on their margins—

Portrait of Robert Browning painted in 1874 by his son Robert Barrett Browning

Sarianna Browning

F. J. Furnivall

Browning taking tea with the Browning Society. A cartoon by Max Beerbohm

Thomas Carlyle. A portrait by Whistler painted in 1872

he and "Sarianna" always speaking of her as if she were something almost supernatural in excellence—talent—and modest unconsciousness etc. etc.—Well—we have often met and talked of all kinds of things. I have told him . . . of the old *sore* "his obscurity"— but I fear it is of no use—he assumes or asserts that he can't help it—that he must write according to his nature or something to that effect. He seems to think that he was never read (always excepting by a *few*) till the generation *next* his own sprung up—and says that he is content with the audience he has *now*. And indeed he *seems* so—The books *sell* pretty well—but nothing like what they ought to and would do if he would *condescend* to be a little more clear.

Despite Browning's efforts, Smith Elder would not run the risk of financing Domett's poetry so he himself paid for the publication—and got back £34 of the £127 it had cost him. He visited and liked Hutton of the *Spectator,* who gave the book a favorable notice. Hutton was a keen Browningite and had just introduced *Fifine at the Fair* in a review which Domett said was the best key to its understanding.

But Browning's own letter (written from Fontainebleau October 18, 1872), of which he allowed Domett to make any use he chose, was the greatest encouragement, especially after Sarianna had reassured him that it was not merely the voice of friendship (she had heard her brother say to a visitor exactly the same things he had written to Domett). "Browning says," Domett tells "Arcturus":

I don't know, though I cannot but care a good deal, how the Poem may have been received and valued: but I am sure it is a great and astonishing performance, of very varied beauty and power: I rank it under nothing—taken altogether—nothing that has appeared in my day and generation, for subtle yet clear writing about subjects of all others the most urgent for expression and the least easy in treatment: . . . such treasures new and old of language and such continuance of music in modes old and new. . . . The Poem is worth the thirty years work and experience and even absence from home;

and whether people accept it now—or let it alone for a while—in the end, appreciated it is certain to be.

Browning wrote, still from Fontainebleau, to commend Domett and his poem to Tennyson and sent on Emily Tennyson's reply to Domett, who copied it for his friend in New Zealand. It gives us a pleasant glimpse of the woman whose conversation reminded W. G. Ward in its sincerity and simplicity of the John Henry Newman of Littlemore and Oxford, and of whom R. C. Jebb remarked that she had "the gift of making one feel that goodness, intelligence and good breeding are a Trinity, of which in her, one can worship the unity."

> It would indeed [she wrote] have been to us a signal misfortune had we been staying a month at Fontainebleau and not your month. I think it quite bad enough that we were there a few days and not your days. . . .
>
> My Husband's patience having been tried beyond endurance by certain proof sheets, he has rushed off with Mr. Knowles to look after them from his house. He will . . . I am sure, not only for your sake but for the sake of the poem itself, . . . feel much sympathy with Mr. Domett and I hope so much that . . . his pen may be moved to record it which is very rare by way of letter writing.—That you may not wish it were even so with his wife I will say farewell. All good be with you ever, affectionately yours,
>
> Emily Tennyson

Tennyson himself wrote twice to Domett, first acknowledging receipt of and then praising the poem for "Intellectual subtlety—great power of delineating delicious scenery, and imaginative fire" but found in it "an embarras de richesses which makes it rather difficult to read—to me at least." Browning tried to dissipate his friend's doubts as to whether this was not "damning with faint praise." He "says it is a great deal to get out of Tennyson." One would certainly think so! But Domett was obviously subject to moods of discouragement to one of which Browning reacted vigorously. "My dear Domett, you shan't have the last word. You have no right to envy anybody with whom you declined to compete in the race. You stepped aside after other objects while I kept plodding on at the particular one I proposed myself. I daresay you have got as much good out of life as I—that is in my enjoyment of writing—for as to the folk's appreciation of it, you don't overvalue *that* I am sure..."

This was written in 1876, but Domett had already been back in England four years: he arrived the year that Isa Blagden died, and one feels that, with the warm welcome recorded from both brother and sister, there might have been in him a partial replacement both of Isa and of Julia Wedgwood. But, judging by Domett's journal, it does not seem to have worked out.

Of Browning he discourses at great length: they meet often, walk together, both call on impulse and miss one another, there being then no handy pre-telephoning. Yet one feels, though Domett did not notice it, that there was no real meeting of minds. Browning discussed the selection he was making of his own poetry which should express, he said, the life of a sort of man beginning with one set of likings and fancyings, ending with another. He told Domett that *Fifine* was "the most metaphysical and boldest" thing he had written since *Sordello* and that he felt doubtful as to its reception. Yet oddly enough he forecast *Red Cotton Night-Cap Country* enthusiastically saying: "I have got *such* a subject for a poem if I can do justice to it." On this poem Domett reports, while partly disagreeing, the comment of R. H. Hutton:"He did not think there was a single line of poetry in it." Both *Red Cotton Night-Cap Country* and *The Inn Album* make Browning's own comment to Domett on choosing unpleasant subjects a little surprising: "As if," he said, "a painter should choose no colours to work in but blood red and lamp black."

The directors of the Chicago and Alton Rail Road were at this time inviting the vast American public to read Browning together with their timetables! Domett read aloud with feeling a passage from *Paracelsus* with which the directors had started a complete series—and Browning criticized what he felt to be an error in his own youthful writing.

"Hypercritical" Domett felt it—but he himself did not hesitate to criticize what was being written and published today. I have told in an earlier chapter how Browning impressed him with *Hercules Furens*, and he sent him everything as it appeared and received with perfect amiability all Domett's comments. But the old intimacy never seems fully renewed, nor perhaps could Domett enter into Browning's more metaphysical side as fully as into the world of the classics they had both lived in as boys. And with all the friendliness there seems little of the eagerness to meet and talk called out by Julia.

In the autumn and winter of 1873 a new hope was dawning in the matter closest of all to Browning's heart. Pen had come to the decision—encouraged by praise from Millais for a sketch he had made—to take up seriously the art in which he had always dabbled: he would try to become a painter. Nothing could have more rejoiced his father, who immediately sought the best advice as to a teacher. Felix Moscheles, Browning's artist friend, believed Pen to be really gifted and he recommended Heyermans, a Dutch painter living at Antwerp. To have Pen busy and happy was everything. And in June 1874 Browning could write to Story:

> My best report is to be of Pen. It is now four months and a half since he has been at steady work, and there must be immense good in that. His master, Heyermans, evidently *is* the master, and, from Pen's letters which are unremitting, I can see he is happier than he ever was in his life. What a load this lightens me of. Who can judge better than you? He has never once budged from his butcher-shop lodging, and it is I, this time, who begin to be anxious that he should change the air and otherwise relax a little. If no other scheme presents itself, I and my sister will join him in an excursion some-whither in the autumn.

Very soon we find the father planning exhibitions of Pen's pictures, getting them varnished for him according to directions, arranging sales for paintings exhibited at Grosvenor House and the Paris and Brussels Salons—Pen would presently win in Paris a medal giving him the right automatically to exhibit there henceforward.

Browning's own fame and the personal friendships no doubt helped, but such things do not win medals—or praise from men such as Leighton and Millais, concerned with their own reputation as judges, or from the critical *Athenaeum*. Nor would Rodin have accepted him for a pupil in sculpture as he presently did. *"C'est étonnant,"* was the comment of another Frenchman, the Slade Professor of Fine Arts at University College, on Pen's rapid early progress. Soon he was established in a studio and Browning remarked happily that Pen could live for a year on the proceeds of one picture. Not that he showed any disposition to do so: right down to his marriage and after, "Pen's bills [writes Gertrude Reese in her interesting study *Browning and His Son*] found their way all too easily to Warwick Crescent." But for the moment the father was content: the only anxious question was: How long would Pen continue to work? Browning pushed this question to the back of his mind. He was in the same state of bliss as when his son had got into Christ Church, was winning friends, and coxing in bump races.

Pen's own feelings are described at two stages by the aunt and niece, once famous, now forgotten, who wrote poetry jointly under the name of "Michael Field." In a book of reminiscences called *Works and Days* we are told that, when they first visited the Brownings, Pen was "a jocund youth of thirty, who seems to find life delightful . . . full of amusement and mockery." But when many years later they stayed with him at Asolo he had become a pathetic figure crushed by the feeling that his success had not been his own, that his pictures were admired and bought solely because of his father.[3] It is true that Pen was always diffident of his powers, but he seems to have enjoyed his success as long as it lasted, which appears to have been just as long as he went on working.

A touching if rather comic story is told of Browning's efforts, when Pen's work was rejected as coarse by the Academy, to persuade the Grosvenor Gallery to break their rule against accepting Academy rejects. When the man in charge saw the poet with tears running down his cheeks, he was so touched that he approached the founder of the gallery and won entry for Pen.

Rodin was justified when a few years later a bronze exhibited in

Brussels and Paris was described as *"empoignant . . . grandement vu et éminemment sculptural."*

There was of course a school of doubters: Sir Sidney Colvin writes of the rather meager results of a talent in which the father took so much pride. But if it rested with Browning to achieve it Pen would be either a great painter, a great sculptor, or both! At Texas University are letters to Heyermans during and after Pen's pupilage, letters to Lehmann after his purchase of a vast picture in 1876—a "prodigious incitement to Pen's energy." Probably Browning had recently proposed Lehmann for the Athenaeum, for he writes: "I should accept the despatch of books and papers as a proof you are clubbable, nay clubbed."

There is also a curious letter to Pen arguing strongly against his exhibiting the picture Lehmann had bought. It depicted a monk reading a more than doubtful book and Browning felt the clergy should be attacked for what was commonly their failing but not for what was *not.* Lehmann was "a quondam Jew and professed infidel, he would delight in the scandal and said so." Lehmann had wanted indeed to make the attack more obtrusive by entitling the picture "The Celibate." All this would harm Pen and ensure rejection by the Academy.

It is interesting to note how Pen tended toward pictures that attacked Catholics—in reaction perhaps from the feverish piety of his childhood. " 'Hating Priests,' is one thing," wrote Browning, "and charging them with what, as a rule, they don't commit is another." The letter is a perfect example of stating a case too often: it might justifiably be called nagging. Pen had actually been against exhibiting on the ground that the picture was not good enough—he wanted to wait for one of which he had higher hopes. But Browning, while praising Pen for seeking advice, was (surely most irritatingly) determined to prove that the *subject* of the picture should be the ground of the decision. Promising finally to pay a number of bills, he adds a reminder that Pen on his side had promised economy. "I shall believe that when I see better proofs of it."

Pen was living more and more abroad; for a while he left Heyermans, a letter to whom in 1877 shows Browning happy in the hope that Pen was about to resume "those relations which ought never to have been interrupted." There are letters also to a man with whom Pen shared a studio, letters about his holiday with a group of young students in the Black Forest.

Increasingly Sarianna had become her brother's chief companion, sharing many of his friendships, especially those with Milsand, Anne Egerton Smith, and Mrs. Bronson. A pleasant correspondence in the University of Texas collection, part of which is published in *Letters of Robert Browning*, pictures another friendship which lasted until Browning's death. The Rev. J. R. Williams of Christ's College, Brecon, sent him in 1874 a translation he had made into Latin of one of his poems. The poet was "greatly honoured . . . greatly delighted" with the "Ovidian music." Williams persevered and more than a year later Browning felt "it was indeed worth my writing, for the delight (and wonder) which your *curiosa felicitas* has given me."

Sarianna became included in a friendship which embraced also the vicar's "wonderful son," in whose Oxford successes (the Newcastle scholarship, the Craven) they rejoiced and with whose bad health they sympathized intensely. And on one St. George's Day Browning will have "no mere after tea visit," but will dine at any hour that suits his friend. On this day, "long and fondly supposed to be Shakespeare's Day also—what generosities of visiting and congratulation are inappropriate to the festival."

Browning's friendship with George Smith belongs even more to his private life than to that of publication or Society—and this above all in Smith's relations with Pen. Evidently he was one of the many friends won by the young man's warmth and charm. Browning writes excitedly to him in August 1875 how Pen "painted my portrait in four days,—life-size profile—certainly the best *likeness* ever taken of me. . . . I had a letter from Robert along with yours—and he speaks of having painted eleven hours a day for the last two days—this time at a ruined castle. Is not this good news?" (The effort to re-christen Pen "Robert" was probably made to give him an added dignity. It did not last long.)

That eleven hours a day was good Smith clearly doubted, but Browning reassured him; it was just a burst of exceptional energy.

Certainly it would *not* be good as a daily practice. A few months later
he was writing: "Do come and see the pictures if you can. If you see
Millais ask his opinion about them—which I prefer he should give you:
it might seem suspicious in my mouth."

Millais advised and encouraged from the first, and both father and
son abounded in gratitude—expressed chiefly by the former. But, apart
from the problem of getting Pen's huge canvasses hung at the Academy,
Browning felt a wish as their numbers increased for a separate Barrett-
Browning exhibition. He held this first at Warwick Crescent, and
later told George Smith with some amusement of a newspaper paragraph describing the fatherly devotion with which he kept in his house
seventy of his son's immense canvasses. For many fewer, the house was
inadequate even as a temporary exhibition place, and Smith solved the
problem by lending a large room. He seems further to have met the
boat bringing the pictures to London, for Browning writes in March
1879: "The Captain is to be 'spoken to,' the mate 'tipped,' and they will
be ready for the exercise of your unspeakable hospitality. Pen is as
grateful to you as he should be."

Three years later he is writing: "Could you have the kindness to
allow M. Rodin (the sculptor) to see the portrait in case it is at Waterloo
Place. Pen is desirous that his master should judge of it."

Meanwhile Browning had sent out printed invitations, each with a
little note from himself, inviting Tennyson, Carlyle, Domett, Lord
Houghton, Millais, Leighton—all and every friend to rally round the
young painter's works. A story ran that either here or in public exhibits
he would occasionally stick the label "sold" on an unsold picture. Anyhow to Smith and others he would write eagerly of genuine sales:
"Pen's picture was purchased by a Mr. Fielden of Dobroyd Castle,
Todmorden— a perfect stranger to us—on the first day of the Exhibition." (This was at the Academy in 1878.) "The effect cannot but be
good on a fellow too much given to self mistrust."

A great deal of gratitude passes back and forth in this friendship—
Browning demurring at Smith's enthusiastic thanks for some service
unknown—"you who have served me so long and efficaciously,"—and
himself expressing enthusiastic gratitude for every check received. He

read his poetry aloud at the Smiths' house, he took Smith and a cousin to Mrs. Procter's, who in turn sent on a letter from Browning with a comment expressing her own enjoyment of the evening—she who was famous for refusing a second entry to the unintelligent.

But on one point the two men by no means saw eye to eye. Browning, as we have seen, thought Furnivall a valuable if tactless friend; Smith thought him an intolerable busybody. Furnivall's desire to "possess" Browning was unpleasing to many of his friends, and Smith was not soothed by such things as his advertising a shilling edition of a Browning selection, on the strength of Browning's having told him that Smith, Elder were considering the issue of a "cheap" edition. I wish we had more of Smith's side of this correspondence, but one brief undated note is revealing. "I have no idea how the Academy got their information —but from the tone of the paragraphs I conjecture that it was written by Mr. Furnivall. It would be difficult to say exactly how much that gentleman's impertinent interference with your works has cost you, but it is no inconsiderable sum."

Brother and sister remained at Warwick Crescent until close to the end of his life, when the house was scheduled for destruction: Pen made it his headquarters when in England.

Warwick Crescent was a quiet spot in those days, almost countrified, with the canal for Pen's boat and a small garden for Browning's pets: two, sometimes four, geese. There was also an owl, but that had a tiny room built for it and was given increasingly the freedom of the whole house. Late in the tenancy the plot was beautified by his friend Mrs. FitzGerald's gardener. It had been, Browning said, a "little patch of wretchedness," but it was big enough to be worth stocking with shrubs, and there was a Virginia creeper which found its way indoors and was trained around the inside of the study window.

After Browning's death William Grove, his manservant for seven years and helped by him to start in business as a photographer, was interviewed for the *Pall Mall Budget*. He described the poet's daily life— early rising, long hours in his study: "When I photographed him, I took him in an attitude I have seen him in thousands of times, his head leaning on his hand. He would sit like that for half an hour sometimes, and then take up his pen to jot something down." Breakfast was light and lunch also—usually "just a pudding." But he always ate a good dinner. "His favourite wine was Carlowitz or claret, but he drank very little of either. Sometimes when he dined out he would drink a little port, but never more than one wine."

After lunch came afternoon calls and private views, and he walked often across Kensington Gardens. "His friends? Well, I should have to give you a list of two or three hundred. Carlyle was a great friend, and so was Dean Stanley, Mr. Gladstone, Mr. Mundella, Sir Frederick Leighton and his sister, Watts, Tadema and a host of others. Tennyson came two or three times a year, and always on Show Sundays, to see Mr. Barrett Browning's pictures."

It is interesting that the only woman Grove mentioned should have been Leighton's sister, Mrs. Orr, called by Browning after Isa Blagden's death his dearest woman friend. For, owing to letters kept and stories told by women, to the biographies by Mrs. Orr and Lilian Whiting, the published memories of Mrs. Bronson, of Lady Ritchie, of Fanny Barrett Browning, perhaps above all the immense correspondences with Julia Wedgwood, Isa Blagden, and Mrs. FitzGerald, an impression prevails that almost all Browning's intimates were women—and that the three months he yearly spent out of London meant only a change from the city's social life to that of English country houses or foreign villas.

Actually this did begin to be true toward the end of his life, but earlier the holidays were for the most part a blessed solitude in which he and Sarianna walked daily. He records even after reaching his seventies five hours or more of morning and afternoon walks; once at least they did seven hours without even pausing for rest or food. Sometimes they took a cottage by the sea where he would bathe as well as walk; sometimes it was the roughest of inns in the mountains.

Joseph Milsand, his close friend since 1851, usually stayed with him in London in the spring. They would meet at other times in Paris or for a country holiday by the sea. Milsand was a French Protestant of remote English descent. His family, by now completely French, had migrated to Dijon from New England in 1718. He had intended to be a painter and embraced enthusiastically Ruskin's art theories, writing a book called *L'Esthétique anglaise,* the working out of which led him to feel that the pen was (anyhow in his own case) mightier than the brush. Something was said in my first volume of his fascinating article on Browning in the *Revue des Deux Mondes,* and the poet valued supremely his criticism and appreciation, trusting him with the revision of his proofs—something not even permitted to George Smith.

At St. Aubin in Normandy, they met in 1870 and their friendship finds an echo in *Red Cotton Night-Cap Country:*

> Milsand who makest warm my wintry world
> And wise my heaven, if there we consort too.

But the outbreak of the Franco-Prussian War brought with it the usual spy scare and Milsand had to get his friend off to England in a cattle boat.

Browning appears to have agreed with Carlyle that France had provoked the war but, deeply distressed over the hunger in Paris, he asked Smith to buy for the *Cornhill* (created and owned by Smith Elder) a poem called "Hervé Riel," which recalls the days of the ride from Ghent to Aix, the check for the poem to go to the relief of the starving city. George Smith generously gave £100, which Browning sent to his old friend.

But later comes a letter refusing to let Smith print "Ned Bratts" in the magazine—it was, Browning said, too long. "Oh 'Ned Bratts' would ruin you—so he shall not."

Was this solely concern for Smith or had Browning slipped back into his lifelong dislike for periodical publishing?

Up to his death in 1866, old Mr. Browning and Sarianna had made their home in Paris for many years, and Milsand had become increasingly close to the whole family. Part of the correspondence with Sarianna is now at Baylor University—tantalizingly only a part, leaving many unanswered questions.

It begins in August 1877 and shows Pen coming to Paris for further art study, especially study of the nude. Milsand is sad that he cannot be there to welcome him, but on his return he has strange developments to discuss.

Pen's start had been unusually successful, partly as we have seen through his own talents, partly through his father's efforts. But, realizing fully his need for further studies, he had doubtless felt also the pull of the capital. Milsand's next letter is two months later.

Pen had been painting and modeling diligently and his father's letters had been full of a steady satisfaction, with only an occasional faint undertone suggesting anxiety—chiefly over Pen's doubts of himself, and the lack of communication in his too brief letters. But at this point there was trouble—and apparently trouble of two kinds.

Heyermans was in Antwerp, many of Pen's pictures were painted in Dinant; now he was in Paris; we do not know how long he had been studying under other artists. But we learn from a Sotheby catalogue that on at least one of his pictures he was described as "élève de MM.J.P. Laurens et A. Rodin."

Milsand writes on October 19, 1877, answering a request for advice clearly from Browning though passed on by Sarianna. He is embarrassed at being asked, but feels that while it is most important that Pen continue his studies from the living model, it is doubtful whether this can be accomplished in Paris. He must certainly change studios, and after what has passed, even this is unlikely to succeed.

"We must bear in mind his hopes and his good intentions, crushed by M. Laurens; we must bear in mind too Pen's moral state. Whether through his own fault or not, he is like a man who has been thrown two or three times from a housetop onto the pavement."

Milsand does not feel Pen to be blameless—in part a reference to a disagreeable letter he had written to his father. The letter had, however, been overtaken by a good one. And Milsand entreats his two older friends not to attribute to "a deliberate lack of good faith all the inaccuracies of which Pen may be guilty. The anger a word may provoke spreads like a blot of oil: the true meaning is lost of the phrase that wounds."

There was something else, it seems, besides the trouble with his teacher, for the next day Milsand writes again, after a two-hour walk with Pen. Telling him he was aware of the tension between father and son and that his own wish was only to help toward peace, he had been greatly embarrassed to be shown by Pen yet another letter.

> I told him again that I loved his father and his aunt. . . . I understand perfectly your feelings and Robert's. It is cruel indeed to be disappointed in one's hopes, desires, the very purpose of one's life. But you know what I went through. I was unable in conscience to bow to the wishes of my mother: I merely postponed my marriage and it would be impossible for me to persuade any man to break or keep engagements which he alone can weigh. I shall advise Penn [sic] to work, I will do my best to make him understand and respect your feelings: I have told him that his father had a perfect right to demand that the sacrifices made to further his career should not be directed to any other purpose—above all one contrary to his wishes. It was up to him, Penn, to profit by the opportunity given him for life studies. But I could not and would not go further than to tell him I thought his primary duty was to concentrate on establishing himself in a profession.

Full of "desolation" for both parents, as he almost seems to have felt them, seeing faults in "Penn" (so he always spells the name) and seeking to calm him, Milsand trusts that they will understand his attitude of neutrality. He is *"de tout coeur à Robert et à vous."*

One would guess from this that Pen, probably deeply shaken emotionally by whatever had occurred in the studio, had sought and found consolation after the usual fashion of youth. And the indefatigable Furnivall later got hold of a story that Pen had married a Belgian wife. Browning wrote: January 5, 1882:

> It is mere gossip grown out of just this fact that more than four years ago [he] formed an attachment to a young lady of perfectly unexceptionable character and connexions. I objected to a marriage, on many accounts quite irrespective of these, and communicated with the lady's father (who parenthetically is wealthy) and the

project was dropped on both sides. This occurred at a time when Robert's pictorial career was just begun and would have seriously affected it: and wholly dependent on myself as he was with little prospect of becoming otherwise, he had no right so to dispose of his actions in that matter: and my objections were felt to be reasonable—I believe on both sides.

What does "both sides" mean? Apparently not Pen, who, besides his letters home and confidences to Milsand at the time, retained a feeling of bitterness which came out years later in talks with "Michael Field," who felt that Browning, if Pen's story was true, had "a bad blot on his scutcheon." This may of course be the case, or again the stories told to them by Pen may have abounded in "inaccuracies."

The solid facts were that Browning, who though comfortably off was by no means rich, was already paying for Pen's lessons and maintenance in the various places where he chose to stay, was handling his business and exhibiting his pictures in London, and settling all the outstanding debts of a very expensive young man. He was asked to add now the cost of a wife and family with the practical certainty of a slackening in Pen's efforts to achieve success in his career.

Belgian parents would almost certainly feel the force of these objections. It was, as Milsand had said, Pen's responsibility to go on with the engagement or to break it off—but if he wanted to go on he would have to show some signs of becoming able to support a wife. "Both sides" may indicate only a conference of parents: it may mean also a Pen convinced against his will—and later believing he was of the same opinion still. He had, the father assured Furnivall, retained "the friendship of all the parties concerned."

Milsand continued to write regularly. He saw Pen frequently but usually other people were present and no private talk possible; all his friends were charmed by the young artist. Two months more and Pen was working at Dinant again—but apparently making no effort to renew the broken engagement. Again a little hurt by Sarianna's tone, Milsand echoes Browning's own view at the time of the Oxford debacle: There was no bad will in the young man but just weakness, *"une*

incapacité de résister à des entrainements." For her own peace he longs
to make Sarianna share this conviction.

The flavor of the whole episode is curiously similar to that of the
end of Pen's Oxford career—both father and son losing their tempers
and then being reconciled.

On December 30 Browning was writing to Mrs. FitzGerald:
"Altogether a dispiriting Christmas time: no Pen, no jollity of any
kind." But with the new year must have come a revival of hope and with
it of cheer, for on January 21, 1878, "*Votre petit mot sur Pen m'a ravi,*"
cries Milsand ecstatically.

12 The Browning Society

*"Disciples" who at meetings Browning-clubbish
Talk such rubbish!*

PUNCH

WHILE *La Saisiaz* grew out of the debate in *The Nineteenth Century*, that periodical itself grew out of The Metaphysical Society. James Knowles, its founder and editor, was the inaugurator of the Society—although (said Tennyson) he did not "know a concept from a hippopotamus!" But he did know very well what was interesting to the intellectual world of the hour. The idea was a brilliant one and unusual in that era—that men of all religions and none should gather on a friendly footing for the discussion of ultimates, religious and philosophical.

Huxley and Froude, Cardinal Manning and W. G. Ward, Gladstone, Martineau, Dean Stanley were all members. A brief but violent clash between Ward and Huxley at an early meeting brought home to everyone (says Froude) that the Society could not last a day under such circumstances. Later Huxley, still the opponent, but now the warm friend of Ward, feared its "dying of too much love." The waiters, they found, had turned "Metaphysical" into "Madrigal," as later they would turn its successor the "Synthetic" into the "Sympathetic Society." The philosophers did, it would seem, sing in more dulcet tones to one another than did most poets. Tennyson was a keen member but I was amazed to find Browning's name among those mentioned to John Stuart Mill when Ward was commissioned to ask him to join, and I have found no trace of his having spoken at or even attended any meeting. He would probably have feared too much being asked to explain his own poetry.

Knowles had gathered his members among the distinguished and the learned. Another Society founded more than a decade later was much larger, much more of an *omnium gatherum* and posed a more complex question for Browning. For in 1881 Dr. Furnivall and Miss Hickey jointly founded the Browning Society which spread widely and produced a great deal of literature, some of it poor or mediocre, with occasional papers of real excellence. Hardly any of its members were Browning's intimates: these were inclined to make mock of it and to commiserate with him over its absurdities. But he felt that the Society was doing him a great service.

To Miss West (later Mrs. Dowden) he wrote in November 1881:

Exactly what has touched me is the sudden assemblage of men and women to whose names, for the most part, I am a stranger, who choose to incur the ridicule sure to come readily to the critics who dispose of my works by the easy word "unintelligible," instead of saying safely to themselves "*I* understand it—or something of it—anyhow!" That there would be exaggeration in the approval was to be looked for, they react against a good deal.

As for Dr. Furnivall, I am altogether astonished at his caring about me at all. I suspect it is a late discovery with him, like that of Fontenelle when, chancing upon some out-of-the-way literature, he went about asking everybody "Do you know Habbakuk? He's a genius!" I think him most warm-hearted, whatever may be the mistakes about me of which his head is guilty; and as Lear's last instance of ingratitude is that of the mouth biting the hand for lifting food to it— so, it seems to me, would as signal an one be, the writers of books that are commonly pronounced unintelligible, objecting to the folk who propose to try that question.

Max Beerbohm's cartoon of Browning taking tea with the Society (a thing he never did) represents the reaction of a large section of Browning's own world. Oscar Wilde young men predominate, with a sprinkling of earnest old ones and (only three) women, of whom two are concentrated and one is yearning. Browning sits in their midst, the cheerful figure of dinner parties and port wine. Could he, his friends asked, want this kind of thing? On the ground that he could not, Jowett refused to join. So did Sidney Colvin, so did Edward Dowden and Fanny Kemble. Tennyson by one account agreed to take the presidency and then, finding the Society was a subject of mockery withdrew his consent. But Furnivall speaks as though he had refused from the first—and refused rather disagreeably.

The thing was unique—to bestow in a man's lifetime the kind of honor, to undertake the kind of research bestowed on an acknowledged classic long after his death. "My dear Mr. Furnivall," said an unnamed duke, "I think it is 300 years too early for a Browning society."

No wonder Browning had not taken it very seriously when Furnivall, calling on him with Miss Hickey, mentioned the idea. "He laught heartily," says Furnivall, "and talkt of something else."

But Furnivall went straight home and spent the night writing to possible members, receiving some of their replies by the following evening. Sir Frederic Leighton joined, Henry Irving, Milsand and Domett, Eleanor Marx, daughter of Karl, Dorothea Beale and Frances Buss, pioneers in higher education for women.

A verse was current laughing at that advance guard of a growing army. Men, including those of the Working Men's College, would share their privileged education with no women. The rhymer declared:

> Miss Buss and Miss Beale
>   Cupid's darts do not feel.
> How different from us
>   Miss Beale and Miss Buss!

Some early members of the Browning Society would only later become temporarily or permanently famous: Sharp, author of Browning's first biography, better known as a minor poet under the name Fiona Macleod, J. J. Wise, the bibliographer whose Ashley Collection at the British Museum is world famous, and whose less reputable activities are expressed by the title of a book on him called *Forging Ahead*, Arthur Symons, and Edward Berdoe. Bernard Shaw joined for the sake of debating practice, not having at the time read a single line of Browning, but now apparently mastering with astonishing speed everything he had written.

The common picture of the Society as a scene of gushing admiration was very far from accurate. The "clergymen and ladies" spoken of with praise in the inaugural address were doubtless often blind admirers and such remarks might even be heard as Berdoe's: "Browning was not born a mere man, but a Buddha on the highest peak of the Himalayas of thought." But vigorous criticism was more common than adulation. Dr. Berdoe, wrote Shaw in *The Star* for October 1888, "disputed with Dr. F. J. Furnivall the distinction of being the 'fightingest' member of the Browning Society, which is probably the most pugnacious body of its size in existence."

Shaw himself was no reluctant fighter. Concluding his probably final speech, he said he was sorry if his "remarks had been almost uniformly abusive, and could only say that the writer of the paper richly deserved it."

Furnivall's own career was an extraordinary one and Sir Frederic Leighton was unfair when he described him as "that self-trumpeting person." Trumpeting he certainly was, but of the causes he had taken up rather than of himself. Educated at Cambridge, destined by his father for the law, he had thrown himself with equal enthusiasm into social work and Early English studies. He had already founded the English Text Society, the Chaucer Society (himself editing a six-text edition of the *Canterbury Tales* and a similar one of Chaucer's minor poems) and the "New Shakspere" Society. And after the Browning came the Shelley Society. He was working both on the first Oxford Dictionary and on a concise edition of it, later abandoned. Meanwhile he was teaching at the Working Men's College, establishing sculling clubs for his pupils, taking them on a walking tour of France, setting on foot dances and social events for them and their girls. He had two unusual club rooms: the British Museum Reading Room where members of the Browning Society could find him all day, and a tea shop (the ABC) in Oxford Street for weekends and evenings, where he expected university professors to mix on equal terms with waitresses. He turned this un-assuming spot, says the editor of *Frederick James Furnivall: A Volume of Personal Record* into an eighteenth-century coffee house, and the contributions to the volume from his young disciples confirm his tre-mendous power of educating and inspiring them.

The reverse of the medal was Furnivall's heartily quarrelsome dis-position, which we have already seen in the Pigsbrook-Swinburne af-fair. His quarrels were hearty, because he could not see why he should not fight violently and be quickly friends again, because too his fights were on the whole impersonal. His worst personal offenses were com-mitted on the river, in his insistence, for example, on getting out of the lock first even if he had entered it last. We have descriptions of him down to the age of eighty-two flourishing a huge boathook as he forced his way through the other craft, finishing his Sunday stint of fourteen miles rowing with a cold shower in the boat house.

At Browning Society meetings his aim was commonly to stimulate discussion whichever way it went. He admired Browning deeply but had little use for the Christian religion. "Being," said G.B.S., "what was called a Muscular Christian (slang for sporting parson) [he] could not forgive Jesus for not putting up a fight in Gethsemane."

Furnivall's enthusiasm and curiosity were not tempered by tact or discretion. As I tell in my first volume, he had "discovered" the inn-keeper whose (possible) existence had so stuck in Barrett throats, he also "discovered" Jewish and negro strains in the poet's ancestry. This apart from the question of accuracy, mattered little, but what must have mattered quite a lot was his eager disinterment of old Mr. Browning's unhappy lawsuit. Of his relations with the poet he idealized it was said that his was "the kiss of death." But, from a man who hated any sort of intrusion into his private life, Browning's comment to George Smith is admirable in its humor: "In spite of his blundering, Mr. Furnivall means beyond a doubt to do me all the service he is able: it is the old story of the friendly bear who broke the teeth of the man with the stone he meant to brush away a fly that had settled on his mouth."

And to all the friends who commiserated with him on the meddlings of the Society—suggesting that it made him look a little foolish—he answered steadily, that it had come into existence to encourage the reading of his poetry, had increased his sales, and had announced to all those who held him unintelligible: "we understand him and will show that you may."

"The many," comments Charles Michael Hancher, in his excellent study *The London Browning Society, 1881–1892* "who expected Browning to take offence at applause from literary amateurs, failed to take into account his long-standing distaste for literary professionals." "I'm not a literary man," he said to Domett, explaining that he never attended the annual Literary Fund Dinner. To another friend he wrote:

how extraordinary is the "ordinary" way of considering a poet's method of work. I write airily "quoth Tom to Jack one New Year's Day,"—and one "student" wants to know who Jack was,—another sees no difficulty there, but much in Tom's entity—while a third, getting easily over both stumbling-blocks, says—"But *which* New Year's Day?" Since all this must be done for me by somebody, I congratulate myself on having somebody so energetic as Mr. Furnivall to do it.

He welcomed, says Dr. Hancher, "the Browning Society as a kind of vindicating popular revolution against the decrees of an entrenched and incompetent literary establishment."

He goes on to show how, although Browning, like Joyce, has suffered from too much inferior admiration, "the Browning Society and its members elicited from Browning a body of information and critical comment about his works so large as to be without precedent in the history of English literature."

It was a little unkind of Mrs. Orr, whose *Handbook* to the poetry came into existence owing largely to the Society, to suggest that it tended to increase what she termed the "morbid development" of the poet's influence on certain women and even men. But after all she had been one of his many rumored second wives, and had perhaps a touch of the excessive sensibility with which she discredited others.

The *Handbook* has been described as one of *the* literary puzzles of the nineteenth century. For at times Browning seemed to endorse it totally—even telling people to read it to find out what he had meant in a given poem; yet at others his own account simply contradicted the book's interpretations. One explanation lies in Browning's very real dislike, widely testified to, of talking at all about his poetry: the *Handbook* offered a path of escape.

Much information and comment was also elicited by letters from Furnivall. This was a very different thing from the talking about his poetry to which Browning so strongly objected. External and factual explanation he was always prepared to give—but never the "explaining" which would have meant putting into prose what he at least could say only in poetry. Let others supply the prose if they would: what he had written he had written.

Furnivall and Mrs. Orr had been at first good friends, but when the *Handbook* appeared, Furnivall spoke of it so disagreeably that Browning felt obliged to protest. He estimated it "very differently." And what can his feelings be when its author "is simply the dearest woman friend I can boast of in the world? It has long been a genuine sorrow to me that there should have arisen, from whatever cause, a painful disturbance in the old amicable relation between that friend and the other to whom I am so much beholden—yourself."

No doubt one of Furnivall's quarrels had started between the beginning of the book and its completion—perhaps over the debate in 1882 when Mrs. Orr suggested that the Society should study Browning for five years and then shift to other literary topics. This seemed high treason to Furnivall—and he was partially vindicated when he could claim in 1884 the existence of at least twenty-one lesser societies, including several in Chicago and one in Melbourne. "By Browning's death," says Dr. Hancher, "it would not have been unreasonable to expect to find a Browning Club or Society in any urban or intellectual center in the English-speaking world," many of these going their own way and not even troubling to communicate with London. But the London Society at its peak could boast a membership of between two and three hundred. Time's revenges can be sweet as well as bitter—and one wonders that Browning could not at that point forget the existence of an Alfred Austin.

Besides Furnivall there were in the London Society two men whose names for very different reasons still mean a great deal and whose relationships with Browning were important—Wise, the first editor of his letters and the perpetrator of forged editions of his wife's poetry, and Bernard Shaw who made in the Society's discussions more penetrating remarks than can be recorded in this brief account. The three men, Furnivall, Shaw, Wise, could not be more unlike each other which is one reason why they mirror that very mixed affair, the London Browning Society.

By far the most interesting member was Bernárd Shaw, and, considering what he would himself later accomplish for the English stage, it is interesting that he should have formed so high an estimate of Browning's unsuccessful plays when the Society revived them. *Luria* was acted in modern evening dress against a background of curtains and Shaw found in it an argument for the return to the open Elizabethan style of production. Earlier he had praised both *A Blot in the 'Scutcheon* and *Colombe's Birthday*, taking issue with the critics who were saying just what he said of "Caliban"—that Browning's genius was not dramatic: "The tragedy is powerful enough to raise the whole question of what a dramatic play is."

In a later review describing both this performance and one of *In a Balcony* as "only partially successful" he declared that with *Colombe's Birthday* "The much-ridiculed Browning Society have made their enemies their footstool at last." The speeches were lengthy and the whole performance was "persistently addressed to the higher faculties of an educated and thoughtful audience. Both of these features materially contributed on Thursday to its success, which was complete and unequivocal."

The most interesting point in Shaw's criticism lies, not in the highly disputable question whether Browning's plays could ever become stage successes, but in the fundamental reason for his own enthusiasm. In the review of yet another performance of the *Blot* he introduces a variation. "Browning," he writes,"when the mere action of his play flags, lifts and prolongs apparently exhausted situations by bursts of poetry, sometimes of rare melody and grandeur."

If one thing more than another has killed Browning societies—and indeed killed Browning's poetry—it has been the impulse he starts in us all to discuss his ideas rather than to listen to his music. Shaw said of *Paracelsus* that it was remarkable for its music but not for its philosophy: "Whatever [Paracelsus] aspired to, he seemed to attain *nothing*." But claiming for himself, with no risk of contradiction, the possession of a musical ear Shaw writes of the poem as "remarkable for its music; and towards the close, when the writer was in full swing, the music was extraordinary."

This unusual view Shaw supported with references to musicians of genius. The greatest had been attacked when introducing a new kind of music—Beethoven, Handel, Mozart. The supreme instance was that of "the old fashioned censure of Wagner for producing formless cacophony instead of measured music." The attack was similar on Browning's novel forms in poetry. "It is but the protest of the unaccustomed and prepossessed ear." And Shaw foretold a day when in the twentieth century the partisans of some yet more advanced poet "will probably pooh-pooh Browning's verse as obsolete sing-song." While, as to his alleged obscurity: "If it was laid down that a poet must be plain to everybody, you came down to Dr. Watts at once."

Professor Hancher points out how—in the background of Shaw, and his fireworks, of the many highly intelligent papers read, of the plays sometimes even brilliantly produced—the energy, drive, near-genius of one man is apparent. "Dr. Furnivall almost single-handed" had created the Browning societies with their immense effect on the poet's fame—and on his sales. Readers of papers have related how Furnivall forced them into reading, officers how they found themselves appointed overnight by a leader who would brook no refusal. Shaw read no papers, but he spoke at all the twenty-two meetings he is known to have attended. Members of distinction were not even dunned for the modest yearly dues of a guinea; interesting visitors were immediately asked to read papers. Furnivall himself would always fill in by reading a paper or leading the discussion. And like a gadfly he tried to sting Browning's publishers into supplying cheap editions of the poems. This was not only for the sake of the Browning Society; Furnivall was one of that small band of scholars whose democracy is sincere and total. He was as convinced that his young laborers and waitresses could understand Browning as he was that the miserable wage of the era made it impossible for them to buy his books at current prices. He did not get his shilling edition from the exasperated Smith, but his insistence—and his societies—did help toward an increasing number of cheap selections.

With his many interests it is impossible to call Furnivall a man of one idea, but the doggedness and energy he put into his rowing, the zeal expended on Early English texts found their culminating point in this enthusiasm of his later years.

One of Furnivall's protégés in the Browning Society was young Thomas Wise who, then aged 23, joined it in 1882, and through the Society got to know Browning himself. The story has often been told of how lacerated this bibliophile felt when, calling on Browning, he found him destroying a trunkful of letters including priceless autographs. Wise said afterward he believed he could have got Browning that day to give him one of the tiny numbers in existence of the first edition of *Pauline*. As it was he finally managed to buy one at what then seemed a high figure—and received a postcard from Browning:

"Thanks unwise Wise."

But before this purchase Wise had begged the Browning Society to sponsor him in issuing as perfect as possible a type facsimile. For this purpose Browning, though reluctant about the project and steadily refusing to write an introduction, did lend his own copy. But he declined to see the proofs and consented only to the reprint as "a concession to the whim of the more than friendly members of the society." Wilfred Partington, author of *Forging Ahead*, believes that it was this "page-for-page type imitating" started by Wise for the Shelley Society with *Adonais* and now employed on *Pauline* that "most probably started Wise on his series of typographical forgeries." He was certainly excited by what he had done, claiming in his introduction: "a sentiment attaching to the very form in which a book of this description first appeared which is entirely wanting if the same work is perused in another dress."

I have told the story in my first volume of the deceit largely instrumental in Wise's exposure—a so-called first edition of Elizabeth Browning's *Sonnets from the Portuguese* which he issued after Browning's death. But even in the poet's lifetime Wise managed to put over similar imaginary publications with two of Elizabeth's earlier poems. Browning expressed grave doubts both of *The Battle of Marathon* and *The Runaway Slave at Pilgrim Point.* "I never heard of a separate publication. . . . I fear this must be a fabricated affair." Wise boldly sent him the pamphlet of *The Runaway Slave,* the appearance of which was so entirely convincing that Browning wrote: "The respectability of the Publisher and Printer is a guarantee that nothing surreptitious has been done." Clearly, too, he trusted Wise and perhaps mistrusted his own memory for he went on to form a theory as to how this puzzling thing might have occurred. For a while during this correspondence the bold and skillful forger must have held his breath. Yet he took such risks over and over again.

The horror felt by the book-buying and selling world when these fabrications were exposed was not shared by Bernard Shaw. True to his reputation for perversity, he criticized the critics, writing a commentary included with the replies to it in a later edition of Partington's book. The author's conclusion had been that a mixture of greed for money and for the kudos of discovery, so dear to the heart of every collector and dealer, were Wise's motives. But Shaw wrote:

> Not at all. His sense of humour had a good deal to do with his choice of this particular form of practical joke; which did not promise to be as lucrative as it proved. He forged nothing; all his literary material was quite genuine. He did not forge first editions; he invented imaginary ones. His fictions hurt nobody, and gave keen pleasure to collectors. Why should we be angry with him for making people harmlessly happy? Foolish people no doubt, preferring first editions full of mistakes to final corrected editions. But quite harmless like T. J. himself.

Would the British Museum, which had accepted and even bought many of these creations, would the bibliophiles and booksellers who paid exorbitantly for them have echoed Shaw? Before the great discovery was made Wise had "invented" some scores of nonexistent editions of Dickens, George Eliot, William Morris, Stevenson, Swinburne, Tennyson, Matthew Arnold and others. He had also done immense work in bibliography and gathered the unique Ashley Collection, now in the British Museum. For all this he had won an Honorary Fellowship of Worcester College, Oxford, an honorary M.A. from the University itself, had been President for two years of the Bibliographical Society and had been elected to the Roxburghe Club—the most exclusive institution of book collectors in the world. He was near his end when the first situation impossible of evasion opened like a gulf before his feet, chiefly through the discovery made by two booksellers of the fact that paper and type both belonged to a later date than that claimed for the pamphlet. Wise's wife began to answer his letters, announcing that his doctor forbade him any exertion.

Thomas Wise died under the cloud he had himself created, but his case remains unique in the honors bestowed on him when underground rumblings of suspicion were already audible in the book world. Nor does a man guilty of such deceit often accomplish at the same time so much solid work or win cooperation from men of such standing as Edmund Gosse, John Drinkwater, Augustine Birrell, E. V. Lucas and others who contributed introductions to the eleven volumes of his Ashley Catalogue. For the sake of that collection alone one might forgive Wise all his sins except for the vendettas he carried on against anyone else who could be discredited on suspicion of forgery. This was obviously part of his cover-up, but there was a strong streak of meanness in a man ready without hesitation to sacrifice his friends if thereby he could save his own skin. Wilfred Partington conceals nothing of Wise's meanness, but gives us also a picture of his achievements. He begins his book with the motto *De mortuis nil nisi verum* and ends it with the remark that Thomas James Wise "staked for himself a threefold claim in the annals of fame as *The Builder of the Ashley Library; The most prolific of British bibliographers, And the forger of the nineteenth century pamphlets.*"

Shaw like Browning was fascinated by the psychology of deception

—but it is highly improbable that the two men would have agreed about this particular deception, had Shaw written a play or Browning a dramatic monologue on Wise. Browning was dead long before the exposure. Dead, too, was the London Browning Society, but other such societies still went on chiefly in the United States: there are several even today—New York, California, Boston. This last is singled out by Professor Hancher as still working seriously on the poems and the man whose lifetime did not suffice to answer every riddle.

13 Age
Not Crabbed but Crowded

For all his "difficulty" Browning was, with his lovers, the familiar and intimate, almost the confidential poet, fairly button-holing the reader with the intensity of his communication and the emphasis of his point.

HENRY JAMES

IN 1882 Browning celebrated his seventieth birthday and received the honorary degree of D.C.L. from Oxford. But neither this nor the same honor already bestowed by Cambridge meant as much to him as his Balliol Fellowship—"perhaps all the more," he wrote later, "that I am an adopted child, and not an heir with his natural rights to sit at the dais, and be welcomed as a Fellow."[1]

At the D.C.L. ceremony at the Sheldonian a jocose undergraduate let down from the gallery above his head a red cotton nightcap, and *Punch*, describing him as *"The Ring and Book-maker from Red Cotton Night-Cap Country,"* parodied "At the Mermaid"

> But, in spite of all the stir made,
>   Put the robes upon the shelf:
> I've my corner at "the Mermaid"
>   With "rare Ben" and Shakespeare's self.

Before the founding of the Browning Society or the Oxford honors, Browning had published *Dramatic Idylls*, Vol. I in 1879, Vol. II in 1880.

Tennyson said to Allingham, "I wish he hadn't taken my word Idyll," and the complaint was not as absurd as it appears. For Browning's idea of an Idyll was wholly different from Tennyson's. Although he had disappointed Carlyle by refusing to write in prose, he saw more vividly even than the old philosopher the dark side of humanity's dilemma. Three of the heroes in *Dramatic Idylls* are a dog, a stag, and a horse. Brilliantly Browning reacts in "Tray" against what he called "that infamous practice—vivisection." To his old friend Frances Cobbe he wrote: "I would rather submit to the worst of deaths as far as pain goes, than have a single dog or cat tortured on the pretence of sparing me a twinge or two."

In "Donald" man and stag meet on a narrow shelf of rocks: it is equally impossible for either to turn back or to pass the other. The man lies down, the stag carefully walks over him, leaving him unhurt— only to be slain when at the man's mercy. Reading "Ivan Ivanovitch," "Halbert and Hobb," "Ned Bratts," I am haunted by the memory of that grim book—Wanley's *Wonders of the Little World.* Surely it did something to the very young Browning which came to the surface in the old. Yet Browning, says Chesterton, like the founder of Christianity, discovered the honest man even inside the thief. Clive is a magnificent study, so is Martin Relph, but on the whole his earlier characters, Sludge, Blougram, and the rest, are more alive, more truly men and women—*convincingly* striving with convincing problems. In the second volume of Idylls is also the beautiful "Pan and Luna."

Anne Thackeray tells us that Browning loved quoting bad poetry and knew by heart an incredible amount of doggerel—and his own impossible rhymes were now increasing. The very worst example noted by Dowden was "Pietro of Albano," which he felt resembled "the jolting in a springless wagon over a rough road and a long."

"Pen is here," wrote Browning from London to George Barrett in May of that year, "very well, though he has been much affected by his hard two months' study of modelling and anatomy in Paris." But there were results on which the father expatiates, ending with his usual gasp of delight: "So much for him,—dear good and absolutely satisfactory fellow, as I most thankfully as well as truthfully can declare him to be."[2]

It was natural to boast to George, but all Browning's letters now abound in similar little cries of joy. "He gives me much delight." "The dear fellow is not idle as you see."

Perhaps he deceived himself when he told a friend that he would sacrifice his own success if thereby he could win triumph for Pen—but he certainly got far more agitated over criticism of the pictures than of his own poetry. William Jones Hoppin, First Secretary at the American Embassy, noted in his journal how, viewing one of Pen's performances, Ruskin remarked: "You see I have been in gloom and fogs and want something bright. I want light—I want blue and vermillion but I don't find them here." "All of which," Mr. Hoppin remarked, "disgusted Browning."[3] As his friend George Smith once said, his affection for Pen was "almost painful in its intensity and absorption."

In 1883 *Jocoseria* was published—and one finds Domett now definitely sympathizing with "the vast numbers his obscurity repels"—and wishing his friend to "condescend to attract" them "by 'completing his incompletion' and letting his meaning 'pant through' the beauty of his poem a little more decidedly and distinctly." But whatever influence Domett had earlier he had little now. Blue pencil or scissors would have been invaluable with the longest poem, "Jochanan Hakkadosh." Comparing it with "Rabbi ben Ezra," one becomes sadly convinced that Browning had imaged the wisdom of old age infinitely better before arriving at it.

If he had died immediately after *The Ring and the Book* it would not have been possible to neglect him as the world did for so many years, to quote his inferior work as typical, to range him, as was for a while fashionable, below the charming but far less deep or original Matthew Arnold, to neglect him in courses of literature for the young (who, in my own experience, can be enthused by him as by few other poets).

Milsand wrote twice about his friend's work, first on *Paracelsus* and *Christmas-Eve and Easter-Day*, the second time on *Men and Women,* which we remember he called "supernatural." And in the second study he explained the lack of popular acclaim. The public's ideal, he said, was the poet "who thinks and feels like everybody else" but has "the talent to do better than anybody what they all agree is the best thing to do. . . . A new fashion in manhood is like seeing a ghost at midday."

It was this immense novelty in Browning that had first impressed Milsand. One is driven, he declared, in evaluating this poet "to prophecy," as though concerning a new religion. The laboratory of the literary critic, like that of the scientist, is stocked with enough reactives for normal analysis and he can indicate to the public how most writers are constructed. But this would be useless with Browning—"all his adventures have been in countries unmarked on the map . . . he has unveiled a fragment of the unknown."

But now with his strength inevitably diminishing Browning was allowing himself to be caught in a stream of social life which must have drained his vital energies. A main interest in this period is the degree to which he did struggle against something of which he only occasionally recognized the inevitable evil. He was slow even to admit the sheer physical results.

Many years ago, her "Prince of Mystics" among the poets had suddenly shown himself to Elizabeth Barrett as the young man of fashion. Did he ever appear to her in the lemon-colored gloves, or did those belong only to his twenties? Anyhow in his early thirties he was still dancing the polka and "cellarius" all night and returning home for breakfast with an aching head, not to be coaxed into poetry. Such a husk of a life she had called it—hardly life at all.

Of the different kind of social life now swallowing him Browning had used the same metaphor, saying of the gypsies, "As though they held the corn, and left us only chaff." Glimpses of the greater personality were apt to show themselves even when Browning was outwardly the merest man of the world. But only when listening to his reading of the poetry was one forced to believe in the poet. "The intense fervour of the man," wrote Octavia Hill, "dominated the company into a hush of awe."[4]

The poetry was less now indeed, not only because the man was older but because the man was less. Read or reread it chronologically and you find the authentic Browning echoed by the Corregidor, the Rabbi, the Pope. You still see the struggle for a freedom (needed by artist and saint alike) in *Fifine,* but you find in *The Inn Album* only the "saturated man of the world." It is not merely because evil is allowed to speak in the later poems—it always had been; it is that the answer of goodness and greatness is dying away.

Yet having said this one must immediately qualify it, for there is no volume down to the end of his life without some note of the old greatness. Indeed an anthology could be made from those later volumes alone, showing him still a major poet. But it would not be a large one. Herford it is who speaks of his "God-intoxicated intellect" from *Pauline* right through to the Pope in *The Ring and the Book.* And he sees Browning after his wife's death remolding "the mental universe which her love had seemed to complete and her death to shatter into a new lesser completeness. . . . A certain relaxation of poetic nerve . . . notwithstanding the prodigal display of crude intellectual power."

In Italy life had been on the austere side: food and drink simple, sleep often broken, long solitary walks and musings, surrounding beauty of art and nature, a great love given and received, a great awareness of a surrounding spiritual world. Returned to England, Browning at first prized his solitude. But he could do nothing by halves. The letters turning up in their multitude, the stories told, depict a life poured out on details; the lengthy dinners of Victorian days, multitudinous engagements. Strengths indeed are visible as well as weaknesses: politeness to the most intrusive, kindness which refused to neglect anyone or reject any request that he could grant. But social life for good or ill does appear to be eating away those elements, poetic and religious, which demand a measure of simplicity if not austerity of life. A measure of recollection, a measure of solitude.

The misfortune was that it was only in the years of this "lesser completeness" that the "importunate hands" of which Henry James speaks began to "crown and re-crown" him. Browning evaded this crowning, joking over it, refusing to talk of his own poetry, reading aloud by preference that of others. Tennyson, it was said, hid behind the Bard, Browning hid behind the man of the world.

In 1880 Browning had joined the newly formed Wordsworth Society and Professor Knight wrote to ask his opinion on an edition he was preparing, giving Wordsworth's original text and putting his later changes in footnotes. This plan Browning considered "incontestably preferable to any other. It would be so, if the variations were even improvements . . . seeing what was good grow visibly better. But . . . in every case the change is sadly for the worse. . . . If ever diabolical agency was caught at tricks with 'apostolic' achievement . . . surely you may bid it 'aroint' 'about and all about' these desecrated stanzas."

Eight years later, asked by Knight to co-operate in a Wordsworth selection, he discovered that "in my heart I fear I should do it almost chronologically—so immeasurably superior seem to me the 'first sprightly runnings.'" With the best "will in the world" he could "try hard to like" the later, while with the earlier "I never can be tired of loving them."[5]

It will be remembered that he had felt the same with Tennyson, and with Morris—yet never does he seem to have questioned that in his own work there was a steady advance. When Smith was preparing a new edition as late as 1887, Browning, "on a sudden impulse," altered *Pauline* as much as was possible without shifting type; "not a line has been displaced, none added," but the printer would have "less trouble with all the rest of the volumes put together than with this portion."

Pauline was of course an old sore, but all the poems, though altering them much less, he had corrected "very carefully."

He had planned on notes for this edition, but on November 12 he wrote, having changed his mind: "I am so out of sympathy with all this 'biographical matter' connected with works which ought to stand or fall by their own merits quite independent of the writer's life and habits, that I prefer leaving my poems to speak for themselves."

"As for the 'notes,'" he wrote on November 24, "well they can stand over, and if I do not supply them, depend on it, some veracious biographer *will*." And in December: "I have been trying to write a note or two, and fear I must give up the attempt: it is so repugnant to my feelings—now of old date—to talk about my own works,—the writing of which has been trouble enough."

The care not to shift type was one element in a most unusual contest between author and publisher—Smith bent on having the best possible edition, Browning equally bent on sparing him expense. If existing copies were sold cheap (what would today be called remaindered) "your loss on the transaction should be supplied by deducting the full amount from the proceeds of the new edition which go to my share." And they should use Chapman's plates, "a very good piece of printing and publishing." The few errors "may be suffered to stand" as against the destruction of plates and books. "It has been only like your constant generosity to make such an offer. . . ."

George Smith was an intriguing personality, depicted by Charlotte Brontë as John Graham Bretton in *Villette,* where his mother figures too, as Mrs. Bretton—some of her very words and phrases were, Smith said, used in the book; Charlotte, talking to Mrs. Gaskell, owned to both portraits. Left in charge of the firm in 1844 at the age of twenty-two by his father's death, Smith was a man of great business acumen and tireless energy. Charlotte Brontë's first visit to him took place that same year. She found him dictating to one secretary while two more were copying letters. He worked all and every day: there were, he said, no Saturday half-holidays for Smith, Elder. His earlier relations with Charlotte resembled those with Browning. She was grateful to the man who had accepted *Jane Eyre,* which came to him in a wrapping revealing its previous journeys to several other publishers. Like Browning, she begged Smith to be careful of his interests, having at first little confidence in her own success.

George Smith and his mother entertained Charlotte repeatedly, took her to the opera and to parties, persuaded her to join the family in Edinburgh, invited her to come to Europe with them. Miss Gérin suggests in her biography[6] that there was some stirring of feeling in the man who had begun by a cool appraisal of Charlotte as longing for beauty and willing to exchange all her genius for it. She was small, plain, be-

spectacled, and eight years older than he. Her fame was great and growing, but she was appallingly shy and unforthcoming—reducing to
silence a party gathered in her honor at Thackeray's house, awkward,
ill-dressed, and totally inexperienced in the ways of a very worldly
world. Whether Charlotte would have accepted Smith remains a question: after all Paul Emmanuel, who was Monsieur Héger, meant infinitely more to her than John Bretton, who was George Smith. But
Villette is, as her biographer suggests, a story of loneliness even more
than a story of love; the three sisters had been the whole world to one
another and after the death of both Emily and Anne, Charlotte's life was
solitary to a painful degree.

When *Villette*, after many delays, was completed, Charlotte was
deeply hurt at Smith's coolness about it; but she does not seem to have
realized that, even if unfair, Smith had something of a case. First there
was his own portrait and his mother's. And then there was the fact that
the theme of "two loves" had shocked the great Thackeray, who would
later refuse a poem of Elizabeth Browning's as liable to bring a blush to
the Young Person's cheek. Many years later again Mrs. Meynell would
write of the "tempestuous purity" of the passions in Emily Brontë's
Wuthering Heights, but at that date the tempestuous passion of the
Brontë sisters, however pure, was suspect to English propriety.

All this was more than forty years behind him when Smith, long
married and established as one of the two or three leading London publishers, could dispose of such funds that George Lewes wrote of George
Eliot's *Romola:* "he made a proposal to purchase Polly's new work for
£10,000. This of course included the entire copyright. It is the most
magnificent offer ever yet made for a novel." (Lewes always called the
stately George Eliot "Polly" in his diary. One entry runs "danced with
Polly to warm her feet, after ineffectually walking up and down for the
purpose.")

It has been said that Browning's permanent content with George
Smith as his publisher lay in the fact that Smith never asked him to
break his rule and let him read the works until they were in corrected
proofs. This contrasts curiously with Browning's sending him a long
outline of *The Inn Album* and saying that it was by Smith's advice *after*

reading the poem that he had decided to bring out *The Ring and the Book* in four instead of two installments. George Murray Smith was not only his publisher, says Mrs. Orr, but his valued friend.

He appears, at least once, to have asked Browning to give a reader's judgment, for Browning's reply begins: "I have known the author of the MS. a long while . . . his opinions deserve a thorough examination." The book was apparently a working-out of the idea that Shakespeare's prose could be read as verse. Browning remarks that Landor had shown the same thing with Milton, but he points out, with some examples, that to do it with the proper beat and rhythms may

make absolute nonsense. In brief, I believe Shakespear, when at work, to have been so accustomed to the main time and tune of blank verse that even when "put out of it" for a minute or two, he would keep it in his head, ready to step into it again in a moment; as a waltzer, interrupted, would trip a few paces hastily before regularly *dancing*. . . . The whole discovery amounts to this—that Shakespear in his prose balanced the periods as he did in his verse. See what a regular period is this last, made without study at all:

> The whole discovery amounts to this,
> That Shakespear in his prose balanced the periods,
> As he did in his verse!

I hope what I have said is intelligible enough: but I could talk the matter over with you at any time if necessary.

If (as the dating would seem to show) this was the "service" for which Smith had overthanked Browning, and which Browning offered to repeat whenever called on, the offer was a generous one. For his daily life was demanding ever-increasing effort put out by ever-decreasing powers, while in the background lay the sense of time's inexorable passing.

The weight of old age grew heavier with the approach of eviction from Warwick Crescent, with all its piled-up rubbish—and treasures—

of a quarter century; with the burden taken up gradually, but now overwhelming of daily social engagements; with the development of Pen's career, Browning deeming himself lucky when that young man attended to its creative side, he as "manager" getting pictures varnished, displayed, and commented on. The business of daily life still included the meticulous account-keeping, which had made Elizabeth smile.

There was the steady stream of visitors to Warwick Crescent, some of whom came once, and others, like Dr. Corson from Cornell University, with whom a friendship quickly sprang up. Professor Corson had been a precursor of Dr. Furnivall: he was in England when the first Browning Society was being planned and told Furnivall "of what I had done at Cornell University, the previous four or five years, in a Browning Club composed of Professors and their wives, and in my university classes."

On their first meeting Browning showed Corson the drawing room upstairs and then "as if I were a young brother put his arm over my shoulder and so descended with me, talking all the while at his usual rapid rate . . . an expression of unconscious cordiality and good fellowship."

Corson noted the two sides of Browning's life, "the unrivalled brilliancy" of the London seasons, his presence in "all the great houses," the nightly dining out, yet the time eagerly bestowed on a fellow enthusiast. "His scholarship was extensive, and, I would add, *vital,* it not having been imposed upon him at a public school and university."[7]

Even more exhausting than society, fashionable or intellectual, was a vast time- and energy-consuming correspondence. Anne Thackeray has described calling one day to find Browning looking unutterably weary surrounded by "a milky way" of letters, all of which he proposed to answer. Once, as the eighties drew on and with them Browning's seventies, we find him speaking of tearing up unanswered six or seven letters, but the general picture is of real trouble taken with every correspondent. Returning from Venice, where mail had been forwarded up to the last safe date, Browning wrote to Furnivall of finding *eighty-four* letters awaiting him at home.

His replies are apt to turn up in any library in any country. At

Trinity College, Dublin, I found recently a pile of the brief notes of the kind the telephone has today almost abolished—thanks, acceptances, refusals. But also one of those careful letters to an aspiring author, over which Browning took so much trouble. For the college student there is, I feel, enough value in this criticism, advice, and warning from a poet to those attempting poetry to make it worth quoting almost in full.

I hope you have not found the delay in replying to your letter excessive: I was much indisposed last week, and many calls on my attention besides: but I have at last read the poems you pleased to desire my opinion about. Of course, I respect you too much to fear that there will be any offence in the frankness I use. I cannot see anything in what is now submitted to me which warrants my saying either "that you will ever succeed"—or the reverse. What you send are an evidence,—no very uncommon one,—that the writer has feeling, musicality, and aspiration: but there is no sufficient individuality, much less originality, in the verses to constitute them "poems"; do you understand? There is wanting the little indefinable touch which makes each poem the peculiar property of the writer,— encloses it, as it were, from the common utterance of youth and sensibility. At the same time, all writers have to *begin,* and one would be bold were one to say decidedly who shall *not* advance. . . .

If you "sing" only for a relief,—for singing's sake,—nothing can be more proper than that you should continue to cultivate the art. It is a difficult one, or where would be the merit of obtaining proficiency therein?

Clearly in this case Browning did not feel that detailed advice or criticism would be of any value, but he was prepared to go to considerable trouble in helping promising beginners. One young woman (Kate Tomkins) working for a living wrote that after his letter "difficulty seems almost an incentive . . . *now I know that it is worth while to go on.*" Yet he had certainly been frank. "I shall try," she says, "to set right the enormities you so *kindly* and *carefully* mention."

How much labor the "milky way" involved may be glimpsed from a selection of letters *to* Browning published in the *Baylor Bulletin* series of *Baylor University Browning Interests*. For Kate Tomkins and the unknown young lady of the Trinity College letter were two of many— some who would remain unknown, others who would win fame. "It is certainly presumption," wrote Louise Moulton Chandler, "in a poor little swallow to want to sing to a great poet." "May I ask your kind acceptance," wrote Wilfrid Meynell, "of my wife's little volume of poems *Preludes* which she is too modest to send you herself."

W. H. Mallock attributes "what success I may have attained" to Browning's advice which "woke me up from dreaming merely about seas and waves and flowers and made me turn to men and men's life." J. P. Mahaffy, the noted Greek scholar of Trinity, Dublin, sends a book in proof and, gratefully incorporating Browning's corrections, writes: "The only danger is that you will expose yourself to new demands from importunate beggars."

Beginners send their manuscripts (a much worse burden than a typescript) and one letter thanks Browning for a successful introduction to Smith, Elder. Relatives and friends send requests for an opinion before publication or after. Violet Paget (Vernon Lee) having met Browning twice "ventures" to send a volume of her step-brother's poetry that it "should have the honour of being on your table, or, in default of that, the honour of lighting your kitchen fire, which is also a distinction *sui generis*." And William Black remarks: "As I suppose it is *de rigueur* for every unhappy versifier in this country to send you his book, of course I must do so also." Apologies follow—and an invitation to dinner (at which doubtless the poems were to be discussed).

Requests arrive for permission to dedicate, which also vary greatly in tone. "I cannot fail to be conscious," writes a novelist frankly, "that your name on the dedication-page . . . would lift my story out of the mass of sensation novels." A poet writes more confidently, offering the dedication of "a poem which has been a dear companion to me for years. . . . Would you find in that gratification and honour?"

Other requests pour in. "I am invited to lecture in America . . . you are great there." Might this lecturer use Browning's name in a *"private circular*. P.S. I believe the Yankees would estimate a favourable word from a man like yourself, Tennyson or Lord Stratford as worth all the Newspaper Notices."

Will he join a deputation from the Authors' Society to Disraeli; will he in addition to his own support of antivivisection laws send on a circular to *influential* friends? Will he write personal letters to them: "A word from you," writes Frances Power Cobbe, "will be worth ten thousand other voters." Will he, "from your pen of your large hearted sympathies," help to bring about a meeting at Oxford to protest against anti-Semitism in Germany and persecution of the Jews in Russia? This (long) letter ends quaintly: "Pardon these remarks. They are intrusive but they are ardent."

Will he support F. T. Palgrave for the Poetry Professorship at Oxford, G. O. Trevelyan for election to the Athenaeum? Mahaffy thanking him for support to be chosen provost of Trinity writes "As they have appointed a man of 65 . . . your good word may come in of use to me bye and bye."

Will he support appeals for various pensions? Will he bring Carlyle to dinner? Will he dine to meet "my friend, your enthusiastic admirer?"; to discuss Beddoes?; to meet Sir John Pope-Hennessy, "who was once a somewhat picturesque figure in parliament and is now governor of Hong Kong"?

One comes to realize more and more with what shrinking Browning must have opened his mail each morning. He seems to have had a sincere interest in helping young poets, and the letters from Palgrave and Lyall indicate correspondences on the nature of translation and on Persian poetry in which Browning was receiving as well as giving. The introductory remarks by Dr. Armstrong also suggest that this volume may be disproportionately full of sweetness and light. He has omitted, he says, anything that might hurt any living person's feelings. It would be surprising if Browning's outspokenness had not appeared at times and produced equally outspoken replies. It is provoking too that so few of these letters match with their opposite numbers in Browning's own published correspondence.

He seems to have done almost all that was asked of him, with one notable exception. *Never* would he speak in public, and Auberon Herbert apologizes for having asked him to do so on behalf of a scheme to put farm laborers on small holdings. This letter, and the whole bundle relating to the Rectorships of St. Andrews, Edinburgh and Glasgow stand out startlingly against the background of what one of Browning's early friends called his "energy" of kindness. He was entreated again and again to let his name be put forward. "How I do immensely hate," he wrote once to Isa Blagden, "this compelled falsity of speech-making."

Scots are a persevering people—and everything was tried in *at least* nine invitations. Jowett's intervention was invoked and given several times, also that of Dean Stanley. Pen was written to, telegrams were sent, and a deputation of young men (to each of whom he gave an inscribed volume) came to London to entreat him personally. But Browning was adamant. He once told Mrs. Orr that he sometimes felt as though he could not enter a room full of people and engage in conversation, but that experience had convinced him he could. Would that he had tried, in speaking also, to build up experience! One feels, reading the correspondence, that there was a real cruelty in disappointing his ardent youthful worshipers. Yet each man knows his own limitations—or else, like Dickens, he dies young. Was Apollo right in seeking longer years for Admetos or were the Fates sometimes laughing up their sleeves? "You can have no conception of what it is," Browning said to Anne Thackeray. "I am quite worn out with writing letters before I begin my day's work!"

Strange that, with this burden so heavy upon him, he should have added to its weight by a number of regular correspondences. With Furnivall, Professor Knight, Pen's teachers, there were definite matters to discuss, but after Isa Blagden's death a similar though rather less intimate exchange of letters began with Mrs. FitzGerald, and later again with Mrs. Bronson.[8] There must also exist (or have existed) letters to Mrs. Orr, to whom he was closer than to either of the others, visiting her when in London—and reading aloud to her—on two afternoons a week.

It is one of the great advantages that we have both sides of the correspondence with Julia Wedgwood (an interesting exception to Browning's destructive habits). There are some striking points of difference between the two others: with Mrs. FitzGerald one sees Browning at once more intimate and less effusive than with Mrs. Bronson. They shared a wider knowledge of literature (that indomitable lady was even studying Greek in her old age). He could and did expect of her a fuller understanding; he tended, as with Isa, to let himself go, while with Mrs. Bronson one sees a careful consideration of what may be sensitive feelings. He rebukes Mrs. FitzGerald in one letter at some length for (a) underrating her own powers of mind, (b) trying to illuminate a poem of his by learning more (from a Hebrew scholar) concerning the surrounding circumstances and people; and this because (c) his poems, carefully examined, are self-explanatory. (This last point is much elaborated.)

It is a curious letter and the sort of thing he permitted himself only with real intimates; it is in fact a scold. One fancies that both Isa and Mrs. FitzGerald understood Browning's moods and smiled indulgently where less understanding friends would have been (with justification) irritated.

A comment by George Eliot on Browning's poem about Elisha would have soothed the harassed poet. "I presume," she writes to a friend, "you did not read the context yourself but only had the two concluding verses pointed out or quoted to you by your friends. It is one of the afflictions of authorship to know that the brains which should be used in understanding a book, are wasted in discussing the hastiest misconceptions about it; and I am sure you will sympathise enough in this affliction to set anyone right when you can about this quotation from Browning."

The touches of unreason make up, however, a very small proportion in the published correspondences, which have been hailed as among his best and which reveal both warm sympathy with his friends' lives and something of himself over the years.

The best things in the letters are the little personal touches: getting the old echo on his first return to Asolo in 1878 and noting how a group of children fail to get it, "perhaps the mighty secret will die with me"; triumphing over "three hundred pounds or guineas from a stranger" for Pen's first exhibited picture; finding Ferdinando in Venice—"the dear old fellow gave us a genuinely Tuscan dinner—having beaten his brains about its achievement for days before"; seeing "dear Carlyle— *not* so changed as I was led to expect. He is silent now unless spoken to —but when he does speak all the old soul is in the little he says. 'He much desires to be released from this world if God please.' " "Poor little Bice Trollope" had died with her first baby. "It seems so lately ago that I was walking with her and Pen and their ponies at Florence, frisking like two butterflies. She was just of Pen's age."

When Mrs. FitzGerald's mentally afflicted son dies, Browning's letter is perfect in its understanding of the mingled feelings about the "life" that has ended, while "what true life has not begun? . . . Of your own part in helping your child through the darkness I need not speak . . . . Bunyan's weary pilgrim whose last words were 'Farewell, Night—Welcome, Day' were never more appropriate. . . . May they be as befitting in the mouths of us all 'who needs must pass the river.' "

One could pick out many more quotations worth making, yet the outcome of a sustained reading of all the collections of Browning's letters is a slight disappointment—of being, one wonders why, rather "let down."

One reason is perhaps the magic in Elizabeth's letters, which cast so much light on their joint life. There is no magic in Browning's correspondence, it has all gone into his poetry. When he gets into deeper issues, one rushes back to the great poems speaking vigorously what in prose he can only stammer. Browning's letters are often interesting, but in the mass, one regretfully uses the word pedestrian.

14 Browning and the Carlyles

> The difference between Orthodoxy or My-doxy and
> Heterodoxy or Thy-doxy.
>
> THOMAS CARLYLE

THE CHIEF PROBLEM in writing this volume is a chronological one. There is so little movement in Browning's later life, one year seems almost exactly like another, marked only by the publication of his poetry. And the subjects of interest demand to be treated separately if they are to be intelligible. About this chapter I have hesitated—but Carlyle is so woven into Browning's life, so interesting a contrast with him and so fascinating a personality that I have ventured to depict more fully than is usual this one man in the life of another: after all I am writing about Browning's world as well as about the man himself.

It was between the second series of *Dramatic Idylls* and *Jocoseria* that Browning lost this friend, who despite wide differences of outlook had given him much support in dark days.

Carlyle died in February 1881: within a month of his death appeared his *Reminiscences*, edited by Froude, the first of several biographical volumes. It was written in a depressed mood after his wife's death and was full of self-blame. The propriety of its publication—above all such rapid publication—was fiercely questioned. All London was talking about it—and doubtless "gossiping" about all Carlyle's friends. In 1881 Browning wrote: "I am astonished at the notion, as to how it could possibly arise, that there was ever the slightest 'falling out' between Carlyle and myself."[1]

And to Mrs. Raynor Belloc, mother of Hilaire, he wrote of the book:

> I do indeed regret deeply the conception, execution and publica-
> tion. . . . I knew the extraordinary limitations of my dear old friend
> —and of his "woman" too. . . . But we must not ourselves prove
> ingrates for a deal of love, or at least benevolence, in deed and wish,
> —*I* must not, anyhow—so, instead of "burning Carlyle and scat-
> tering his ashes to the winds," I am on the Committee for erecting a
> monument to "True Thomas"—whose arm was laid on my shoulder
> a very few weeks ago. . . . He wrote *Sartor*—and such letters to me
> in those old days! No, I am his devotedly.[2]

When DeVane wrote his book on the *Parleyings* Browning's letters
to Mrs. FitzGerald had not been published. We see from them that it
was *Letters and Memorials of Jane Welsh Carlyle* that, in 1883, affected
him most seriously—chiefly the revelation of Carlyle's ingratitude to
some of his best friends (Foster and Allingham particularly), the general unkindness and sneering at so many people,—plus an exaggerated
appreciation of Lord Ashburton's "gift of a horse" and "invitation to
'the Grange.' " Browning had, he says, read "with so much pain and
indeed disgust that I willingly say just *that* and no more." On which
Mrs. FitzGerald comments: "Yet I think he *does* say something more?"
—for Browning's disgust is decidedly vocal to the extent of a full printed
page, ending with the remark: "We must un-Carlylize ourselves and
put up with it."

No two figures could have appeared more dissimilar in the London
world of the seventies than these two men. The ancient peasant—
wrapped in a plaid or an old dressing gown; the middle-aged man of
the world so carefully and fashionably dressed. The prophet accepting
his role, consciously pontificating, the metaphysical poet who hated to
discuss his own poetry, whose appearance and conversation belied his
genius. The man who sat at home to be worshiped or, enthroned in the
house of some great lady, accepted the homage of her circle; the man
who mixed on equal terms with the world, accepting its conventions and
obeying its rules. The man depicted by Froude as cultivating misery

and the man of whom Mrs. Orr declares that, despite a sense of life's pain which made him state that he would not live it again, he "cultivated happiness."

Carlyle said of Browning: "But there's a great contrast between him and me. He seems very content with life, and takes much satisfaction in the world. It's a very strange and curious spectacle to behold a man in these days so confidently cheerful."[3]

Carlyle's liver had probably a large share in this contrast—he spoke of a rat gnawing at the pit of his stomach, declared himself "tormented as never man till me was." Yet too he admitted to his parents that "when I shout 'murder' I am not always being killed."

Browning was preoccupied with other men and women of all kinds and conditions. Carlyle, though he could describe people brilliantly, was perhaps wrestling too exclusively with ideas: above all he was passionately aware of the importance of his own message to the world, the safeguarding and giving of which made him self-centered to the point of selfishness.

The picture emerging of two married lives and all that it conveyed in the understanding of sex, in the penetration of character, presents the most marked contrast between two geniuses who all but spanned the century with their lives and who both became prophets to their generation. For while Browning waited hand and foot on his wife, Carlyle expected Jane to wait hand and foot on him. It was only after her death that he realized with deep grief how unhappy he had made her. For he had really loved her—not certainly with the passionate devotion of Robert for Elizabeth, but with an inward tenderness he never showed save sometimes in his letters. "Her inmost life," Froude quotes from her intimate friend Geraldine Jewsbury, "was solitary— no tenderness, no caresses, no loving words, . . . a glacier on a mountain would have been as human a companionship."

Of himself Carlyle spoke in his *Reminiscences* as living habitually in "an element of black streaked with lightning." "One's imagination," he said, "is a black smithy of the Cyclops, where strange things are incessantly forged. . . . Alas! How much happier I should be not talking or talked to."

And so it was for days on end at Craigenputtock, where for six years they lived in the depths of the country, where she baked bread, sometimes even cleaned grates and scrubbed floors, in gaps between the incompetent servants who normally performed these rough tasks. "The unheard of *mésalliance*," writes Froude of the marriage between Carlyle and Miss Welsh of Haddington, "had been the scoff of Edinburgh Society." One friend of both husband and wife expatiated to Carlyle on the dismay he felt at "Titania falling in love with Bottom"— for Jane was of a fairy-like elegance with lovely eyes, giving an impression of a greater beauty than was technically hers. She had handed over her small fortune to her mother for life, and the first years of marriage in Scotland and even in Chelsea were of greater hardship than she could have dreamed possible. Carlyle's manuscripts came back, with at times contemptuous rejections; his articles for periodicals became hard to place and were tardily paid for. But she never lost faith in the genius for which she later admitted she had married him and in which his own belief made him bitter indeed at the world's blindness but never faithless to himself and his message. Indeed in all his penitence for the suffering to which he had exposed his wife a curious undertone can be heard: "How cruel it was on her," he wrote after lamenting the "chaotic mountains" of material that he must take into his "poor soul and in that furnace fairly smelt the grains of gold out of it . . . so cruel, alas, alas, and yet inevitable." She was, he cries, a "heroic thrice noble and ever loving soul"—but again and again one hears in that word "inevitable" the underlying conviction that, however painful, it was the order of things that human sacrifice should be offered to genius—his own life most certainly which abounded in sacrifice, but also hers.

Jane sewed and cooked and made the house elegant, transacted Carlyle's business, kept accounts, paid bills, argued with tax collectors, supervised painters, drove away the cocks next door when they interrupted her lord's sleep. But in Chelsea she had around her distinguished men who found her—some of them—an even greater attraction than her husband. Mazzini came constantly to sit at her feet. Maurice came, filled with admiration for Carlyle, but making Jane feel "as if one were dancing on the tips of one's toes (spiritually speaking). And then he will help with the kettle and never fails to pour it all over the milk and sugar." Then there was Monckton Milnes, who on her recovery from a severe illness kissed her weeping with delight; as did Forster, with "great smacking kisses of joy." There was a strong element of the flirt in Jane. She was a witty and delightful hostess, and the Hanson biography shows us that the earlier years at Chelsea and the last months before her death were not so black as Froude painted them. She felt herself to be the deepest comfort to her husband as she threw her arms around him grieving and lamenting his loss when (so we are told) Mill's housemaid had burned the first volume of *The French Revolution*. And when Carlyle said that Jane had "a sort of spite against Mill and his wooden set," it was perhaps more that horrible accident she was resenting than the loss of Mill from their circle to "the half angelical half demoniacal Mrs. Taylor." She breathed courage into Carlyle as he began the renewed agony of a rewrite, and when he had finished it she scorned his fears that the book would be "trampled" by his public "under foot and hoof." "Pooh, Pooh!" said Jane, "they can't trample that."

Nor could they; but before money began to come in Harriet Martineau and a group of friends started Carlyle on a series of lectures. Jane gave him brandy, inspired him with confidence, and left him at the door; he would not let her stay in what he called "the place of execution." The lectures and *The French Revolution* together were the turn of the tide and about 1838 Carlyle noted that they were "what is called 'rather rising in Society' " and he added the comment "certain of the aristocracy did seem to me still very *noble*." But Jane had some good reason to sigh "*Ach Gott!* if we had been left in the sphere of life we belong to, how much better it would have been for us in many ways."

The Baring couple, shortly to become Lord and Lady Ashburton, struck up a violent friendship with Carlyle. The lady in particular was given to collecting literary lions, each shortly ousted by the next. "Well, Tennyson," said an outgoing favorite, "all I can say is my advice to you is to rise with your winnings and be off." But while others passed away Carlyle was permanent. Sent for at first, as Jane complained, "like a clergyman to give consolation in trouble," he became more and more a day to day visitor at Bath House, an ever-welcome house guest at Addiscombe, and later The Grange. It was made clear that Jane was valued solely as his appendage; and she was not comfortable in a circle where she had to think of how she was dressed, had to cope with wits not as quick by any means as her own, but exercised by people who had acquired a talent (compared by Carlyle to dancing a minuet) for passing lightly from topic to topic, and used a skill *un*observed by him for planting the exquisite barb with which one woman can slight and humiliate another.

But what really broke Jane was her husband's enslavement. "A man cannot hold his genius as a sinecure," she had said through the solitude and toils of her life, but now to see Carlyle, who had no time for conversation with her, going night after night to Bath House: this was what shattered her world. She had waited patiently for his success and here was what it had brought.

Did she know that he was calling Lady Ashburton "My Beautiful Lady," "Principessa," "friend sent me by heaven"? "Best and beauti-fullest of Heaven's creatures," he wrote, "I kiss the hem of your garment."

This was the Lady Ashburton who had so melodiously read Browning's *Men and Women* one Christmas at Addiscombe, but after her death Lord Ashburton married the famous Louisa with whom Browning's relations have been so much discussed. She loved Jane and understood her as one Scot (she had been a Miss Mackenzie) so often does another, and opened for her the serene last months of her life. It is now Jane who is writing: "Dearest, sweetest, beautifullest." "Oh Lady, fair and dear . . . you bear and strive and love and are more like an angel than a grand lady." A visit to the Ashburtons' house, transformed from a place of torment, has become "such a good break in the long, dreary, Chelsea winter, and stirs up one's stagnant spirits, and rules up one's manners!"[4]

Froude had not wanted Browning's letters from Carlyle for his book and he remarks that neither he nor Tennyson belonged to the Cheyne Row circle. If this meant dropping in like Leigh Hunt three or four evenings a week (he had, he claimed, almost become "a Lar") to be fed Scotch porridge and listen to Jane's Scotch tunes, it could hardly happen save to a near neighbor. Tennyson lived in the Isle of Wight, Browning first within a ride, when he did indeed visit and was visited by Carlyle, but then for a long time remote in Italy. If it meant an agreement with Carlyle's views it would probably be truer to think of him as Carlyle wrote concerning an earlier friend, as having "long discussions and argumentative parryings and thrustings . . . in brisk logical exercise." They had "parted usually in good humour, though after a game which was hardly worth the candle."

Just as Browning in *La Saisiaz* had prolonged his intellectual interest in the symposium on immortality so I think his interest was mainly intellectual in contrasting Carlyle's views with his own in the "Parleying with Bernard de Mandeville."[5]

DeVane has shown convincingly (in both *Handbook* and *Parleyings*) that Browning must have written this "Parleying" on a vague memory of *The Fable of the Bees*, given to him by his father in 1833 but written more than a century earlier, and a more recent reading of de Mandeville's *Vindication* in which he endeavors to offer a different interpretation of his paradox by a conciliatory tone and an "ostensible position on the side of virtue." It was indeed a "grotesque situation. . . . Had Browning realized the true purport of de Mandeville's thought few men in England would have been more outraged." And DeVane quotes Coleridge: "Can anyone read de Mandeville's *Fable of the Bees* and not see that it is a keen satire on the inconsistencies of Christianity, and so intended?" Leslie Stephen, from an agnostic angle, was equally horrified at a philosophy expressed though "not quite in plain words" which would "leave nothing but a bare hideous chaos." Stephen saw de Mandeville accepting the theological view that without a God and a heaven there can be no virtue and grinningly replying "I accept your conclusion that virtue is a humbug. Let us laugh but not in public."

One could hardly exaggerate the strangeness of calling in a man like de Mandeville to refute one like Carlyle, a worldly de Mandeville asserting the truth against the prophet who, dark as his views were of possible happiness, stern as they were on man's sole duty to labor and die laboring, had never uttered in his life a sophistry or suggested a compromise with ease or worldliness, or any lowering of the highest ideals. But it was ideas more than men that Browning was depicting and the ideas on one side were as certainly those of Carlyle as the opposition ideas were *not* those of de Mandeville but of Browning himself.

They had often argued before—and no quarrel *need* be inferred when he writes: "whose groan I hear with guffaw at the end/Disposing of mock melancholy." Browning must in their long friendship have shared Mazzini's experience of Carlyle, that "from his lips, at times so daring, we seem to hear every instant the cry of the Breton mariner— 'My God protect me! My bark is so small and thy Ocean so vast.' "

It had been so long a friendship, and it seems pretty clear that even after the blow of 1883 Browning's feelings went up and down. When two years later Norton asked for the letters unwanted by Froude he wrote: "the goodness and sympathy which began so long ago continued unabated to the end of the writer's life. I repaid them with just as enduring an affectionate gratitude. . . . His love was altogether a free gift, and how much it has enriched my life I shall hardly attempt to say—certainly not at this moment when I write in all the haste of approaching departure from home. . . . "

Norton still wanted more than the letters, but Browning wrote again: "I cannot undertake to write any account of our beloved friend at present. I feel just as you do respecting the misunderstanders, but am hardly able to say my whole mind aright just now, from abundance rather than lack of matter."

There were most certainly, as DeVane says, "many things that had to be fitted into his old conception of Carlyle" after these publications. Reading them through is so moving that we need no Browning to convey their effect in the great dramatic monologue he might earlier have achieved. Anyhow Browning was wholly unlikely to depict his friends. Dickens' portrait gallery included Leigh Hunt in Skimpole, Landor in Boythorn, an unfortunate acquaintance in Miss Mowcher, his father in Micawber and his mother in Mrs. Nickleby; Browning's intimates were perhaps thankful that he stayed with the Sludges and the Blougrams. A confiteor written by another was unnecessary for a man whose years were passed writing it for himself—so eloquently that we need only gather the fragments from those five volumes to have the picture before us in all its pathos. No one could judge Carlyle more severely than he judged himself. And he imposed his own penance in collecting and annotating the letters, writing the memoir which painted a highly idealized Jane, unrecognized by Browning or even by Froude, whose interesting conclusion is, despite his vivid picture of Carlyle's faults, that Jane's was the stern and his the tender heart.

It was not an aspect of either which struck the casual observer to whom they both appeared "too clever by half," that half being the constant criticism and sarcasm poured out on their acquaintances. A Welsh boy leading her donkey in the Malvern Hills said: "Mrs. Carlyle, you would be a vast deal more amiable if you were not so damnably clever," but Jane never approaches the devastating quality of the vast majority of Carlyle's judgments scattered through his own books and Froude's records. Newman had "the brain of a moderately sized rabbit," Keble was "a little ape," Mill "essentially was made of sawdust," Harriet Martineau had "a mind reduced to these three elements: Imbecility, Dogmatism and Unlimited Hope. I never in my life was more heartily bored with any creature." Sydney Smith was "a mass of fat and muscularity . . . shrewdness and fun, not humour or even wit, seemingly without soul altogether. The rest babble, babble." Of Mill's friends he says: "No class of mortals ever pleased me less. There is a vociferous platitude in them, a mangy hungry discontent; their very joy like that of a thing scratching itself under the itch." Macaulay: "a poor creature with his dictionary literature and erudition, his saloon arrogance. He will never see nor do any great thing, but be a poor Holland House unbeliever, with spectacles instead of eyes to the end." Gladstone was "a man ponderous, copious, of evident faculty, but all gone irrevocably into House of Commons shape . . . tragic to me rather."

Another "ape" was George Eliot's George Lewes, so christened by Jane, his talk being described by Carlyle as "a tempest of twaddle." (Later he was more approved and, declared Margaret Fuller, "was allowed sometimes to interrupt Carlyle a little, of which one was glad.")

Swinburne had once admired Carlyle but now in a poem "After

Looking into Carlyle's *Reminiscences*," he wrote of "Three deathless names by this dead snake defiled." And after a "Last Look" he addressed the dead philosopher as Malvolio "sick of self-love." The three defiled names were Coleridge, Wordsworth, and Lamb. Swinburne cries:

> ... men watched thee snarl and scowl
> And boys responsive with reverberate howl
> Shrilled, hearing how to thee the springtime stank
> And as thine own soul all the world was rank.

It is easier today to feel the pathos of a revelation of which Froude seems to have wrongly estimated the effect on the contemporary world. Most of the people named with such scorn were at least living memories, loved or respected by many readers, who had not, like Froude himself, become inured to Carlyle's fashion of speech. "Courage, my poor little Jeannie," Carlyle once wrote to his wife. "Had I been other for you too it might have been easier But I was not other, I was even *this*. Let us both cry for help to be better for each other."

For the most part of his mind had, through life, been concentrated on whatever book he was struggling to write. Now his neglects, roughness, lack of consideration were revealed to him as he pored over Jane's letters, meditating on a past so much of which had gone by strangely outside his consciousness. With no less concentration than had held him on *The French Revolution*, on *Cromwell*, or on *Frederick the Great* he determined now to write about Jane "that some memory and image of one so beautiful and noble should not fail to survive by *my* blame, unworthy as I was of her, yet loving her far more than I could show, or even than I myself knew till it was too late—*too late*."

Writing the memoir, which Froude decided to publish as a chapter in his *Reminiscences*, in the "poor house" which Jane had made "so beautiful and comfortable," he looked back on their

> hard battle against fate: hard but not quite unvictorious, when she left me, as in her car of heaven's fire. My noble one! I say deliber-

ately *her* part in the stern battle, and except myself none knows how stern, was brighter, and braver than my own. Thanks, Darling for your shining words and acts. . . . And I was Thomas the Doubter, the unhoping . . . in continual gloom and grimness, as of a man set too nakedly *versus* the Devil and all men. Could I be easy to live with? She flickered round me, like perpetual radiance, and in spite of my glooms and my misdoings, would at no moment cease to love me and help me. What of bounty too is in Heaven!

Jane he declares was "careful always to screen me from pain, as I by no means always reciprocally was; alas no, miserable egoist in comparison. . . . Oh it was noble, and I see it so well now, when it is gone from me, and no return possible."

And again: "I have no book a thousandth-part so beautiful as thou; but these were our only 'children,'—and in a true sense, these were verily ours; and will perhaps live some time in the world, after we are both gone."

Jane pervades Carlyle's *Journal* too and is constantly present in the other essays that make up the *Reminiscences*, while Froude quotes copiously in his biography of Carlyle, who had entrusted to him the choice of what and when to publish, desiring only that Jane should be known to others as he had known her and, reading her letters, was still learning to know her. And he could not but cry out his message to others "Blind and deaf that we are: oh, think, if thou yet love anybody living, wait not till death sweep down the paltry little dust-clouds and idle dissonances of the moment, and all be at last so mournfully clear and beautiful, when it is too late!" And again: "Five minutes more of your dear company in this world. Oh that I had you yet for but five minutes, to tell you all!"

Among that "all" was doubtless one element to which Carlyle gives a sentence "*Ay de mi!* it is a mingled yarn all that of our 'Aristocratic' history, and I need not enter on it here."

Browning must have read all this and one surely sees in imagination the resultant struggle in his own feelings. He had loved Carlyle, had, early in their friendship, loved Jane too, but with her marked dislike for him it was unlikely that he continued to feel much warmth for her. He said to "Michael Field," "No, you would not have liked her much. She would have tried to pick holes in you." His first instinct was obviously the defense of his old friend. Yet nothing could be more totally repugnant to his feelings than what Froude told, what Carlyle himself was lamenting, in that friend's behavior to his wife. This was an absorbing drama he was witnessing—a man making love to the dead wife as he had not to the living.

The climax was reached in Carlyle's self-crucifixion: had man ever left such a record? And after all Jane *must* have brought him trials as well as loving service: she was a tough little creature spiritually and intellectually, however frail her body; her letters bear witness to both facts. Carlyle had indeed been grievously neglectful with that total absence of mind which has been defined as "presence of mind on something else." It was only when the something became a someone that Jane's world turned black.

The contrast with his own marriage, the whole question of this aristocratic world into which he, like Carlyle, had been almost forcibly dragged, but into which he was fitting more and more completely, which Carlyle had in the end almost wholly rejected—all this must have been absorbing enough to make it hard for Browning to say his "whole mind aright." There was indeed "abundance rather than lack of matter."

It is of course possible that Browning was, as DeVane suggests, affected in his judgment by Carlyle's continued attitude of the ancient sage to the young disciple, having patronized him in his beginnings and unable to abandon this attitude. But I doubt it, because of the immense warmth with which he wrote of his old friend before these shocks began. They had certainly drifted apart during the long Italian years and Carlyle had on his return freely (sometimes unreasonably) criticized Browning's poetry. But he had also praised warmly—both praise and criticism openly given and apparently light-heartedly received.

William Allingham recounts in his *Diary* of November 5, 1875, meeting Browning in Cheyne Row. Browning reminded Carlyle of the long ago days when he would come to their house and "talk Scotch" to his mother. "You told me the Scotch name for buns—*cookies*."

"C. 'I hear you've been bringing out several new Books lately. I always read your Books and find them well worth it, but I have not seen these.'

"B. 'I'm afraid of you in that way! I'd sooner trust my body to you than my book!' "

Carlyle talked afterward to Allingham of how much he had liked the young Browning: "a modest youth, with a good strong face and a head of dark hair. He said little, but what he said was good." Carlyle had, at the time, written to his friend Sterling of "little Paracelsus Browning, a dainty Leigh-Huntish kind of fellow, with much ingenuity, vivacity and Cockney gracefulness." While Carlyle uses the word "Cockney" in a friendly spirit, FitzGerald declaring Browning a cockney defined the word to Tennyson as the affected and overstrained style "of Londoners on subjects with which neither their Birth nor Breeding (both rather plebeian) has made them familiar." Leigh Hunt's style he found "Cockney Pastoral" and Browning's "Cockney Profound and Metaphysical."

As we have seen, Carlyle had been immensely enthusiastic over Browning's first translations, but when it came to the *Agamemnon* he asked Allingham, "*Can you understand it at all?*" For his "soul's salvation" he "couldn't make out the meaning."

And on a later visit he declared, "R. B. admitted that all said it [*Agamemnon*] was of no use." Browning told Domett of not calling on Carlyle for a while, for fear of a meeting with someone or other whose name Domett says, "I did not care to ask." But that this was a passing episode we also learn from Domett, who records visits in his diary, as does Allingham, sometimes with pain. For Carlyle seems never quite to have shed the ill nature he repented of. Allingham, the "star" in whose sky he knew Shelley to be, records sadly his triumphant: "Browning came on my birthday. . . . He agreed with me about Shelley and his poetry." Carlyle despised Shelley and Allingham listened "with pain," but preferred in his journal to blame Browning rather than the old philosopher, who, with Tennyson, stood on the highest pedestal accorded to the living.

He had long so stood with Browning, but by the mid-eighties the process of de-Carlylizing had gone a good way, as we may gather from the gossip set down by Daniel Curtis in Venice. In these talks Browning was primarily critical of the idealization of Jane Carlyle by her husband, who "spoke as if she had stepped down from the stars to marry him. What was she after all? The daughter of a small Scotch doctor in an obscure country village. She did no more work than was good for her."

Browning had known many a curate's wife, gently bred, living on the same income working just as hard, and saying nothing about it. The type of girl Jane brought untrained from Scotland, her mother's bed brought from there also, created her troubles—the "vermin" especially over which she wailed. People had evidently told tales to Browning. A Miss Williams Wynn had advised Jane to burn her journal. Jane had once thrown a cup of coffee at Carlyle. She had in Browning's opinion no beauty except her eyes and her hair. He sketched in the air a markedly turned-up nose and described her complexion as resembling pickled walnuts. Again he told the often-told story of the kettle, with a little more to it than we get from Mrs. Crosse. It had happened on his first return to England and he had not seen an English tea table and service for some years, so got confused when she said, "Now Mr. Browning be useful and hand the kettle from the hob." Awkwardly he held it, not knowing what to do next. She cried "fill the teapot," which he did and again was left with the kettle in his hand. "What am I to do with it now?" "Put it down," which he did on the carpet at his feet. But to Mr. Curtis his explanation of Jane's annoyance was that she chose to think he was putting on airs, the affectation of a fine, traveled gentleman. The damaged carpet Browning had not apparently noticed.

But even about Carlyle the note struck is not a kind one. He felt the couple were too concentrated on themselves—they had no children to worry over, no real sorrows and cares; Carlyle was arrogant, accepted all attentions as simply due to his genius. Allingham devoted two hours a day to walking with him. His services were acceptable, but Carlyle regarded him only as a sort of faithful dog who might be kicked (with a gesture).

Browning was convinced that Carlyle had mastered his subject always, that his power of description was immense—Waterloo, the

Prussians coming up—"You'd think you were there yourself"—and Carlyle "if you listened without contradicting him, talked better than he wrote." Browning had only once argued with him, pointing out that, after "crying up Force" all his life, he had the man he had been demanding (Louis Napoleon) and was now calling him upstart and usurper. "Carlyle had nothing to answer."

While not, like Carlyle, overbearing in conversation, Browning had many a monologue inside him and Curtis depicts him "sitting— stretched out in a low chair, hands behind his head or in his trousers pockets. If someone else offers a remark or a rejoinder he listens for awhile, then raises his voice and 'overtalks the interruption.' "

There is little in these notes of the deeper things Browning shared with Carlyle, and one wonders whether in any case Curtis would have been capable of recording them. But on the poet's reading he reflects an immense experience shared with the Storys and other friends. The power he felt lay not in the strong, audible, though unmelodious voice, not in tricks of elocution, of which there were none, but "the interest and attraction is *his* interest, the *si vis me flere, flendum est tibi.* . . . When he reads his poetry he ceases to be the Browning of Society . . . and becoming Browning the poet is seen, as it were, under the afflatus by which he is inspired and carried away . . . his voice features and manner reflect the great quality of his verse and he is his greater self and his own best interpreter."[6]

It was the poet at bottom more than the man of the world who disliked the Carlyle confiteor. Browning was the living half of that almost magical union which had so enchanted Mrs. Jameson. There were of course, there must be in even the happiest marriage, "paltry little dust clouds and idle dissonances" but need his old friend thus seat himself in the stocks to be pelted by the populace? Browning I think, despite his Christian philosophy, had a good deal about him of the old Roman and pagan outlook. Although he had experienced contrition I doubt if he could ever understand self-abasement, more especially as he grew older. He *must*, one feels, have been moved as he read, but one can well conceive of a profound conflict of feeling which made it impossible "to say my mind rightly."

Froude tells us of Carlyle's unwearying charity and kindness to those who, after his protective wife's death, literally swarmed around him seeking help, lying often in wait for him outside his house if the bell had gone unanswered. Jane had been generous and he continued all her charities, adding many of his own. He did complain in old style of the "extraneous fools from all quarters: penny post a huge inlet to that class." But charity was, says Froude, his only luxury. Though he now had thousands instead of the earlier few hundreds, his life remained as simple as of old. Jane's birthday he celebrated by a gift to a Scotch pensioner: "poor old Betty, who, next to myself, remembered her in lifelong love and sacred sorrow."

His contacts with the realities of world politics remained as strange as ever: he supported Prussia vehemently in the war of 1870 and hoped that Germany "the peaceablest, most pious, and in the end most valiant and terriblest of nations" would now be "President of Europe."

But world matters were increasingly becoming peripheral: Carlyle wrote that not even this "grandest and most beneficent of heavenly providences"—the Prussian victory—could "kindle" him more than briefly. The journal of October 11, 1870, runs: "Infinite longing for my loved ones—towards Her almost a kind of mournful worship—this is the one celestial element of my new existence; otherwise in general 'wae and weary'—'wae and weary.' "

His hand was becoming feebler and to his niece Mary he dictated what was of a public kind, but he still continued to write in his journal, and two years later we read again of "serious penitent reflection, and of a sorrow which could be called loving, calm and in some sort sacred and devout. Pure clear *black* amidst the general muddy gloom. . . . Close by lies the *great secret*. . . . Perhaps something! Perhaps *not* nothing after all. God's will there also, be supreme. If we are to meet! Oh Almighty Father, if we are, but silence! silence!"

The overwhelming quality of a trust in God which yet held this uncertainty was shot through during these years with flashes of a deeper intuition. Arranging Jane's letters in 1869 he had written: "Perhaps this mournful but pious, and ever interesting, task, escorted by such miseries, night after night and month after month—perhaps all this may be wholesome punishment, purification, and monition, and again a *blessing in disguise*. I have had many such in my life. Some strange belief in an actual particular Providence rises always in me at intervals, faint but indestructible belief, in spite of logic and arithmetic, which does me good. If it be a fact, as Kant and the clearest scientific people keep asserting, that there is no Time and no Space, I say to myself sometimes, all minor 'Logic' and counting by the fingers becomes in such provinces an incompetent thing. Believe what thou must, that is a rule that needs no enforcing."

And on October 14 of the same year "stepping out after midnight and looking at the stars" he felt with "a strange new kind of feeling . . . God Almighty's own Theatre of Immensity, the Infinite made palpable and visible to me, that also will be closed, flung to in my face. . . . And then a second feeling rose on me, 'What if Omnipotence, which has developed in me these pieties, these reverences and infinite affections, should actually have said: Yes, poor mortals. Such of you as have gone so far shall be permitted to go further. Hope! Despair not!' I have not had such a feeling for many years back as at that moment."

Combatting with real rage the atheism that he felt this "poor protoplasm generation all seemingly" were determined to try for a while, he knew that they must return to God "or go down altogether into the abyss. I find lying deep in me withal some confused but ineradicable flicker of belief that there is a 'particular providence.' Sincerely I do, as it were, believe this to my own surprise, and could perhaps reconcile it with a higher logic than the common *draught-board* kind. There may be a further *chess-board* logic says Novalis."

Charity, contrition, the dumb cry of the soul to the God he trusted even "should he slay me"—for fourteen years these had been the dispositions of Carlyle's soul. At the age of eighty-five he died, on February 4, 1881. Froude was there within an hour: "He lay calm and still, an expression of exquisite tenderness subduing his rugged features into feminine beauty. I have seen something like it in Catholic pictures of dead saints, but never, before or since, on any human countenance."

Carlyle had foreseen and frustrated any effort to bury him in Westminster Abbey. After one funeral there he had remarked to

Froude, "There will be a general jail delivery in that place one of these days." And he had objected to the Anglican burial service—"The grain of corn," he said, "does not die; or, if it dies, does not rise again." So with no religious ceremony, for in Scotland the prayers. were then offered in the home. before or after, in what seemed to Froude a miserable hugger-mugger affair, a crowd come from curiosity only, newspaper reporters standing on the tombs, boys and girls bright with ribbons climbing on the churchyard walls—"Scotland laid her greatest and best in his solemn sleeping place." Froude for a moment could not but regret the Abbey funeral, the splendor, the great ranks of mourners he had been obliged to reject. "But for a moment only. It was as he himself desired."

15 Back to Italy

Full of a generous and indomitable spirit, free from the whining and cavilling to which poetic philosophy so often inclines; throbbing with that remembrance of delight which is perhaps better than any delight itself; not covetous but not despairing of more . . . a poet who is also a man, which duplicate advantage poets have not always possessed.

GEORGE SAINTSBURY

B ROWNING never succeeded in bringing himself back to Florence, but the pull of Italy was strong and in 1878 he had returned to Venice, least associated in his Italian past with Elizabeth. It became the terminus of every summer holiday for eight out of his eleven remaining years.

This meant a curtailment of his solitude. Venice was a social city for Americans and English: there would be dinner parties here too, though simpler ones than in London, poetry readings, and the "sitting" for portraits by ambitious beginners.

A warm friendship grew up as we have seen with Mrs. Arthur Bronson, who has told how much was here renewed of the old Floren-tine days.[1] Browning would explore such byways as the ocean city contains, would haunt the curiosity shops for bargains. There were splendid sunsets, and the Public Gardens, where he could make friends with captive bird and beast. In the worst of weather he walked on the Lido—and began to dream of a project which in 1885 kept him in Venice beyond his usual date. He writes in November of the Palazzo

Manzoni: "I buy it solely for Pen, who is in love with this city." They had separately seen and longed for this "most beautiful house in Venice. . . . Pen will have sunshine and beauty about him. . . . I and my sister have secured a shelter when the fogs of life grow too troublesome."

Visiting Florence I was shown by the Marchesa Fossi pictures of her singularly lovely mother, formerly Edith Bronson, who, as well as *her* mother, had become very dear to Browning—one does not wonder when reading the introduction Henry James wrote to Mrs. Bronson's account of "Browning in Venice."

No one better than James could evoke Venice for us, and it is the American in Venice who especially concerns him. In Mrs. Bronson one seems to see one of his exquisite young women grown old, but one wishes he had added "Edie" to the picture. Most people come to Venice, he tells us, for the healing of their troubles. "Mrs. Bronson's case was beautifully different—she had come altogether for others." Whether or not he is right in seeing this in her coming, he had certainly seen it in her abiding. "She cultivated their dialect, she renewed their boats." She lit the lamp "of the tutelary Madonetta; she took cognisance of the wives, the children, the accidents, the troubles." And for all these she became "the established remedy." She had a "perfect tenderness for Venice," increased by her friendship with the ageing poet. "The rich and interesting form in which she found it in Browning may well be imagined." In his poems "he had more ineffaceably than anyone recorded his initiation from of old."

Next to her house, Casa Alvisi, stood—and still stands today—"a somewhat melancholy old section of a Giustiniani palace," annexed for her friends. And there Mrs. Bronson herself records what she calls Browning's "Spartan-like daily life," the cold bath at seven in the morning, the long walk with Sarianna, who was dearly loved, the Marchesa told me, both by Mrs. Bronson and Edith. But they did not much care for Pen, described by Mrs. Bronson as Browning's idol, "his vulnerable point, the heel of Achilles. People who praised . . . his only child found the direct road to his heart."

The owners of the Manzoni hesitated, hoping for a better price, but Browning was told the foundations were insecure. A lawsuit ensued

and Browning, back in England wrote: "There was really much done
. . . consultations, citations and so on—documents in duplicate." As he
had withdrawn, the expenses for both sides fell on him, plus some
"previous and subsequent work" by his own lawyer. The total bills
amounted to £12.7 from the vendor's lawyer and £12.2.6 from his own.
"I doubt if litigation is not more costly here."

The failure to buy the Manzoni came as a surprisingly bitter disappointment to Browning, but meanwhile he had completed and dated
from the "Giustinian-Recanati" a volume entitled *Ferishtah's Fancies*.

We find in Browning's poetry an immense insistence on body as
well as soul; in thinking and still more in loving:

> Captures from soarings high and divings deep.
> Spoil-laden Soul, how should such memories sleep?
> Take sense, too—let me love entire and whole—
> Not with my Soul.

All his thoughts of reunion with Elizabeth are of a bodily meeting—
the ghost is to take on flesh and become the living woman. Yet, talking
of death, he would speak of the body as just the "old clothes" of the soul.
Never does he seem to say "I believe in the resurrection of the body."
For "life everlasting" the soul is somehow to become itself complete,
itself physical.

> Then a light, then thy breast,
> O thou soul of my soul! I shall clasp thee again,
> And with God be the rest!

The nearest he gets to resolving this apparent ambivalence of
thought is in *The Ring and the Book*, where Pompilia sees the angels as
not marrying in the human sense yet finding themselves one. Browning
is often represented as seeing heaven merely as a stretched-out earth,
and, while this is not wholly true, it is true that he did not work out his
own meaning but gave us, as poets will, momentary visions only of the

eternal activity in eternal tranquility brought to men by the direct vision of God.

Another paradox is more curious still: the Browning of old age is almost aridly intellectualist (in "La Saisiaz" for instance), and yet only in old age does he say those things seized on by critics as proving despair of the intellect.

> Wholly distrust thy knowledge, then, and trust
> As wholly love allied to ignorance!
> There lies thy truth and safety.

Ferishtah's Fancies is surely, apart from the lovely lyrics (written, Mrs. Orr believes, on consecutive days), the worst Browning ever.

"If the pessimism of the present day," the *Athenaeum* wrote, "is to be confronted and answered, it is not by such optimism as this."

And, indeed, there is something infinitely depressing in the cozy approach to life's anguish, wholly uncharacteristic in the creator of Guido and the Pope, of Sludge, Andrea, and Lippo Lippi. But it is hardly fair to quote this one book (as is so often done) without going back and forward to see what Browning's full mind was. It emerges as something very different from Ferishtah's exhortations to unlearned love.

Robert Langbaum in *"The Ring and the Book: a Relativist Poem"* answers the theory that Browning is anti-intellectual, substituting love for thought; it is for a wider, deeper kind of thought that the poet stands, when, as Langbaum puts it, the Pope "relies not upon logic to make his judgment, but upon talent, intuition, insight, the advantages of his own character gained through a long experience of life and people."

Taking Browning's poetry as a whole you find this is what he believed: intellect is not the *only* faculty man should use—the whole person must be involved in the approach to reality. He wrote to Mrs. FitzGerald of the doctrine Schopenhauer "considered his grand discovery—and which *I* had been persuaded of from my boyhood—and have based my whole life upon—that the soul is above and *behind* the intellect which is merely its servant. . . . The consequences of this

doctrine were so momentous to me—so destructive of vanity, on the one
hand,—or undue depression at failure, on the other—that I am sure
there must be references to and deductions from it throughout the whole
of my works."

But the poet's approach is not the logician's, as he had shown when
he wrote "Transcendentalism." To another poet he cries out:

> ... Song's our art:
> Whereas you please to speak these naked thoughts
> Instead of draping them in sights and sounds.

Often and often does the young Browning answer the old—and
never more triumphantly than when, in "Transcendentalism," he sees
the gulf between two ways of approaching truth. For while "settling
on the sense most to our mind" or discovering "subtler meanings of
what roses say" we "find life's summer past." Meanwhile, the true
poet—

> He with a "look-you!" vents a brace of rhymes,
> And in there breaks the sudden rose herself,
> Over us, under, round us every side, ...
> Buries us with a glory, young once more,
> Pouring heaven into this shut house of life.

It may seem off the point to bring into the realm of intellect Browning's
violent changes of mood. But he himself used the same metaphor as
Elizabeth about his sensitivity when he described how faith and doubt,
each "shakes the soul": "we called the chess-board white,—we call it
black."

Probably only a believer can understand Browning fully, but that
believer must himself have been shaken by chill doubt.

> "You must mix some uncertainty
> With faith if you would have faith be . . ."
> No. The creation travails groans—
> Contrive your music from its moans, ...

> "How were my case, now, did I fall
> Dead here, this minute—should I lie
> Faithful or faithless?"

When two years after *Ferishtah* (1887) the *Parleyings* appeared Furnivall detected in them Browning's view that the soul must grow in its grasp of truth as the body in its powers. Browning, in his reply, speaks of the soul interchangeably with the intellect, not as of something "above and behind" it. We have not got Furnivall's letter; Browning's reply is dated February 23, 1889.

> The meaning of the passages is much as you say—entirely so, indeed. "Neither body nor mind is born to attain perfect strength or perfect health at its first stage of existence respectively, in each case, by the want of and desire for the thing as yet out of reach, they get raised towards it, and are educated by the process—as would not happen were the body strong all at once—or the soul at once perfect in apprehension."

Furnivall evidently begged for further elucidation, and Browning wrote again on March 2:

> I should prosaically state the meaning thus: I do not ask a full disclosure of Truth, which would be a concession contrary to the law of things, which applies equally to the body and the soul, that it is only by striving to attain strength (in the one case) and truth (in the other) that body and soul do so—the effort (common to both) being productive, in each instance, of the necessary initiation into all the satisfactions which result from partial success: absolute success being only attainable for the body in full manhood—for the soul, in its full apprehension of Truth—which will be, not *here*, at all events.[2]

This did not mean that Browning would have placed the power of knowing *above* that of loving. Love remained supreme—not ignorant love but "love made wise."

Chesterton was as much misunderstood as had been Browning himself when he pointed out that the poet's philosophy was based on a hope, springing from the imperfection of man—and from what could only be described as the imperfection of God. This has been called blasphemy (Henrietta Barrett felt it so in "Karshish") but the meaning is profound enough, developed by Browning above all in "Saul," as David sings of the incarnation and death of Christ. Without this transcendent happening man had the power to do for his fellow men what the almighty, impassible, eternal God literally could not do—love to the point of suffering and dying.

> "Would I suffer for him that I love? So wouldst thou—so wilt thou!
> So shall crown thee the topmost, ineffablist, uttermost crown—
> And thy love fill infinitude wholly, nor leave up nor down
> One spot for the creature to stand in!"

"Karshish" and "Cleon" both illuminate this realization of a love which, as Browning pointed out in several letters, *needed* the incarnation to become visible to man. Power might be seen through creation, love could be realized only in redemption.

None of this did Browning ever unsay. But the bursts of song came now almost wholly on one subject, the key which had unlocked life for him. And he never hides the moments of chill doubt any more than the sunset-touch or flower-bell of life's "grand perhaps."

> Only, at heart's utmost joy and triumph, terror
> Sudden turns the blood to ice: a chill wind disencharms
> All the late enchantment! What if all be error—
> If the halo irised round my head were, Love, thine arms.

Mrs. Bronson wrote of Browning in Asolo as well as in Venice. At her delicious house, built into the city walls and called La Mura, he would read to her and her friends, choosing chiefly Shelley, Keats, Coleridge, or Tennyson. With his own poems he would read the graver parts "in a quiet, almost introspective way as if he were thinking it out again."

He would talk to her of "the indelible association which these hills bear with the names of Shelley and Byron. . . . His face always lighted with pleasure when he spoke of a poet's fame, or heard of honors, even if only in the form of a tablet on a wall, to prove that the great dead are not forgotten." He sought out the old landmarks and told Mrs. Bronson what they signified. History was alive to him. Canova "would have been a greater man at a greater period." El Barco, a former residence of Queen Caterina Carnaro, had become a farmhouse, but he found frescoes there of the period of Giorgione, and the very soil around was sown with spear tips. He would break off his musings to exclaim. "Pen must see this. Dear Pen." And they must always get back in time to view the wonderful sunset from the loggia of La Mura.

When a touring company came there Browning went every night to the theater, which was in the old castle. The company acted fifteen different plays, some being performed in the prison, where the orchestra could be heard from the cells. Browning was popular in Asolo, she says, generous to the peasants and their children, grateful for the smallest attention; and if later visitors found his memory green it may not have been solely because his son now lived and reigned there.

Pen had long been most satisfactory as well as most dear when in 1887 (now aged thirty-eight) he announced his engagement to an American, Fannie Coddington. He had (he told his father) proposed and been refused as long as fourteen years earlier; now he had begged an invitation from some friends Fannie was visiting in England and had courted her again.

Fannie said later that it was the likeness to his father that won her: "the same kind and gentle manner." She had lately lost her own father and Pen's sympathy was precious. His memories of her father's kindness, too, and of their happy times together "touched me and shortly after that we became engaged."

Three months before the wedding in June 1887 came the upheaval for Browning of the move from Warwick Crescent to De Vere Gardens. It is probably true that the vast destruction of letters at this time largely resulted from his horror over the Carlyle publications. Tennyson, at the same date, destroyed his own early letters from fear of indiscreet publicity. But surely the change of residence had a good deal to do with Browning's holocaust. Because of the inherent danger of keeping everything, the move would have forced him into rereading the accumulation of a lifetime. As with his father's papers so with his own: wholesale destruction would seem preferable to the wearisome distress of rereading, especially for a man who, as Mrs. Orr has noted, both felt the pain of memory with unusual acuteness and cultivated present happiness as a duty.

A year after Pen's wedding Browning wrote to Fannie's sister, Marie Coddington: "I am certain that their happiness is 'catching'—and would communicate itself to you—as it did to us who have been close to it so long." And all allowance made for his power of idealizing, one feels that Pen and Fannie were very much in love for a while. "Both parties [he wrote] have decided happiness on the brain just now." A number of letters to Pen in the Balliol College library give a pleasant picture of the start of the marriage that ended so sadly, showing too Browning's joy at having gained the daughter he and Elizabeth had once hoped for. "I can never," says Fannie, "forget his affectionate and warm greeting. . . . He completely opened his heart to me." He never, she notes, used the word "in-law." Arabel Barrett had been his sister, Fannie was his daughter.[3]

Pen, he writes, "who is *shy*, would delight" in her choice of a small country wedding. Lady Wolseley had said to him at Hallam Tennyson's splendid show in Westminster Abbey: "Mine was the desirable wedding in the country, with nobody but ourselves, and after the ceremony we walked together in the fields *and how happy* we were." And to Pen: "You will have a quiet rational beginning of your life." The letter to Pen comments also on the idea of an instant decision to live abroad: "All I objected to was your coming to any hasty determination. . . . It would be as easy to *visit* one country as another—trying the advantages of both places. Of course, I have a wish that you should get the repute and the rewards which you certainly might in England as well as Paris or Belgium." But all this would become clearer "after a few weeks of your intimate life."

Other letters from the two left in London follow the young couple.

Eight charming young sisters from Australia had called, wrote Sarianna, "crazy to know your father"; and the English damsel who made her fiancé pass a Browning examination had given him such high marks that "they are to be married on Saturday, and your Papa has received an invitation. . . . He intends to go."

Browning had not, he claimed, solicited a single vote, yet Pen had been elected to the Athenaeum by 173 votes to four—and those four, the secretary said, were the minimum of mistakes at any election. He can have made no enemies in that small Society world thinking itself so large that people like Sarianna could write of London "emptying" at the end of every season.

However necessary Browning's repeated exhortations to work, they must have got on Pen's nerves, and although he often said he would now leave all this to a better counselor, Fannie, he never in fact did. In October he wrote hoping that happiness would be an incentive, that "the fire of art" was not quenched "by the overflow of oil in the shape of enjoyment, but I hand over the preaching and teaching now to the far more effective inspirer." Yet a couple of months later: "Do your gaieties altogether preclude painting? Fannie darling, 'stir him up with a long pole' as we used to say in school!"

There *was* a picture to be shown in the salon in the spring of 1888— and a bust too—which got there only by Browning's efforts: "Pen should have spoken earlier," but he got the case and dispatched it. And Sarianna wrote that she and Browning "feel quite stuck up at the Salon success," much better than the Academy, and she hopes he will not give up his Paris studio.

But Pen's mind was on other matters: an immense palazzo was in the market—the Rezzonico—and he was bent on its purchase. Browning was all in favor if "dearest Fannie" wanted it. All he cared for was their health and happiness, and "that you deserve it by hard work, and falsifying the ordinary notion . . . that too much prosperity is a hindrance to an artist's career. Don't be the little man in the big house."

Pen had another kind of genius: he could have made a fortune as an interior decorator. "What Pen Browning has done here," wrote James to his sister, "transcends description for the beauty, and, as Ruskin would say, 'wisdom and rightness' of it. It is altogether royal and imperial—but Pen isn't kingly and the *train de vie* remains to be seen. Gondoliers ushering in friends from pensions won't fill it out. . . ."

Besides restoring and modernizing, Pen was expending the energy that might have gone into his career as portrait painter in adorning some of the Palazzo's immense ceilings with grandiose frescoes. In the third-floor room that became Browning's on his first (and last) visit he painted an eagle struggling with a serpent. Professor Corson's wife called it "a most vigorous conception." It was, she said, "illustrative of Shelley's 'Revolt of Islam.' "

What Henry James thought of the frescoes we are not told, but back in England he wrote to the Daniel Curtises: "I talk of Venice with Browning when I meet him—and he always tells me the same thing—that the 'dealers' have offered Pen the eyes of their head for the mere supererogatory fixtures of his disproportionate palace. And Pen is sketched with paternal fondness as making a kind of *pied de nez*."[4]

Fannie's two (at least) miscarriages and her increasing tendency to invalidism had not yet made them despondent. After all, as Browning pointed out, Elizabeth had had the same problem and yet Pen had arrived safely. But the gradual loss of hope for a family may have been a contributory cause in the slackening of Pen's ambition. Of the success at the Salon Browning wrote: "You have the power now in your hands of winning all the distinction your future work deserves. Nobody can escape jealousies and spitefulness, but you may battle it out as well as anyone."

But Pen was never a fighter.

16 Two Robert Brownings?

Marcel Proust is very persuasive in separating the author in the throes of creation from the domestic animal we meet next day on the boulevards.

OSCAR CARGILL IN THE C. E. A. CRITIC

READING ALOUD the chapter on Browning's public life to a group of friends who had just listened entranced to passages from *The Ring and the Book* I encountered a shocked silence: could this dinner-party figure be indeed the creator of both the Pope and Guido? Extremes of good and evil appeared alike incongruous. Perhaps this is the point in the story of a life to take breath for a long look at the man whose story is being told, see the face that emerges from his poetry and his story and from a thousand snapshots or sketches of the poet reading or the social success dining out.

"One of the latest sensations," Henry James had written (in July, 1880), "was going one day to Lady Airlie's to hear Browning read his own poems—with the comfort of finding that, at least, if you don't understand them, he himself apparently understands them even less. He reads them as if he hated them and would like to bite them to pieces."

But this was only a first impression. Later James felt, as I have told in my first volume, that Browning was no bard like Tennyson but a thousand times more a poet. And this chiefly because although, like Gilbert's wandering minstrel, he was "a thing of shreds and patches" ("heterogeneous and profane," says James), "he revealed in his personal delivery of the fruits of his genius . . . almost to harshness . . . extraordinary life."

James had known more than most Englishmen or Americans of the continental background from which Browning had returned to smoky but welcoming London; he moved in the same circles, had seen hostesses vying for Browning's presence at their dinner parties; he had watched the man whose rescue of Andromeda and years of romance had become a legend.

"The wall," we have heard James say, "that built out the idyll of which memory and imagination were virtually composed for him, stood there behind him solidly enough." And it became James's complaint that "even in his most splendid expansions" the poet allowed no entry through its door: he arrived after much gazing, and a certain irritation, at *his* theory of the private and the public Browning.

During the winter of 1876–77, James, as inveterate a diner-out as Browning himself, had met Froude, historian and biographer, Kinglake, traveler and romanticist, and the historian Motley in the poet's company. Browning, he complained, was "a great chatterer, but no Sordello" and "no more like to Paracelsus than I to Hercules."

To his sister Alice he wrote that Browning had seized the lion's place in conversation with "a sort of shrill interruptingness," that there was in this "a kind of vulgarity" unredeemed by depth. "It is altogether gossip and personality, and is not very beautifully worded. But evidently there are two Brownings—an esoteric and an exoteric. The former never peeps out in society and the latter has not a ray of suggestion of Men and Women."[1]

Leon Edel believes that Henry James's theory of the two Brownings originated in his uneasy awareness that there were two of Henry James. Whether this is true or not, some surprising parallels may be noticed between poet and novelist. Both were Europeans rather than merely American or merely English. Both cared more for the individual than for "humanity," and paid insufficient attention to the social evils of the age. Both tried the theater, and both failed for the same reason— too little action and too much talk. Both had an admiring court, including alike sufficiently remarkable and dull and adhesive women. Both had intense family feeling, both spoke with deep tenderness of their dead mothers, but both had left them to live abroad. Both were in their work intensely observant of detail, admirers of Balzac, yet each with individual genius striking out a new line—to be admired and imitated in their respective fields by a host of others.

Both had what Professor Edel terms "a rage of privacy"; they engaged in "mystifications" to cover their tracks, wanted their correspondents to burn all letters, themselves burned much that we long today to have. In "The Aspern Papers" James gives perhaps the best picture ever drawn of the passionate desire to know, with its uglier aspect of exploitation, and the claims to privacy of the great exploited. For no one saw more clearly than he the two sides of this dilemma—and no one except perhaps Browning was ever more torn between two cravings: for expression and for reticence. "The artist," James said, "is present in every page of every book from which he sought so assiduously to eliminate himself."

"I don't think," remarked Mr. Hoppin in his Journal, "that he talks remarkably well. I believe he keeps his most piquant ideas for his books." It might almost be James discussing Browning. Mr. Nadal, Second Secretary at the American Embassy, said that James was "always talking about class distinctions." Annoyed with a middle-class acquaintance who talked of "one's own class"—meaning his and hers as different from the aristocracy—James said that he did not wish to be "adjudged a place in English society in accordance with English standards." But when Nadal criticized some other Americans for pursuing social success, Henry James replied, "I don't agree with you. I think a place in society is a legitimate object of ambition." With Browning a concert or private view, with James the "first night" of a new play "would seem incomplete if his familiar figure were not to be seen."

"I suppose," writes Henry James to his mother after listing some important dinner hosts, "that William will call me a 'fat snob' for mentioning these names," while William writes: "The way he worked at paying visits and going to dinners and parties was surprising to me, especially as he was all the time cursing them for so frustrating his work. It shows the perfect fascination of the whirlpool of a capital when once you are in it."[2] Of all ambitions that of social success should be most alien to the artist, yet both James and Browning had it to a marked degree: both were artists of the rarest quality, both were worldlings.

And if Browning's crush hat and opera cloak startled his admirers, what would James's have felt about the picture of his infinite variety given by the frankly proletarian H. G. Wells?

He thought that for every social occasion a correct costume could be prescribed and a correct behavior defined. On the table (an excellent piece) in his hall at Rye lay a number of caps and hats, each with its appropriate gloves and stick, a tweed cap and a stout stick for the Marsh, a soft comfortable deer-stalker if he were to turn aside at the Golf Club, a light-brown felt hat and a cane for a morning walk down to the Harbour, a grey felt with a black band and a gold-headed cane of greater importance, if afternoon calling in the town was afoot.[3]

In his early short story, "Benvolio," and in his later important novel *The Tragic Muse*, James develops his theme of double identity: "It was as if the souls of two very different men had been placed together to make the voyage of life in the same boat, and had agreed for convenience's sake to take the helm in alternation." In "Benvolio" we find a young poet who passes from "boisterous many-voiced suppers" to a "little scholar's cell." He is in love with two women—a countess who "represented felicity, gaiety, success" and the daughter of a scholar who had been "cradled in an old folio, three quarters opened like a wide V." With her "he longed to embark on a voyage of discovery on the great sea of pure reason." But tired of reason he would go back to his countess and write a brilliant play for her and her friends to act. "You see, the negative with Benvolio, always implied the positive, and his excuse for being inconstant on one side was that he was at such a time very assiduous on another."

The choice of a play as one of the poet's debasing activities would seem to confirm Graham Greene's theory that James was striking at his own temptation to write plays, since he did so almost solely as a possible source of the money which his novels and tales, despite their immense *succès d'estime*, did not bring in sufficient abundance for his expensive way of living.[4]

Yet is Benvolio really Henry James—or is he an early attempt at penetrating Robert Browning? It would be many years before James would write "The Private Life," but in Benvolio he depicts his hero as sitting in his exalted moods before a picture of Andromeda:

> By the dark rock and the white wave just breaking
> At her feet; quite naked and alone.

Did James know that, as Browning wrote *Pauline,* Caravaggio's "Andromeda" was his inspiration—that his own love story fulfilled Benvolio's dream? James does not quote *Pauline,* but his Andromeda is Browning's.

"Benvolio," Henry James declared, was all but a fairy tale; its theme he developed later, transposed from a foreign and fantastic setting into a novel of English life. One of his characters in *The Tragic Muse,* Nick Dormer, is torn between a political career and the pull of an artistic vocation. With a growing contempt for political life, Nick gives up his career, a fortune from his father's old friend—and a rich wife, to devote himself to portrait painting; but, like Benvolio, he cannot hold steadily to his ideal, is shaken by chill doubts. The most intriguing character in the book is the man who had first helped him to define these doubts. Gabriel Nash is an Oxford friend whose life had been spent drifting around the world, experiencing and remembering exquisite moments, contemptuous of all worldly ethics, preaching idealism, but doing precisely nothing.

In Nash's keen eye one seems to see yet a third Henry James, especially in the hour in which he warns Nick that his art itself—that of the portrait painter—may become a fertile ground for the worldliness he had discarded. He will marry as a painter the woman he had lost by giving up politics, "find a good north room where you can paint . . . do all her friends, all the bishops and ambassadors . . . become a great social institution."

But at this point Nick turns upon his mentor demanding that, in the emptiness of after-season London, he should sit for his own portrait. Nash agrees reluctantly, "uncomfortable, at first vaguely, then definitely. . . . He was so accustomed to living upon irony and the interpretation of things that it was strange for him to be himself interpreted, and (as a gentleman who sits for his portrait is always liable to be) interpreted ironically."

Nash was to return the next day. "The next and the next and the next passed, but he never came back." And Nick, as he looked at the unfinished picture, had the fancy that it soon began to fade, that within days "the hand of time was rubbing it away, little by little."

In James himself the slightly shadowy outsider lived on, but he could present the scene with a cynical self-awareness as profound as it was delicate. In his stories he poses gracefully as the sympathetic narrator; and he has one of his characters tell him, "You're a searcher of hearts—that most frivolous thing, an observer."

For more than ten years James was thinking about Browning and we have every opportunity of watching him while he watched the poet. The final result may be seen in "The Private Life," published after Browning's death.

First we are shown the man of the world—yet not posing as this any more than as poet: "He had his hours and his habits, his tailor and his hatter, his hygiene and his particular wine, but all these things together never made up an attitude. Yet they constituted the only attitude he ever adopted." James seems to have abandoned his view that Browning held the floor at dinner or parties. Describing him in the story as Vaudrey, a famous novelist, he wrote:

> There was a general understanding among us that when Vaudrey talked we should be silent, and not, oddly enough, because he at all expected it. He didn't, for of all abundant talkers he was the most unconcerned, the least greedy and professional. It was rather the religion of the host, of the hostess, that prevailed among us; it was their own idea, but they always looked for a listening circle when the great novelist dined with them.

A group of acquaintances had gathered accidentally in a Swiss inn; there was a famous actress, who wanted Vaudrey to write her a play, and her husband; a famous artist; the frivolous observer—and Vaudrey.

The story centering on the two men, artist and novelist, is contrived by the actress and her friend, the narrator. It is they who take each man out walking and, comparing notes, reach strange conclusions.

Lord Mellifont, the artist, is the natural center of every gathering. Supposed in real life to have been Lord Leighton, he is splendid in appearance, in dress, in his art. But in the seclusion of this Swiss village they discover that he is nothing *but* a splendid appearance. To be left alone means for him to disappear entirely—"He was all public and had no corresponding private life."

But the fascination of this paled for the two onlookers compared with their greater discovery about Vaudrey. Famous from the start of the story, he

> used to be called "subjective" in the weekly papers, but in society no distinguished man could have been less so. He never talked about himself; and this was a topic on which, though it would have been tremendously worthy of him, he apparently never even reflected! He addressed himself to women exactly as he addressed himself to men, and gossiped with all men alike, talking no better to clever folk than to dull. . . . I never found him anything but loud and cheerful and copious, and I never heard him utter a paradox or express a shade or play with an idea.

Can this be the same man whose writing is so great, whose reading of it carries one away—but with, says the actress Mrs. Adney, the strangest impression that he is reading the work of another man. The narrator (i.e., James) going up one evening to his room, having heard Vaudrey's voice in the terrace below, is amazed to see him sitting in the dark at his desk, silent and absorbed, with only the stars for company.

"I've often wondered," he tells Mrs. Adney, "—now I know. There are two of them."

"What a delightful idea!"

"One goes out, the other stays at home. One is the genius, the other is the bourgeois, and it's only the bourgeois whom we personally know. He talks, he circulates, he's awfully popular; he flirts with you."

Mrs. Adney begs the narrator to test this theory, to take the social Vaudrey out for a long walk, while she looks for his poetic double and persuades him again to read to her. With the innate honesty so endearing in Henry James he describes the effect of this walk; first came irritation at having London gossip relayed to him among the Swiss mountains; stories, too, that he knew already. And then: "It broke my heart to hear a man like Vaudrey talk of reviewers."

But gradually James owns to "the irritating certitude that for personal relations this admirable genius thought his second-best good enough. It *was*, no doubt, as society was made, but there was a contempt in the distinction which could not fail to be galling to an admirer. . . . I suppose I wanted him to make an exception for *me*. I almost believed he would, if he had known how I worshipped his talent."

But this could not be, for the other Vaudrey was at that very moment reading to Mrs. Adney. As he read she was falling in love with him.

"If there are two of Mr. Vaudrey," they conclude, "there isn't so much as one, all told, of Lord Mellifont." These discoveries as well as the break in the weather bring to an end the gathering in the little inn, but Vaudrey is puzzled at Mrs. Adney's shrinking from him. Had he offended her?

She could not, she tells James, after knowing and loving the poet, endure the sight of the other. But, muses James, they are one firm in business together, could one even live without the other? "Mere survival would be dreadful for either."

Certainly in contrast to modern speculation, the idea of anything neurotic or twisted in Browning never seems to have occurred to Henry James. Yet the temptation is obvious to search for a psychological twist of some kind, and it might be irresistible if one had not observed that it is usually achieved by some degree of manipulation of the facts. Casting Browning as the strict uncomprehending father, Mrs. Miller described his relations with Pen, omitting all the spoiling and tenderness—the father walking himself into exhaustion beside Pen's pony, giving him a boat for the river at Oxford, taking him to races and dances, paying his debts, hiring studios wherever he wanted to paint. And again, casting Browning as a captive set free by Elizabeth's death, she depicts him avoiding the fresh captivity threatened by his friendship with Julia Wedgwood. But it was *Julia* who broke off the friendship—to Browning's great regret—because (as her close friend put it) her heart had betrayed her.

Many more instances could be cited, and not from one writer alone, for there is something about Browning that makes the temptation to "explain" him almost irresistible. But theorizing is dangerous when one has to deal with facts. Who was it spoke of stabbing a generalization with a fact?[5]

I have no reason to think I understand Browning any better than Henry James did, if as well. There is, however, a kind of half theory which supplements James's and into which the facts tend to push me, always a doubter, yet feeling that it covers more of what we actually know than any other I can find.

In the Browning of loves and hates, of resentments and tenderness, the rather simple character noted by Edmund Gosse lay side by side with an exceptionally complex intellect. Is it possible that the mind in Browning ate up, so to speak, all the complexity of the nature?

A less simple man, I suddenly felt, would never have told his diary-keeping friend Daniel Curtis that he was acceptable to the English aristocracy because he did no work—except write poetry. A less simple man would not have taken at face value all the adulation heaped upon him by that little world of fashion whose ambiguities and self-centeredness Jane Carlyle perceived so keenly and with such bitterness. A less simple man would have watched his step with Lady Ashburton. A less simple man would most certainly not have "cut" an old friend like Anne Thackeray (Ritchie) because she was rumored to be discussing a second marriage for him, would not have shown the world that he was stung by Alfred Austin's attacks.

There is a simplicity, too, in his obvious enjoyment of success, in his open support of the Browning Society, in his delight in his position at Oxford. Browning certainly had his vanities (the vice of a simple man). What he handled badly was an occasional attempt at pride (the vice of a complex one). That his temper was always a hot one and sometimes boiled over unreasonably could be true of any man, simple or complex.

I get no pleasure from the picture of Browning's last decade, with its atmosphere of adulation, especially the adulation of elderly and rich ladies—one giving him a block of railway shares, another lending her house to him and Sarianna when herself called back to the States, another keeping his special armchair inviolate (and after his death tying ribbons across it so that no lesser person could use it). Browning had always enjoyed flirting (to use that expressive Victorian word) with women young or old, and the little fever of admiration from otherwise strong-minded matriarchs was not displeasing to him. And, although the Curtises thought him Spartan over the large cold rooms in the Palazzo Giustiniani, he certainly enjoyed the many luxuries of Mrs. Bronson's hospitality.

Some nineteenth-century customs are, as we have noted earlier, quite unfathomable: that Disraeli's hair should have been treasured at the *Times* office in London, even that Leigh Hunt should as a crowning act of friendship have shared with Browning his precious lock of Milton's. But for a man in his seventies to allow his hair to be cut off and treasured appears just a little too simple. "I enclose you, dearest," wrote Mrs. Bronson to Mrs. Jack Gardner (whose famous museum can be visited at Boston), "a tiny lock of hair—which dear Mr. Browning allowed me to cut at Asolo. . . . The thought flashed over me, he thinks this will be the last time anyone asks for his hair." "Mrs. Jack" put the hair into a moonstone locket—and begged for an autograph, receiving the last Browning ever wrote.

The change from comfortless hotels to the houses of friends, the increasing lateness in leaving London arose in part from the urging of these friends and of his sister and in part from an increasing physical inertia. Sarianna complained over the difficulty of moving him and the pressing invitations came as an immense relief. He tried hard, in the case of Mrs. Bronson especially, to return her hospitality in London; he took great trouble to search out gifts that would give real pleasure (quite a problem with one's richer friends). But in his last years he was often and inevitably at the receiving end. An innate simplicity enabled him to be so with grace, showing indeed an extreme of gratitude and never failing in the correspondence that was obviously their principal desire. And all the time he was liable to let the confusing speech of his complex mind suggest to a later generation a character equally complex.

These are perhaps superficial matters, but the deeper side of Browning's life may be tested with the same results. Was it a complex bit of humbug when he expressed joy over his wife's success, while he himself was ignored? Or was it the natural reaction of a man passionately in love? Was his headlong effort to release his father from what he believed to be a designing woman the act of a complex or of a very simple man? And nothing could be "simpler" than Browning's patriotism. Elizabeth had felt that he was far too preoccupied by the Crimean War when she was panting over the liberation of Italy, and little though he talked on the subject one is aware, in the man, of the boy so many decades back acting in Rowe's absurd "British" play. Browning never looked squarely at the horrors of England's growing industrialism. He could not even have written any survey of his country to match "The American Scene" of Henry James. He probably never questioned Domett's terrible self-righteousness over the colonial treatment of the Maoris; he was opposed to Irish Home Rule. His friendships with Lord Albemarle and Sir Garnet Wolseley suggest what was apparently his creed: a given political party might be terribly wrong, but Britain was sure in the end to be right.

Browning would, above all, have dealt better with his son if he had been more subtle—as Pen himself quite possibly was. For he was his mother's son as well as his father's, with who knows what strains from earlier ancestry or how affected by the transplanting on the verge of adolescence. Pen got pretty well everything he asked for, plus adoring love and a wild exaggeration of his virtues, suddenly shattered by brief despair over his "peculiarities." Browning could have done a marvelous dramatic monologue about him had Pen been another man's son living a hundred years earlier. As it was, Browning, with all that he was continually doing for him, seems to have *understood* him little better than the aristocratic parents of the era did their children, relegated to the nursery, the schoolroom, and the boarding school.

Poet and bourgeois—says Henry James. "Barbarian," cries Santayana. "*Il nous faut des barbares,*" comments André Gide, feeling that Browning was all the greater as poet for being one. "Today we need barbarians," he affirms. "One must ... have a vision of natural life, have vigour, have strength rising even unto rage. The time is over for sweetness and trifling. Today begins the era of passion. Yes, Nietzsche, Dostoyevsky, Browning and Blake are four stars in the same constellation." Gide sees in all four a power arising from joy in living, a vision of good even in evil, "if the evil is not merely an absence of good but a manifestation of energy." This may well, he believes, "be a greater launching and educating power than what is called *good.*" Browning's entire work (he declares) is to show God through souls, each one refracting some ray of the divine spectrum.[6] This is the Browning who will live on—but who or what was the total Browning known yet unknown by Henry James, fully known perhaps only by Elizabeth? She had feared his being misunderstood because the essential in him was often masked by the accidental. Our question still stands: was there a complex nature to match the immeasurably complex mind?

Henry James declares that Vaudrey-Browning never spoke of himself and never seemed even to reflect on this topic, so "tremendously worthy of him." I fancy that of all religious exercises self-examination would be the last that Browning would have practiced.

All surmises end with the feeling that any effort I or anyone can make at reaching his reality is less real than James's fancy. There are truths that only myth can tell, and the truth about a great poet in nineteenth-century England may well be one of them.

17   Parleyings with Certain People of Importance in their Day

Earth's young significance is all to learn.

"PARLEYING WITH GERARD DE LAIRESSE"

MRS. ORR'S biography of Browning is an example of something we have seen displayed recently at a much higher temperature; the family, who had wanted her to write it, keenly disliked the finished product. Pen expressed this dislike with some vigor to William Lyon Phelps. "That was a very bad book," he said, and told Phelps that he and Sarianna had supplied "all available material" but had not been shown the book until in proof. They had offered suggestions and corrections but were told "brusquely" that nothing could now be changed.

It was probably in her reading of Browning's character that son and sister felt her to be at fault, since her ideas on the poetry had been expressed in her *Handbook* published in Browning's lifetime, which they had both liked. Nothing in the biography or in the omissions made later by Frederic Kenyon seems adequately to justify the strength of Pen's annoyance. Mrs. Orr discerned in Browning a hardness which would "melt into inexpressible tenderness," a self-centeredness (essential, she believed, to the creative nature) which would yield to "the largest self sacrifice and the smallest self-denial . . . whenever love or duty clearly pointed the way."

She noted an "impulsiveness—of manner—with much real reserve" standing in a "marked apparent antagonism." He was ready on all his serious convictions to explain them if asked and "if, even on such points, he did not appear communicative, it was because he took more interest in any subject of conversation which did not directly center in himself. . . ."

"The fiery child and the impatient boy had left their traces in the man . . . the peculiar childlike quality which the man of genius never outgrows . . . in its mingled waywardness and sweetness. . . ." A "recurrent touch of hardness, . . . like his reserve, seemed to conflict with his general character, but in reality harmonized with it. It meant, not that feeling was suspended in him, but that it was compressed."

She felt an absence of regard for humanity in the mass, and a certain antagonism to any individual with whom a clash of opinion might mean an "implied submission to the law of other minds." His "dominant individuality" she saw as barring the recognition of others' opinions—but this yielded to "continued indirect pressure, whether from his love of justice, the strength of his attachments, or his power of imaginative absorption."

Accepting "imperfect knowledge as part of the discipline of experience," Browning held as "the central fact of his theology" a "conviction of direct relations with the Creator. . . . The third part of the Epilogue to *Dramatis Personae* represented," she said, "his own creed; though this was often accentuated in the sense of a more personal privilege, and a perhaps less poetic mystery, than the poem conveys. The Evangelical Christian and the subjective philosopher were curiously blended in his composition."[1]

One can, I think, realize how irritating much of this analysis must have been to son and sister. With Victorian discretion Mrs. Orr introduces herself only as an anonymous friend to whom Browning read aloud two afternoons a week from two to four. He would read, she says, anything except English novels. They read biographies and Balzac, English, French, and Italian authors, chapters from the Old Testament. She supports her view of Browning's latterly declining powers which Pen and Sarianna denied by quotations direct and oblique from letters of the same anonymity. One can see the relatives who were with him in

Asolo and Venice, feeling how much more they knew than she of his
state bodily and mental, wondering on what subjects he had shown
hardness to her—*and* melting tenderness.

The supreme point of irritation lay perhaps in the small proportion
given in the book to that central fact which concerned both son and
sister: Browning's family life. To some extent this omission was, like
Mrs. Orr's own anonymity, a tribute paid to Victorian convention. But
her statement that "the parental instinct was the weakest in his nature"
was not likely to please Pen, even though qualified by the remark that
it made his affection for his son the more striking. Browning and Pen
had often irritated each other, but the irritation was brief and superficial, the love deep and lasting.

Mrs. Orr was a highly intelligent woman, even if biased, and her
book is of value, her picture vivid of a mind so many-sided that no one
has succeeded in fully penetrating it. Dr. Johnson was a far easier subject for the biographer than Browning, so was Scott, so even was
Dickens: although the comparison has been used absurdly, there is
something in the idea that Browning's two eyes—of extremely long
and extremely near vision—bore some analogy with his mind. Mrs.
Orr tells us that "he used for all purposes a single eye."[2]

The difficulty in evaluating Browning's later poetry emerges strikingly in the *Parleyings with Certain People of Importance in their
Day* published in 1884. Mrs. Orr had Browning's authority for claiming that the book was autobiographical, but the reviewers had every
right to say, as they did, that the rumors to that effect preceding publication had proved false. There was not, in the usual meaning of the
term, a vestige of autobiography in it—and it was many years later that
DeVane would label it "The Autobiography of a Mind." Browning's
idea was indeed to give the public the one thing to which he felt it had
a claim. His personal life was strictly his own, but the sources of his
thought should be available to the readers of his poetry. The *Parleyings* are an obscure biography of the intellect. They concern his chief
sources of inspiration: music, art, poetry, his political outlook, and his
philosophy of life. After *Ferishtah's Fancies*, the work of a very old
man, it is startling to meet the young Browning so often in this impressive book.

There are in these poems some splendid flashes of natural beauty
in relation to which Mrs. Orr has an interesting theory. Music had in
London taken for Browning the place medieval art had held in
Florence. But after Miss Egerton Smith's death he went to few concerts. They had always gone together and Mrs. Orr conjectured that, as
with Browning's aversion from visiting places where his wife, his
father, his sister-in-law had been his companions, he lost the wish for
music in losing his musical friend. She noted that about the same time
he began to care much more for scenery, began on his holidays to set
natural beauty, in a new way, above advantages to health or other
considerations. I don't think one can read Browning's early poetry and
fully subscribe to this view: it is a *re*awakening that we see of something that in London streets had lain dormant. Nor was there ever
an abandonment of interest in painting, though perhaps the contemporary English painters came to hold too large a place. William Grove
speaks of Browning's constant attendance at private views. There may
not have been as total a giving up of concerts as Mrs. Orr supposes, but
there is certainly a suggestion in each phase that apart from poetry one
source of artistic nourishment could with him supply for another. It
is possible that the change was only one of proportion—and the
Parleyings show a resurgence of them all.

Unfortunately the people chosen for his revelation were in themselves entirely unrevealing to the ordinary reader; they were, as Browning says, well known *in their day,* but no longer. He had known them
in his far-away youth, chiefly in his erudite father's library. Childhood
is the seeding period, and it was logical to be immensely concerned
with all those who had sown the seeds. Add to this that he had lost his
power of creating a dramatic monologue. Nor was he now attempting
to do so. Whatever these men may have said to the young Browning,
the old Browning was simply haranguing *them.* Yet with all this there
are moments when "the sudden rose herself" is seen again.

Bernard de Mandeville and George Bubb Dodington have already
been discussed, one in relation to philosophy and Carlyle, the other to
politics and Disraeli, and I propose to leave Francis Furini and Daniel
Bartoli to the last. Neither belong to Browning's youth and Bartoli
presents a peculiar problem of self-revelation deeper than Browning

realized and perhaps too deep for our reading. It had been one of the great events of Browning's youth to encounter Christopher Smart who, in his view, wrote only mediocre verse until in "Art's response to earth's despair." Confined in a lunatic aslyum he wrote on the wainscot with a key the magnificent *Song to David*—not included by his nephew in the first publication of his poetry because it betrayed "melancholy proofs of the recent derangement of his mind." Dr. Johnson delightfully described the form this derangement took of "falling upon his knees and saying his prayers in the street, or in any other unusual place. Now although, rationally speaking, it is greater madness not to pray at all, than to pray as Smart did, I am afraid there are so many who do not pray, that their understanding is not called in question. . . . I did not think he ought to be shut up. His infirmities were not noxious to society . . . and I'd as lief pray with Kit Smart as anyone else."[3]

The *Song to David* moved Browning deeply:

> A fireball wrapping flesh and spirit both
> In conflagration. Then—as heaven were loth
> To linger—let earth understand too well
> How heaven at need can operate—off fell
> The flame-robe, and the untransfigured man
> Resumed sobriety.

That heaven does break in on earth is a familiar topic with Browning; he had felt its effulgence in *Christmas-Eve and Easter-Day;* in "Two Poets of Croisic" he had talked of it. And supremely he recognized it in the great figures of Scripture: David, of whom he as well as Smart had sung; the risen Lazarus; St. John, whose symbol was the eagle flying in the blaze of the sun of righteousness.

> What were life
> Did soul stand still therein, forego her strife
> Through the ambiguous Present to the goal
> Of some all reconciling future? . . .
> Earth's young significance is all to learn! . . .
> What once lives never dies—What here attains
> To a beginning, has no end, still gains . . .

> With so much knowledge is it hard to bear
> Brief interposing ignorance?

These lines are taken from the "Parleying with Gérard de Lairesse," whose book had inspired Browning in his boyhood. He read it, he says, "more often and with greater delight, when I was a child, than any other," which considering it was five hundred pages long, in thirteen books, is sufficiently remarkable.

Dictated to his sons by de Lairesse, then blind, with seventy illustrations, it had given Browning something that won his eternal gratitude. He confesses to disappointment on mature examination of de Lairesse's pictures, and indeed it was by his book that the painter won fame, his pictures being little known outside Holland and not at all in England. Lairesse in his blindness wrote of earth's beauties from memory, taking his pupils on a walk—in "Holland turned dreamland."

Hearing in his youth the complaint that romance was dead outside Italy, Browning had said he would make an exception of Camberwell (the London suburb that was his boyhood home). The spirits of Keats and Shelley had dwelt for him in a suburban garden; he had walked transported over the heath nearby, he had drunk in inspiration even from pictures of which later knowledge had seen the imperfections. But never would he abandon the painter's teaching "That artists should descry abundant worth/In trivial commonplace."

De Lairesse had transformed nature into "Dream Land"; but Browning, now challenging much of what he had once accepted, will start on a walk of his own, "Having and holding nature for the sake/ Of nature only." This is his claim, but the astonishingly vigorous verse that follows is replete with the gods and goddesses with whom literature had peopled nature. Browning declares:

> ". . . somehow fact
> Has got to—say, not so much push aside
> Fancy, as to declare its place supplied
> By fact unseen but no less fact the same . . .
> You saw the body, 'tis the soul we see."

In a brilliant essay on "Browning and the Question of Myth," which discusses how far Browning anticipates the explicitly mythical element in the writing of Yeats, Eliot, and Joyce, Robert Langbaum analyzes the contrast between the de Lairesse and Browning methods of using "fancy." Where Browning treated subjects taken from the past he "used them as history rather than myth." In "Daniel Bartoli" he deplored the absurd use of a legend concerning a woman saint to draw moral lessons. Browning told instead a true story of a real girl, which more realistically revealed a more real sanctity. In "Gérard de Lairesse" he questioned whether just to tell the old story of Dryope picking the lotos blossoms or repeat the myth with an English girl gathering "fruit not fabulous" but apple blossoms. "Advantage would it prove or detriment/If I saw double?"

This seeing double certainly bothered his contemporaries and he had to convince them of its validity. In this parleying he passes from the fact of spring flowers, not to claim like Wordsworth that his heart "dances with the daffodils," but to find in the flowers a symbol, or myth, of resurrection. It is a remarkable lyric to come from a man in his seventies:

> Dance, yellows and whites and reds,—
> Lead your gay orgy, leaves, stalks, heads
> Astir with the wind in the tulip beds!
>
> There's sunshine; scarcely a wind at all
> Disturbs starved grass and daisies small
> On a certain mound by a churchyard wall.
>
> Daisies and grass be my heart's bedfellows
> On the mound wind spares and sunshine mellows:
> Dance you, reds and whites and yellows!

Langbaum sees this as Browning's approach "towards projecting a total vision of life. . . . Christianity (Browning implies) makes realism possible by confirming our deepest intuition that the vegetation cycle is, indeed, symbolic of our fate after death."

A recurrent problem in discussing the Victorians in relation to the moderns is the change in the meaning of the word "myth." Elizabeth Barrett uses it as a modern would in calling Christianity a "worthy" and "poetically acceptable" myth. For, though herself a believer, she sees Christianity in its profoundest meaning as evident even to those who do not accept the Christ story as fact. In the modern meaning of the word "myth" factual truth is irrelevant, yet the confusing thing is that the adjective mythical keeps its old connotation and from time to time "myth" itself is still taken as meaning legend. Pompilia and Caponsacchi fit Browning's most treasured myth of Perseus and Andromeda, a lifelong haunting which he brought to reality in the central event of his own life; in *Balaustion's Adventure* he is mainly translating the Euripides myth of Alkestis and Herakles, exquisitely rendered through the double prism of his memories and his own creation of the girl, Balaustion. But when he wrote "Saul," "Karshish," "Cleon," was he merely approaching the Christian myth from various angles as "poetically acceptable," or did he believe that he was writing about the central truth which gave birth by anticipation to the old myths?

I fancy that a great deal of the discussion of whether Browning ever wrote the revealing poem of his youthful desires, *and* whether he is to be ranked with the greatest poets in giving us "a total vision of life," depends on how we answer this question. Langbaum feels that *The Ring and the Book* was his "climactic attempt" to "collapse the 'prismatic hues' into the pure white light—in order to make explicit what is implicit in all the dramatic monologues, that the relative is an index to the absolute, that the relative is our way of apprehending the absolute."

We return to the *Parleyings:* Browning meant them, we have noted, as an autobiography of his own mind, not an autobiography in the factual sense. As Langbaum has said, he is in most of them not discussing a poem, a picture, or an event as it appears on the surface, but penetrating to the deeper thing that it is saying. But in "Francis Furini" the merely factual autobiographical is a good deal in evidence.

Some of his son's pictures of nudes had not only been refused by the Academy and Burlington House, but the Treasurer of the Academy,

John Calcot Horsley, had led an attack on nude painting in *The Times*. In the correspondence that follows he had signed one of his letters "A British Matron."

Furini was a Florentine artist (1600–49) celebrated for his paintings of the nude. At the age of forty he became a parish priest and was alleged by his biographer, Baldinucci, to have repented on his deathbed of his "lascivious pictures" and requested that they be burned. "Nay, *that* Furini, never I at least/Mean to believe," cries Browning at the start of his poem. Baldinucci had committed the same sin as Pen's critics: and they and he had received on their heads the boiling vials of wrath which any attack on his son deserved in the eyes of this excitable father.

The phrase "suppressed concupiscence/A satyr masked as matron," would have made only Horsley writhe, but Furini's words to Baldinucci apply to all such critics:

> Did you but know as I
> O scruple-splitting, sickly-sensitive
> Mild-moral-monger, what the agony
> Of Art is ere Art satisfy herself
> In imitating Nature.

Most of what follows is of general application to

> Art's endeavour to express
> Heaven's most consummate of achievements, bless
> Earth by a semblance of the seal God set
> On woman his supremest work. . . .

> God's best of beauteous and magnificent
> Revealed to earth—the naked female form.

Halfway through the poem Browning asks Furini what he would say if he had to preach not to the country flock of his own day but in the London of Browning's. And he provides him with a long sermon on the Evolutionists, of which no congregation would have understood twenty words together. Reading it slowly, we still find it puzzling, a distressing not-quite-linking of arguments which it is hard to see as poetry; again one longs to quote against him his own words " 'Tis you speak, that's your error. Song's our art." One thing clear is that he is not attacking the idea of Evolution, but only the exclusion of knowledge and love from its beginning and progress.

How does Evolution come into a poem on painting in the nude? Simply that the body is involved in both, and in Browning's vision of life the body means so much. He describes what he calls his "point of vantage" on life:

> my soul, and my soul's home.
> This body,—how each operates on each, . . .
> from this I judge.

This fundamentally is what the poem is about. We feel that movement toward today's phenomenologists which we met so long before in *Sordello*:

> Because perceptions whole, like that he sought
> To clothe, reject so pure a work of thought
> As language: thought may take perception's place
> But hardly co-exist in any case,
> Being its mere presentment—of the whole
> By parts, the simultaneous and the sole
> By the successive and the many.

"Furini" ends with Joan of Arc bathing naked. We hardly need to be told, perhaps, that this had been the subject of one of his son's rejected paintings.

In his "Parleying with Charles Avison," Browning again chose an unremembered man, an unknown man almost, even in his own day. Charles Avison (1710?–70) was organist of St. Nicholas' Church, Newcastle. Here he was born, lived, and died, composing little, but publishing in 1752 *An Essay on Musical Expression*. Although a march of Avison's had first stirred his childish musical instincts, Browning seems to have owed more to this book than to his scores: he studied Avison as he had studied de Lairesse.

Browning's biographers dwell on his musical powers: he wrote accompaniments to songs, he had played the piano before his small hands could stretch an octave, while in old age his memories of Russian music amazed a fellow guest of Mrs. Bronson's, the Russian Prince Gagarin. His musical poetry shows both width of sympathy and depth of feeling: "A Toccata of Galuppi's," "Abt Vogler," "Master Hugues of Saxe Gotha"—to take only three examples of widely differing tempo and interest.

We meet a contradiction of this generally held view when Pen Browning told William Lyon Phelps that his father played very badly. In old age he was still trying, said Pen, getting up early in the morning to practice five-finger exercises, but he never achieved any sort of proficiency. But when Allingham, admiring Pen's playing of Chopin, asked Browning if he had ever played it as well, the reply was "A thousand times as well."

Whatever his own performance on the piano, Browning's musical feeling was intense—and this Parleying expresses his belief that through music comes the most profound expression of man's soul. The poet tells a story, the painter

>   from the hand
> Of God takes Eve the life-spark whereunto
> She trembles up from nothingness. Outdo
> Both of them Music! Dredging deeper yet,
> Drag into day,—by sound, thy master-net,—
> The abysmal bottom-growth, ambiguous thing
> Unbroken of a branch, palpitating
> With limbs' play and life's semblance! There it lies,
> Marvel and mystery, of mysteries.

But marvel though it be, sound passes away, canvas and book remain:

> ... Thanks Homer, Angelo!
> Could Music rescue thus from Soul's profound,
> Give feeling immortality by sound,
> Then were she queenliest of Arts!

All the struggles of his youth toward expression are remembered, are experienced again in this very green old age: "May dews chrystalline/Nourish truth merely,—does June boast the fruit/ . . . Autumn comes,/So much the better."

De Lairesse and Avison are of Browning's boyhood and there is in these two Parleyings far more of the young Browning than in the others. From them alone readers might have guessed something of what he was at, but "Daniel Bartoli" utterly puzzled them, and "Francis Furini" almost as much.

The perpetual fight in Browning between an intense desire to tell all and a determination to keep the world out of his sacred places reaches its climax in the "Parleying with Daniel Bartoli." For, despite the order in which he has placed the poems, Browning has gone forward here from the formative influences of his childhood to the romance of his youth wrapped up in a story told by Bartoli—a Jesuit historian of the seventeenth century, whose book was published in London in 1830 by Browning's Italian tutor—and also in the Memoirs of the Marquis de Lassay.

"Mademoiselle Marianne" (Marie-Anne Pajot), a druggist's daughter, had won the love of the Duke of Lorraine; a banquet is taking place to precede the wedding ceremony when a minister of the King arrives and asks to speak in private with the bride. His message is that the King will forbid the marriage unless the Duke will assign his dukedoms to the King after his death. This he refuses to do and Marianne is taken, a prisoner, to the King's Court.

The Marquis de Lassay many years her junior fell in love with and subsequently married Marianne. A brief period of intense happiness was ended by her death. De Lassay "did his best to die—as sun, so moon/Left him, turned dusk to darkness absolute"; he tried solitude, tried "sainthood," but finally "took again, for better or for worse,/The old way in the world, and, much the same/Man o' the outside, fairly played life's game."

So had Browning done, so was he doing. Returning to the Duke we may be hearing once more in this poem the note of bitterness, the searing remembrance of something in his own life that Browning would like to forget but cannot.

> The duke reviewed his memories, and aghast
> Found that the Present intercepts the Past
> With such effect as when a cloud enwraps
> The moon and, moon suffused, plays moon perhaps
> To who walks under, till comes, late or soon,
> A stumble: up he looks, and lo, the moon
> Calm, clear, convincingly herself once more!
> How could he scape the cloud that thrust between
> Him and effulgence? Speak fool—duke I mean!

But of course the Duke did not speak: It seems some profound trouble in Browning rising to the surface in one poem after another. This one is both obscure and challenging.

The literalists, as we have noted, cry despairingly that Browning's own life should never be read into his poetry. He was a great teller of stories and it is irrelevant—and impertinent—to seek hidden meanings.

The biographer can only feel tantalized. When Browning returns to the Duke in stanza XVI it is to talk of man's faithlessness: "Man's best and woman's worst amount/So nearly to the same." The necklace intended for Marianne, may soon appear around some dancer's throat. Physical unfaithfulness may, however, resemble merely "unconsidered munching." The real, perhaps unforgivable, sin is a spiritual betrayal. And in the next stanza Browning is quite obviously no longer talking of the Duke, whose past had been so very unattractive that he would be thankful rather than "aghast/To find the present intercepts the past."

But if not of the Duke's whose is this past, holding an illumination threatened by the present but not wholly lost? Was Elizabeth in this as in so much of Browning's poetry the moon, obscured by some cloud of his own making, was she the "Sea-foam born Venus" he had "won in youth?" And was Lady Ashburton the cloud intercepting the moon, the "bold she-shape/A terror with those black-balled worlds of eyes?"

This question has been asked earlier and seems unanswerable until more information comes to light. But Lord Acton's letter (see page 79) though the gossip he had heard about the event of twenty years earlier was valueless, does give us one bit of real enlightenment. Lord Acton had himself witnessed Lady Ashburton's reaction to the mention of Browning's name, had heard "the fury of her language," had felt it as "a storm unappeased."

This was in 1888—and the *Parleyings* had been published the previous year: one wonders if she had been reading them. For the first time we learn that Browning's own anger was matched by hers. And the one thing we cannot fail to see is that Browning remained to the end of his life deeply disturbed by *something* that had left him a "ghost" of the man he once was, yet hoping to be at last "Called into life by her who long ago/Left his soul whiling time in flesh disguise."

He said that in the *Parleyings* he was giving a sort of autobiography. It concerned especially (he told Mrs. Orr) "the intellectual sympathies and imaginative pleasures of his very earliest youth." But in this parleying he had certainly gone beyond his youth, beyond intellect and imagination to a story of some profound emotion expressed not very intelligibly.

I have found more difficulty with this volume of Browning's than with any other—partly through the willfulness which certainly grew on him of refusing to try to meet his readers halfway. If a man is writing any kind of autobiography the story he is telling should be lucid: this the *Parleyings* most certainly are not.

DeVane is invaluable in the light he casts on the men with whom Browning "parleyed" and the facts and events that cast light on what he was saying. It is a wonderful bit of research covering every poem in the book. Yet these details are not as important in thinking about the *Parleyings* as is the one main fact: these are the work of a man in his seventies, again writing under conditions that he had refused to accept in his forties, when he waited, Elizabeth tells us, drawing, modeling, reading, until his thought had ripened and he was ready to write. Latterly, said Pen, he hated to write—yet each morning he would at least sit in front of his paper trying to force the half-formed thoughts into words which sometimes, alas, came all too abundantly.

The deepest pain in writing means thought struggling out—but it is better than numbness. With age the numbness is more frequent, the arrival of inspiration rarer. What Mrs. Orr says about Browning's problem in finishing this volume is, more than she seems to have realized, another result of age. His ideas, she complains, "would slide into each other when a visible dividing line was required." So it is for all the old as we "sit down and ponder." Memory is at once a telescope and a microscope—relegating the past to an immense distance, bringing it near with a wealth of detail. There is a fascination in reading this book when, after much groping, one sees suddenly that in it "The present intercepts the past," not just once but again and again.

In the Prologue and the Epilogue Browning is looking at life—is setting his life in a framework which shows in what sense his much derided optimism should be taken. The book is dedicated to Milsand who died while it was being written. So did Matthew Arnold, and, naturally enough Browning's own mind was in this last decade of his life constantly aware of mortality; he was questioning at moments the value of life. This he allows the Fates to do in the Prologue—dialoguing with Apollo on whether Admetos will really gain by the gift of added years. Apollo stands firm and aided by wine, brought by the god Bacchus, wins their assent to the giving. But the poem ends with their mockery at Apollo's confidence that throughout his kingdom Admetos will find men and women ready to offer their remaining years to their King. We are back to *Balaustion's Adventure*, as they offer Admetos longer life if father, subject or wife dies in his stead. And they mock loudest of all Apollo's belief that Admetos would refuse the boon if his wife alone were to offer it.

The Epilogue brings, I think, the message that Browning felt his own choice in life had been the right one—not art, not music, but poetry. The written word will outlast all else. And the invention of printing has made it possible for that word to spread throughout the world.

Two voices are the least in which Browning can speak—and the answer to the song of triumph over truth's spread is met by the reply that, through print, lies also

> May speed to the world's furthest corner—gross fable
> No less than pure fact—to impede, neutralise,
> Abolish God's gift and Man's gain!

One feels how ardently Browning would of old have carried on this contest—one of his primary beliefs being that every voice has a right to be heard, that in the end truth will emerge the brighter and stronger for its testing, that truth is often present hidden in apparent falsehood. The complexity of life would have become apparent, its richness have been gathered from the elements his own life had furnished. But Browning was too tired now—and in a curious anti-climax gives us only as an antidote to all ills the appearance of "a man" who was, says a footnote, Martin Luther.

Even if difficult in places, in others disappointing there is beauty in the *Parleyings* and flashes of true inspiration. It is Browning's last major poem; if not as informative as he fancied in some things, it tells us others which he himself did not know were there.

18 Death in Venice

None of his instincts grew old. . . . The subtlest of writers he was the simplest of men.

EDMUND GOSSE

WHAT WERE the feelings of Moses as he came down from the mountain and found the Israelites worshiping the golden calf? He shattered the stone tablets on which the law of God was written—and had to go back and see again, get it inscribed once more in human language. The poet and the mystic both bear the message of a vision which the business of the world is constantly threatening, which they themselves may shatter in moments of despair, may fail to read aright.

Turning from Browning at his greatest moments one sees him not raging like Moses, but adjusting (not always painfully) to daily life, a life which had in it an element of the Golden Calf. From London he writes frequent letters to Pen in Venice: "Poor Domett died last week, to my surprise and sorrow." "Dearest Fannie, you are like yourself to have sent me that photograph. I find none quite so satisfying. . . . How are you—exactly, pray!" "Consider both of you how I and S yearn for news." "I am just now overcome with a sudden press of work—the arrival of the whole of my first volume, which I have to correct thoroughly, at once." "I begin to go out a little—refraining from dinners rather by choice than necessity." Arnold's funeral "was a very affecting sight . . . I carried a beautiful wreath from Millais." "To-morrow, 'Waterloo Day,' I pay the customary visit to Lord Albemarle—his 73rd anniversary of the battle. . . . The dining-out has been somewhat in excess of late—and I should prefer a quiet week to any amount of amusement. . . . Remember the Salon soon closes—you must arrange about your pictures there. . . . Pen, do try salt and water as a gargle for your throat."

Sarianna writes: "Your father had one of his attacks of liver . . . he will not be quite himself till he leaves town. Where we shall go I have not the slightest idea. . . . Your father is horribly disinclined to travel."

"Father . . . will not be quite well till he leaves London. . . . Between ourselves it serves him right for the way in which he keeps hesitating and refusing to make up his mind. . . . Of course London is made very pleasant to him by all the attentions he receives." "People from the country and abroad write to ask leave to see your father . . . I am obliged to be at home, in case he should not return in time himself."[1]

Edmund Gosse by his moving record *Father and Son* became a sympathetic figure to many, but the chief memory of him will remain that of an understanding friend and admirer of contemporary great men—of Browning, of Swinburne. He has described how he and Browning sat together in the Fellows' Garden of Trinity, Cambridge, on a glowing June day of 1888: a shrub of sweet briar, summer foliage, and a pink mountain of double may, beneath a blazing blue sky. The birds, as in Browning's boyhood, "came closer and closer, curiously peeping." Curiously, too, did Gosse see, in the absence of any reference to the surrounding beauty, a disregard for the nature the poet could so accurately observe. But seldom has man brought alive better a great talker of whom all that we ask is that he will continue to give us of his best.

Contrasting Browning's private with his "dinner table" or "picture gallery" talk, Gosse sees a tiger and a domestic cat. With intimates "his natural strength came out," with "the volume and tumult of a cascade . . . rose to a shout, sank to a whisper . . . a redundant turmoil of thoughts, fancies and reminiscences flowing from those generous lips . . . an image of intellectual vigor . . . overflowing . . . with the geniality of strength."

He told Gosse a story, suddenly imagined, which might have become a splendid dramatic monologue, in which an act of apparent "spirited defiance" should prove in reality one of "tame renunciation." He went back in memory over the history of his own beginnings, his period of "long-drawn desolateness" as a poet, his Italian memories. And Gosse noted "not his strength only, his eloquent and ever-eruptive force" but "his humanity: Of all great poets except (one fancies) Chaucer, he must have been the most accessible." Most imaginative genius, Gosse felt, needs "support from without"—but Browning demanded no such tribute. He rather, "hastened forward with both hands full . . . anxious to please rather than hoping to be pleased . . . the whole world was full of vague possibilities of friendship." No one indeed could be more indignant, more resentful toward one "who had proved the poet's optimism to be at fault," but among those who "shared a nearer intimacy . . . is there one left to-day who was disappointed in Browning?" Deeply regretting one recent incident (the attack on FitzGerald described below) Gosse pronounces, "It was the judgment not the instinct that was amiss."

"He missed the morbid over-refinement of the age: the processes of his mind were sometimes even a little coarse. . . . But this external roughness, like the rind of a fruit, merely served to keep the inner sensibilities young and fresh. None of his instincts grew old. . . . The subtlest of writers he was the simplest of men."[2]

Browning went on to his dear Oxford, staying of course at Balliol. "There is a soft sadness about this place," he wrote, "such a perpetual remembrance is it of the fleeting state of mortal things." The Master recalled since last year "ten eminent members of the College whose places know them no more." Even the three brief years of undergraduate life had its melancholy. "Well, we can smile and say—'my all was not laid here!' Now who wrote *that*, Learned Lady?"

The next year, there again—for his positively last appearance—he rejoiced in having Jowett to himself "at breakfast, luncheon and dinner and generally a walk besides. I took him photographs of Fannie and yourself, with which he was much pleased." Pen's picture of his father looked "exceedingly well" and at the Gaudy with "some hundred and thirty old Balliol men . . . they sang beautifully what they call 'my

Balliol song' adapted from one of my poems, and Jowett spoke most kindly. . . . It is singular how I lose at once every symptom of physical trouble, forget what coughing means, the moment I arrive there."

It is pretty certain that even Browning would listen more than talk with the redoubtable Master, whom I myself feel almost to have known through my father's memories. Jowett abounded in stories of Oxford past and present, enjoyed jovial singing—but, rejecting the "Little Fat Grey Man" ("he laughs and he laughs and he sings and he sings") as too secular for a Sunday, asked my father to sing from an Italian opera an extremely vivid love song the solemn sounding music of which had meant more to him than its very suggestive words.

Jowett, unlike Gosse, did not overflow in print, but among the Balliol letters is one to Pen after his father's death: "He was one of the noblest men I ever knew and one of the kindest to me—I value his friendship more than I can express: it was so strong, so unchanging."

The same could be said of Browning's friendship with his fellow poet Tennyson, who had tried vainly to convince Edward FitzGerald of Browning's worth: "I abuse Browning much," wrote FitzGerald, "and get others to abuse him; and write to you about it; for the sake of easing my own heart, not yours." And again: "But *you*, A.T., tell me he is grand and I ought to hold my tongue . . . you magnanimous great Dog, you!"

A. C. Benson tells the story (in the biography of his father the Archbishop of Canterbury) of a friend reading aloud "The Grammarian's Funeral" and then saying, "We'll ask Tennyson whether Browning's writing at large is poetry or not."

"I'll think about it," Tennyson replied, and a week later, as they walked together, "apropos of nothing, he observed: 'I have thought, and it is.'"

This story has no date, but in 1887 Browning wrote an interesting letter to Mrs. Bronson about Tennyson. He began by giving his own light-hearted version of the story that he had been annoyed at getting no invitation for the Queen's Jubilee: "The respected authorities who distribute the admissions to the Abbey for 'the representatives of all classes' not considering that poets are of any importance as having done something towards the illustration of the last fifty years." Dean Stanley, getting tickets for his family, "meant to take me as his grandson." Browning "declined with true thanks." At the very same time the Prince of Wales had asked him for "a poem to be set to music by Sullivan," Tennyson having declined to attempt it.

"This comes," Browning commented, "of engaging to do what no true poet should attempt. . . . Tennyson is as able as ever to write transcendentally when the mood is propitious. I could never understand how he came to wear the livery and take the wages. If he had chosen to say 'I am ill at these numbers, do you try and help me to get it done' I would have tried probably."

Their friendship still meant a great deal to both. On one occasion, wearied out by applications, resembling demands for "opinions" from aspiring poets of which he got "rarely less than two daily," Browning was greatly disgusted at being told "that I had a different character for affability and sympathy for young attempters of verse from that of Tennyson who has brought contempt and hatred on his white hairs by his callousness." This man got "an opinion so definite as to silence him altogether."

The "incident" regretted by Edmund Gosse put something of a strain upon their friendship—besides, almost certainly, shortening Browning's own life.

In the summer of 1889 appeared *The Life and Letters of Edward FitzGerald* edited by Aldus Wright. Browning opened it at random and read: "Mrs. Browning's death is rather a relief to me I must say. No more Aurora Leighs thank God! A woman of real Genius I know but what is the upshot of it all? She and her Sex had better mind the Kitchen and their Children; and perhaps the Poor. Except in such things as little Novels, they only devote themselves to what Men do much better, leaving that which Men do worse or not at all."

One would scarcely need to be Browning to find this all nauseating unless too contemptible even to enrage, but FitzGerald had, through *Omar Khayyam*, won a wide publicity. Browning tried to withdraw by telegram what he wrote on a first impulse. The editor of the *Athenaeum*, enchanted by the scoop, did not open the telegram until the poem was safely in the press and he could aver that it was too late to stop it.

I chanced upon a new book yesterday . . .
                      —and learned thereby
That you FitzGerald, whom by ear and eye
  She never knew, "thanked God my wife was dead."
Ay, dead! and were yourself alive, good Fitz,
How to return you thanks would task my wits.
  Kicking you seems the common lot of curs—
While more appropriate greeting lends you grace:
Surely to spit there glorifies your face—
  Spitting from lips once sanctified by Hers.

Julian Hawthorne considered FitzGerald's remark "whimsical" and declared that no *man* would have written as did Browning. It was "a feminine screech . . . a raving street-walker."

"Your papa was quite ill with the pain it gave him," wrote Sarianna to Pen, who, devoted though he was to his mother, seems to have regretted Browning's outburst. Such words as FitzGerald's he said, "recoil sufficiently on those who use them." No, replied Browning. A new edition of Elizabeth's poems was on the way just when this widely read biography might be "of real influence." And "*my* name only occurs once —he calls me a 'great man': people would have understood why that caused me to be placable."

The Tennysons, he heard, were upset, so off went a letter to Emily suggesting the parallel of what her feelings would be if "dispraise" of Tennyson's poems "had been ushered in by a thankfulness for the relief felt that an illness of their author's guaranteed that there would be no more annoyances from 'Idylls' and 'In Memoriam' (the exact parallel is too abhorrent for me to think out and write down)."

Emily's reply was both affectionate and ambiguous: "We grieve deeply for you and your son," she wrote, "and for FitzGerald's family." This was indeed the element forgotten by Browning in his moment of stormy grief and rage—he too in smiting the dead was striking at the living.

But as he had written: "If the blow I received was thoughtlessly dealt my counter-blow was quite as unpremeditated."[3] Surely even a dull imagination must glow with a reflection of the young fire blazing in an old man's heart. Tennyson's biographer notes with delight how wandering in the lanes as a very old man he said to a friend, "I cannot help being troubled by the terrible excitement of the Spring." Here was for his fellow poet a deeper, more troubling excitement: perhaps poets are never old in spirit. Browning had been especially worried by the fear that the shocking letter had been written *to* Tennyson—Fitz-Gerald, he characteristically remarked to Pen, had always been "Tennyson's lick-spittle." Relieved to find this was not the case, and longing if need were to re-establish the old footing between them, he wrote again on Tennyson's eightieth birthday.

> Let me say I associate myself with the universal pride of our country in your glory, and in its hope that for many and many a year we may have your very self among us—secure that your poetry will be a wonder and delight to all those appointed to come after. And for my own part, let me further say, I have loved you dearly. May God bless you and yours!

Tennyson replied:

> I thank you with my whole heart and my whole being for your noble and affectionate letter, and with my whole heart and being I return your friendship. To be loved and appreciated by so- great and powerful a nature as yours will be a solace to me, and lighten my dark hours during the short time of life that is left to me.

Browning drew from this letter very real comfort after all the attacks leveled at him and the letters he had felt obliged to write. Sending a copy to Pen with injunctions of strict privacy, he wrote:

> I want you to know that T. is not the man to sympathize with a poor creature like FitzGerald, whom I punished no more than he deserved—heartily wishing he were alive in the body—not, for the first time, alive in his words which only now go forth to the world: I *did* nothing—only said what I would certainly have done had they been spoken in my hearing.[4]

There is a curious mingling of the strands in these last months—an unconscious completing of a life's pattern. Last letters to Mrs. Fitz-Gerald, to Williams, and to George Smith were sent from Asolo—city of Sordello and of Browning's own youth. Often he had dreamed of returning there, had found it impossible to reach, had awakened in nightmare distress: and we remember again his strange, profound dread of revisiting any place where he had lived and been happy with those he loved, or even whence they had departed! Hatcham with his mother, Florence with his wife, the villages he had summered in with his father could never be revisited—he could not so much as walk through the street where Arabel Barrett had died, and wrote quite seriously of the decreasing range open to him as death swallowed more and more of his closest friends.

But to Asolo, escaping the nightmare, he had gone now several times. This last year of his life he finished *Asolando* there, naming it after the town—and noting in a dedication to Mrs. Bronson that *Asolare* signified in English "to disport in the open air, amuse oneself at random." To Mrs. FitzGerald two days earlier he had written of the loss of Pippa's silk industry to "places nearer the main railway," of the falling leaves, the turret "rather the worse for careful weeding . . . the echo is sadly curtailed of its replies; still things are the same in the main. Shall I ever see them again, when—as I suppose—we leave for Venice in a fortnight?"

Staying at the Rezzonico was a friend of Fannie's, Evelyn Barclay, who kept a diary and has left a fuller account of Browning's last days than the commonly quoted one from Fannie's little book. She later became Mrs. Giles and describes how on this visit Browning allowed her future husband to sketch him—"He was most cordial and kind, always making it appear as if he were receiving a favor instead of granting it. Every day he got letters from people for this that and the other and he always answered them all."

One of his correspondents was a schoolgirl, Constance Armfield, who was studying "Prospice" for a competition in reciting. She begged for elucidation of the poem and received Browning's answer just after hearing of his death. "Prospice" is a poem of 1864 or earlier and the much quoted Epilogue to *Asolando* is a pale echo of it—diminished like the echo at Asolo, and the notes diminish it still more. One feels sometimes like cursing the fools who *would* ask these questions, but after all she was only a schoolgirl. "There my dear young lady, I have done the little that was necessary and hope it may suffice. Affectionately yours Robert Browning." But it was a curious incident coming just then; and the verses must have haunted him:

> Fear death?—To feel the fog in my throat, . . .
> The power of the night, the press of the storm . . .
> Bear the brunt, in a minute pay glad life's arrears
> Of pain, darkness and cold.

Browning would sit, says Miss Barclay, in what was called "the Pope's Room," which looks on the Grand Canal—partly, perhaps, because Jacko the parrot had his abode there. After every meal Browning would bring him cake and fruit. Father and son were at one in their love of bird and beast. Browning had even kept tame snakes as a boy—and it may be that the snake Pen had modeled from in his Dryope was another resident at the palazzo, certainly the shrieking birds were, which later got on the nerves of both Fannie and "Michael Field."

Evelyn Barclay's diary relates how Browning used to read aloud to them all and tell them stories of people he had known. And on November 19 came a sort of full-dress reading at the Curtis house when he read *standing* from 4:30 to 6:30 with only one short interval. It was too much and she noted with what difficulty he walked upstairs. The twenty-first and twenty-second the weather was very bad, but Browning went for his accustomed walk, and on the twenty-third was eating little and coughing a great deal. The whole household was probably vainly endeavoring to persuade him to take care—for, says Miss Barclay, the servants were devoted to him for his thoughtfulness and consideration. Pen had taken both Wilson and her husband into the Rezzonico: Ferdinando was perhaps still a skillful cook, but Wilson probably a cherished guest to Pen rather than a servant. Browning was engaged that day for a tea party and insisted that he must go since it had already been postponed once for his convenience. Very nearly did he fulfill the prophecy that he would die in a dinner jacket—for again he insisted on the twenty-seventh on going as planned to a dinner party, but, too ill to stay, came back early, and the next day almost fainted returning from the opera.

On the twenty-eighth, says Miss Barclay, she begged him to see a doctor but he refused, remarking "they are all fools." Pen finally summoned the doctor whom up to then Browning had refused to see and moved his father's bed to the mezzanine to save him the seventy-two steps to his room on the third floor. Later they carried him upstairs again to Fannie's room, the sunniest in the house. The doctor diagnosed bronchitis, but more serious was a weakness of heart. He ordered poultices and "Fanny, Pen and self" sat up all night making them. "He was most patient, always saying 'How good you are to me. Thank you.'" A nurse was engaged on December 2, but that night he got much worse and the nurse awakened both Pen and Evelyn to help her. They got a second doctor a week later, but by now it seemed to be hopeless. Often delirious, Browning was yet able to understand the telegram which arrived on the day of publication (December 12): "Reviews in all this day's papers most favourable, edition nearly exhausted." There is a curious contradiction between Mrs. Orr's statement that after the trained nurse came Miss Barclay left, and Miss Barclay's diary. For she records Browning's awareness and appreciation of the telegram—and then gives us his very last words, "I am dying. My dear Boy, my dear Boy."[5]

Pen had thought to bury his father in Florence by his mother's side, but an order had been issued closing the cemetery. An Act of Parliament he found would have to be passed to allow its use. Meanwhile friends in London had been hoping for an Abbey burial, and, despite its crowded state, the Dean of Westminster found a place for Browning in Poets Corner just below Chaucer's tomb and close to Spenser's. Venice had begged for the honor of keeping the body that Browning used to call his "old clothes," but when the municipality learned of the decision for Westminster Abbey they conveyed Browning's body to their mortuary island of San Michele, where it lay until Pen could arrange for the transfer to England, effected privately and at night.

A magnificent funeral barge was towed by an Italian admiral's launch and followed by an immense crowd of gondolas—the chief officers of the city, the family, a multitude of friends. The glowing sunset Browning had so often delighted in illumined their arrival at San Michele.

The strangest anticlimax followed: the coffin was sent to London in charge of a courier, while Pen, his wife, Sarianna, and Mrs. Orr (who had rushed out to Venice), followed by a later train. Whatever arrangements had been made broke down and the courier waited all day at the station for a hearse to convey the coffin to the Abbey.

This strange situation arose from no lack of enthusiasm in England. Among the pallbearers were the Master of Balliol from Oxford, the Master of Trinity from Cambridge, Leighton the painter, Archdeacon Farrar, and Hallam Tennyson representing his father the poet laureate. "Half London was there," said Edmund Gosse with a pardonable exaggeration of the six hundred ticket holders who included Huxley, Froude, Meredith, Holman Hunt, Burne-Jones, Leslie Stephen, Whistler, Lord Wolseley, Kinglake, Lord Houghton, Bret Harte, and Henry James.

I have said something in my first volume of the feeling overwhelming James that with Browning there arrived in the Abbey a strikingly new presence, someone belonging, yet alien to his own age, with his "heterogeneous vocabulary," his "boldnesses and overgrowths, rich roughnesses and humors . . . that might well alarm any pale company for their formal orthodoxies."

But surely James had forgotten, or perhaps did not know, that his friend was to lie close to the grave of Chaucer. For it was to Chaucer that Landor had compared him and so later has Ezra Pound. Edwin Muir believed Browning was "second only to Shakespeare—and Chaucer in his rich variety" and there is little pale orthodoxy in either Shakespeare or Chaucer. Browning surely belonged remarkably little to the Victorian era, reaching back to the age of Chaucer and forward— to whom? That he has affected subsequent poetry no one doubts and surely he will affect poets still unborn.

Again it was Swinburne who spoke, blotting out for posterity both the sordid details of the newspaper ("charcoal in the graves as a sanitary precaution"), and the gush ("that great temple of Silence and Reconciliation"). And Swinburne seems to see more vividly than the Abbey pomp a mourning world around the gondola as it carried the coffin into the sunset:

> Who, seeing the sunset-colored waters roll,
> Yet know the sun subdued not of the sea,
> Nor weep nor doubt that still the spirit is whole,
> And life and death but shadows of the soul.

Thus he wrote in a sequence of sonnets. For, whatever his moods about the poet, he had a rare understanding of his poetry.

In the Abbey Elizabeth's verses were sung, forbidding the tears to fall, for God had in death given His crowning gift: "He giveth His beloved sleep." The idea was of course a touching one, but the sentiment wholly unsuitable to the man they were burying. Swinburne saw this death differently:

> He held no dream worth waking: so he said,
>   He who stands now on death's triumphal steep,
>   Awakened out of life wherein we sleep
> And dream of what he knows and sees, being dead . . .
>
> The clearest eyes in all the world they read
>   With sense more keen and spirit of sight more true
>   Than burns and thrills in sunrise . . .
>
> The works of words whose life seems lightning wrought,
> And moulded of unconquerable thought,
>   And quickened with imperishable flame.[6]

EPILOGUE
Robert Barrett Browning

The Italy of the Rezzonico was not, in spite of "A Toccata of Galuppi's," the Italy we felt and cherished in [Browning]—not a place consonant with the charged messages . . . an impression not dispelled by the beautiful cold, pompous interior, partly peopled though the latter be, in its polished immensity, by every piously-kept relic of Casa Guidi and of London years.

HENRY JAMES

"YOUR LOSS," wrote Henry James to Mrs. Bronson, "was really the first reflection I made after I heard we should never see Browning again." Yet "even that sympathy was submerged in my sense of its being a supremely happy and enviable death . . . In the fulness of years and honors. He was very much in our life here—that of all of us who knew him and met him often and liked him, as I did, as I always had. Even this big, brutal, indifferent London will miss him—and that says everything."

Very Jamesian is surely the adjective he half apologetically chooses for the funeral—"charming"—but also—"crowded and cordial and genuine, and full of the beauty and grandeur of the magnificent old cathedral . . . with its dim, sublime vastness, with the boy voices of the choir soaring and descending angelic under the high roof. They were really national obsequies. . . ."

Pen alone remained to satisfy a world-wide curiosity about his parents. He told Mabel Dodge Luhan (best known through her friendship with D. H. Lawrence) that he was never introduced without seeing the start of wonder: "What! That the son of two poets?" For the lovely little boy had grown into a plump rosy man, a little comic, *very* plain and unromantic.

I wonder whether some of the diffidence which had troubled Browning in his son had its source in this change—from Ganymede to Punchinello? Pen usually wore rather strong checks. A photo in an early book of Freya Stark, that notable world traveler, shows him (and Bernard Berenson described him) as a rather rough type of English squire. Mrs. Luhan (in her *Intimate Memories: European Experiences*) adds that he was curiously inarticulate, not in speech only, but in his very joints: and he had a puzzled look as if bewildered by life, by all that had happened and was happening to him. But she describes him as a staunch friend, loyal and trustworthy. The Rezzonico went on for a while with all its splendor. Freya Stark remembers, when Pen lent it to her parents, the magnificent appearance of the gondoliers, the carpets with fringes that hung over the side of the gondola. But the splendor had probably gone to Pen's head.

Mourning another friend, John Addington Symonds, in May 1893, James wrote to Mrs. Curtis: "You will sometimes see his ghost (with Browning's audible spectre) in the bright Venetian air. Poor grotesque little Pen—and poor sacrificed little Mrs. P. There seems but one way to be sane in this queer world—but there are so many ways of being mad. And a Palazzo-madness is almost as alarming—or as convulsive— as an earthquake—which indeed it essentially resembles."

Within a few years of Browning's death Pen and Fannie had separated. Various reasons were suggested, as is common in cases of incompatibility. Pen's extravagance was certainly one of them; Fannie's failure to produce a child was another, and perhaps a greater. To any Browning, family life meant much. Then there were Pen's animals, ranging from dogs that barked and birds that shrieked disturbingly to snakes, which alarmed Fannie. Many stories are told of this peculiar taste of Pen's: that he paid 1000 lire for a snake in Venice, that he bought a python for 300 lire at a fair near Asolo. He would sometimes carry his snakes to England and frighten the customs men when he opened the basket. The python he would drape around his model—but finally had to shoot precipitately when it started constricting.

Even more than the snakes did at least one of the models upset Fannie. Becoming more and more of an invalid, she had engaged as nurse-companion a beautiful blonde called Ginevra of whom she became so fond that she wanted to adopt her. But then Pen began to model from her and Fannie to be jealous—perhaps (says Mrs. Luhan) with reason, for his two statues of Ginevra show more feeling than any other of his work. But the painting and modeling were coming to an end: there were other things Pen wanted to do with his life.

His father had been planning the restoration and rebuilding of a house in Asolo. Pen carried out the scheme, and went on buying, owning eventually five houses in that tiny city. He restarted the silk industry, which had died, or rather had moved away from Asolo to places with better transportation. Presently he would settle, more or less, with his Aunt Sarianna at Asolo, but we still find him in Venice or Florence, or moving about. The silk spinning failed, but he tried again with lacemaking and this continued throughout his life. Ginevra, who had been housekeeping for Pen and Sarianna, became superintendent of the industry. She married Pen's manager, and their son showed me with pride a faded but impressive photograph of a very beautiful woman.

Clara Hahn, now aged ninety-five, remembers vividly meeting both Pen and Fannie in 1893 at San Martino di Castrozza. She thinks it was shortly before they were separated; "they were very reserved, bowing only to the other visitors." But with them was Wilson, now an old woman, who so many years ago had helped Elizabeth to escape from Wimpole Street. "Rather stout with great natural dignity," Clara Hahn describes her. They talked often, but Wilson told her, "One of the reasons I like you is because you never ask me questions." She said no word about Pen or Fannie, Robert or Elizabeth, except in one connection: she would talk endlessly of Pen's childhood. She described the elaborate outfits which, she said, gave people the idea that the child was "royalty." She spoke of her own efforts "to bring him up a man" as thwarted by the immense spoiling by both father and mother.

There was a pleasant small incident. Clara, wanting to climb, was rejected by the guide unless she would agree to wear the trousers she did not possess. "I'll see to it," said Wilson, and arriving with a roll of cloth and a pair of Pen's plus fours for a pattern, she cut out and stitched a sufficiently satisfactory pair of climbing knickers.

Two years later "Michael Field" paid the visit to Asolo referred to in chapter 11. They found Pen and Sarianna deep in a quarrel with Fannie's sister Marie, who was threatening "outside help" to recover furniture allegedly belonging to Fannie, the loss of which would "wreck" the Rezzonico. They thought Pen "very gentle, very patient, fumblingly good-natured," while Sarianna "hammers on the sore."

They had reached the "Palazzo Pigstye," as Pen called his country house, "under a battery of howls and yaps from five dogs," while brilliant cockatoos, blue, orange, and scarlet, surrounded them. Inside were "old chests and chairs—and bronzes—peacock feathers and sunshine."

The first night there was nothing but praise for their host. "He is a thoroughly good fellow and never so happy as when caressing his dogs. But his devotion to his aunt touches me; and when his father's name is mentioned tears fill his eyes."

The worst of a journal is that the writer cannot put into perspective the daily kaleidoscope of feelings. Pen was perhaps as changeable in mood as his father, quite certainly this curious couple were. A few days later "Pen's neglect of his promise to go up with us to the Torricella Tower is somewhat chilling—especially as he takes a ride instead. But it is useless to think that Brownings will act gracefully. . . . Even our poet was no exception."

But even in the disillusioned mood we get an interesting analysis of the elements perceptible in the "poor little man," whose

sighs are awfully vacant. Pen is most touching in his sensitiveness and humility. He says he is a failure and his own sorry sense of his personal deficiences has driven the poet's son deep within the shell of Barrett common-placeness. . . . His eyes are still his mother's— ardour and timidity almost bewitch in them—yet they are lost under fat brows tortured with rheumatism. He has his father's serious- ness, thinks about life till he is on the road to madness, and escapes with jocund instinctive habits of life, like those of a squire. He looks masculine and is absent to the limits of rudeness; yet never really overbears . . . a painter's tact and vision . . . without having a painter's vitality of touch. . . an irritable temperament and a patient heart. . . . His high birth from poets makes him nervous.[1]

The Curtises were clearly on Fannie's side and their information stirred James's indignation against the "paltry Pen! Never was a great name (two of 'em moreover) dragged through *meaner* dishonors."

Among the saddest elements in the foundering of a marriage is the total condemnation of one party or the other: I am glad that Pen was gentle and patient and even fumblingly good-natured as his aunt hammered on the sore!

Mabel Dodge Luhan tells us something that, if true, may have been a contributory factor in Pen's general disillusionment. He had grown up with Edith Story much like a younger brother. Landor had spoken of them when they studied together as Abelard and Eloise, which was probably the merest jest, Pen being then only ten or eleven. But according to Mrs. Luhan the grown-up Pen had been deeply in love with Edith. She however wanted only to escape from her parents' literary and artistic world, and, in her marriage with Marchese Peruzzi, she was taken into the court surrounding Victor Emmanuel.

Pen married late and Edith was six years his senior, but, says Mrs. Luhan, his old love was never forgotten and he showed it especially in relation with her two sons. The Engineer Cantoni at Asolo (Engineer being used as a title in Italy), son of Pen's manager there, remembered as a boy the visits of these two, especially the elder, Bindo, a handsome, graceful boy who became an officer in Victor Emmanuel's army. Bindo got heavily into debt; his mother, it was rumored, was selling her jewels to help him. Pen helped too, and, far more important, supported Bindo in the final tragedy of his life. Accused of homosexuality, Bindo stood trial and emerged acquitted. But after a second accusation he threw up the sponge—and his commission. In those days and that country this meant total social exile, involving also any man who visited him.

Edith, Mrs. Luhan felt, was cruel when she begged Pen, every time he called on her, to go down to the flat below and talk to Bindo. It was, she remarks, social suicide. It is pretty certain Pen would have gone even without Edith's bidding. One of his many houses was bought from her to ease her situation—and then deeded to Bindo. But neither mother nor friend could save Bindo from despair: he ended in suicide.

This tragedy must greatly have shaken Pen, but one feels both from the scattered memories in Asolo and from descriptions by visitors there that he did as time went on live out his life with a good deal of content.

One sees him through the eyes of children now grown old: those of the Engineer Cantoni brightened as he described the dogs, the peacocks, the parrots, and above all, the milk-white horses. Pen used to drive them, he told me, in various formations, and to make sure I understood he sketched them on paper: two in front and one behind, two behind and one in front, two in front and two behind—and, surprisingly, all five together one behind the other. How he negotiated the narrow streets of Asolo remains a mystery; and though he drove William Lyon Phelps in splendid style, only two horses were involved that day.[2]

Freya Stark, whom I saw in Asolo, told me of his cutting an orange into a face for her—she could never, she said, in memory, separate that orange face and Pen's. He was her parents' friend—and Arthur Young's, who later willed his house in Asolo to Freya.

I met too, in Florence, an old, old woman, Ersilia Nardini, who had gone to work for Pen as a young maid and remained in his household to the end of his life. He lived, she said, *very* luxuriously, he was *very* kind, and of course he was *very* rich. "He had twenty-three dogs, thirteen horses, peacocks and a monkey." The word "ricchissimo" was the one I heard the oftenest—and I provoked a strong reaction by remarking how sad it was that everything had to be sold after Pen's death to pay his debts.

"Debts," exclaimed Cantoni. "There were no debts."

Unkindly I pressed the point that when Pen died immense debts were discovered.

"Not in Asolo," he said. "My father would never have allowed it."

Despite his earlier comments Henry James had a soft spot for Pen.

In his steady correspondence with the Curtises we find a letter of 1899, written when he was visiting Mrs. Bronson in Asolo, in which he sums up the results of much thought and observation:

> Pen was there to dinner 2 of the nights—and showed me all his wondrous property including the boa-constrictor, the new mountain (he *has* literally bought one) and the husband of Ginevra. He didn't speak of his (own) wife, but seemed in gayish spirits—and I had a strange lurid vision of the *fond* of all his conduct. But it's too far to go into now—I find here so many letters to answer. Roughly speaking, it is vanity and pride of possession and proprietorship—the *owning* (the air and grandeur of it) of ½ that little place; and the being, there, the great swell. There!—Fancy playing to *that* gallery. It's wonderful what he owns—and what he has done with it. His talents in this line [are] great. And his box at the Theatre. He's the Asolan Kaiser Wilhelm. There's nothing *over* for Fanny. The Torricella is a marvel. It makes me realize what he is anchored to. Basta.[3]

Mrs. Bronson was certainly kind to Pen if only from memories of his father, and they had one meeting ground which to the animal lover is of overwhelming importance. Mrs. Bronson, like Pen, had many pet birds and dogs which she adored, and in a letter to Mrs. Gardner she wrote of "a Valentine which Pen Browning sent to my beautiful little Contenta...":

> How could you be Contenta if you were not content?
> Things being as they are there's little to lament,
> But if instead of being man I were of race canine
> I'd ask you for your pretty paw to be my Valentine.[4]

One curious gap in our knowledge of Pen is of course the one about which rumor ranges most widely—the extent and object(s) of his love life. His mother had foretold, when he was a tiny boy, that his adult emotions would be tempestuous. The abortive affair at Dinant, the rather tepid middle-aged marriage, even a romance with a girl, once his sisterly companion, hardly seem to fill the bill.

Attention was drawn to this question by the statement in Frances Winwar's *Immortal Lovers* that Pen had two children by Breton peasant girls before he was nineteen. I have not been able to discover what evidence there is for this. It is difficult to check a story of the kind a century later: and Browning's repeated assurances that Pen's idle life was as entirely harmless as idleness could be does cast some doubts on it. Yet Pen's constant state of debt might have meant something other than just tailors' bills and an effort to live at the level of his aristocratic friends.

It is quite possible that when he began to paint he had romantic and sexual relations with his models. Yet I incline to a feeling that, past his first youth as he then was, his attitude to Ginevra may have been as parental as Fannie's. One can hardly see him bringing her to Aunt Sarianna, putting her in charge of the lace school, happily giving her in marriage to the Engineer Cantoni, if his own feelings had been deeply engaged.

Much more probable appears the rumor which Freya Stark told me was current in Asolo that Pen, after his marriage failed, had fathered more than one child in that small city where his extraordinary position might give him almost a *droit de seigneur*. But the idea was indignantly denied both by the maid who had worked for him and by the son of his manager.

At the Casa Guidi, at Baylor University, people have turned up claiming to be descended from Browning, "though not legally." They were, I was told by those who met them, "crackpots." Maybe. But it would be entertaining if one day a major poet were to emerge, English or Italian, claiming to be the great-great-grandson of Robert and Elizabeth Browning. The probability of his proving it would seem to be slight.

Whatever his sense of inferiority, Pen was vastly proud of his parents. The old chapel of the Rezzonico was dedicated anew to the memory of his mother. In 1899, persuaded by George Smith, he published the love letters, evoking a storm of rage from his Barrett relatives. Knowing his father's wishes, he gave many manuscripts to Balliol College, Oxford, keeping only *Asolando* for his own lifetime.

At the age of sixty-three he died of a heart attack in the centenary year of his father's birth.

Pen had rejected with some violence of expression the suggestion that his wife be summoned, but Edith Story was with him when he died and Fannie arrived shortly after his death. Cantoni told me his father could find no will in the place indicated by Pen—no doubt (he added) Edith had destroyed it! Alternative rumors attributed the destruction to Fannie. But a will was in fact produced and probate granted in Italy to Henry Patrick Surtees and Norman Herbert Smith, attorneys of Fannie Barrett, and Edward Moulton Barrett, cousin german of the deceased. The will, which is now in Florence, contained one solitary legacy of 15,000 lire to Carolina Betto—a girl well remembered by Ersilia Nardi, a small and delicate field-worker taken by Pen as a model.

Pen's debts were indeed numerous, amounting to about £21,000 in English money, but even after these were paid an estate remained of about £27,000. Fannie got £6,000 and the remainder was divided among sixteen Barrett cousins. (These figures were given me by Philip Kelley who is editing *The Unpublished Diary of Elizabeth Barrett Barrett 1831–1832* for the Ohio Press.)

Into the total had gone the price of manuscripts, pictures, books and furniture, taken by Pen to the Casa Guidi after the sale of the Palazzo Rezzonico. Only with Sotheby's inspired catalogue in hand or mind can one bring back the past today in those long dark rooms and narrow streets opening on infinity.

But his father's last thoughts had not been of the Casa Guidi or even of his reunion with Elizabeth. In one concentrated moment the love, fears and anxieties of almost forty years had found expression—"My dear Boy, my dear Boy."

Notes

As with my first volume the notes are mainly directed toward either clarifying the text or helping students who may want to do further reading. I have not thought it necessary to give references for every quotation (from letters especially) where the matter is not controversial.

CHAPTER 1   *A Time of Loneliness*

1 The quotations from Browning's letters in this chapter are taken from *Letters of Robert Browning, New Letters of Robert Browning, Letters of the Brownings to George Barrett,* and *Dearest Isa.*
2 The letters to William Story are all in *Browning to his American Friends,* those to Isa Blagden in *Dearest Isa.*
3 *Notes of Travel* (Boston 1840) Vol. IV.
4 Fantastic as Pen's costume was, it was not nearly so unusual as it would be today (or should one say "yesterday"?). Compare the photograph of Hallam and Lionel Tennyson in Charles Tennyson's life of his grandfather. Their age is not mentioned, but they are both big boys and are wearing smocks with large lace collars over very baggy pants. They both have shoulder-length hair.
5 *Letters to Owen Meredith* (Lytton's pen name).
6 From *Tennyson, Ruskin and Browning.*

CHAPTER 2   Dramatis Personae *and an Interesting Friendship*

1 Captain Magellan in his *Voyage* (from *Purchas the Pilgrime*) tells of the great devil Setebos and the higher God believed in by the Patagonians—and of one man who, finding the Cross could overcome Setebos, asked for baptism. This is related by Wise in his *Literary Anecdotes,* a mine of fascinating sidelights on Browning.
2 Edward C. McAleer has an interesting theory that, despite his immense admiration for *Empedocles* it was Arnold Browning was answering rather than FitzGerald. Some part of that poem is written in stanzas similar to *Rabbi Ben Ezra;* and FitzGerald's *Rubaiyat,* published only as a pamphlet in 1859, had made no stir at the time. Rossetti had discovered it (just as he had *Pauline*) and he might of course have shown it to Browning. DeVane, too, thinks that Browning was interested primarily in answering Matthew Arnold. But the ease with which Le Roy Sargent could com-

bine the Rabbi and Omar rather supports the common opinion. Even so, Browning could hardly have been unaware of *Empedocles*.

3 Browning says later of their friendship: "As to the past, it was only incomplete thro' my wife's absence: she never had any woman friend so entirely fit for her as you would have been—I have told you so sometimes."

CHAPTER 3 *Three Generations*

1 See also Alice Corkran, "Chapters from the Story of my Girlhood."
2 For the full story of this, as far as it is known, see my Vol. I, Chap. 14. It is interesting to note that, when the immediate misery of the case was over, the entire sympathy of his children was with Mr. Browning— and that also of his employers. "Poor victim of a villainous woman," wrote Elizabeth to Arabel after establishing him in Paris and enlisting the love and sympathy of the Corkrans, "who if he had been less pure than he is would have escaped the whole trap laid for him. He can't understand any of it . . . struggles against facts and necessities." Mrs. Von Müller had "been to Mr. Browning's Bank and accused them of conspiring to defeat the Court." The Bank had refused to have any dealings with the plaintiff or her lawyers, and had paid Mr. Browning's retirement pension in full. Contrasting the account in the *Times* with all this, one is conscious of some mystery—there is more than a touch of "Bardell v. Pickwick" which is never explained. On December 31, 1858, Browning had written to his Uncle Reuben. He was paying a part of the lawyer's

costs so that his father should feel free to return to England if at any time he wanted to "though I firmly believe he would, in no case, choose to return, and though I have a remarkable objection to diminishing Mr. Potter's costs by one halfpenny" (as it might be Dodson and Fogg's?).

3 The letters about both these deaths can be found in full in Hood, *Letters of Robert Browning*.
4 All these letters are in the Berg Collection, most of them undated.
5 Gertrude Reese Hudson has in "Browning and His Son" (PMLA, LXI, September 1946) given an excellent account of the relationship between Browning and Pen during the years of his education.
6 James Pope-Hennessy's book *Monckton Milnes, The Flight of Youth* gives a delightful description of Pen's host and his surroundings and of the wider world of his period.

CHAPTER 4 The Ring and the Book

1 Other documents have been discovered and edited which Browning certainly never saw. A pamphlet was found at Baylor by W. O. Raymond and a large group were found and edited by Beatrice Corrigan. In W. C. Raymond's book *The Infinite Moment* and in Beatrice Corrigan's article "New Documents on Browning's Roman Murder Case" a full account of these discoveries may be found. The most important new fact we learn is that Pompilia was not illegitimate, but the daughter of a poor widow, Corona Paperozzi, who agreed to let Violante have her.
2 It may be said that this is an illegitimate identification destroying the character of a dramatic mono-

logue. But Browning, writing to Julia Wedgwood, points out that the Pope's judgment is "a new light; I did mean it to be so." Julia in return expresses her wish that all poetry should be not dramatic but "direct utterance of some congenial feeling"; and Browning in his next letter wonders at her not recognizing in this work " 'an utterance of congenial feeling,' all the louder that it is not *direct*.—I hoped it would be heard always, by the side of and *above* all the disgusts and painfulness." She is wrong in thinking that "whatever you count white in Pompilia and Innocent could have come out as clearly without the black."

I could match the Pope's speech in Browning's other poems, which are by no means all dramatic monologues. He *was* immensely dramatic, but he most certainly was not a man without a distinct viewpoint recognizable by a constant reader of his poetry.

CHAPTER 5   *St. Martin's Summer*

1   There is a possible alternative story which the "mores" of the nineteenth century make almost plausible. Lady Ashburton's predecessor had written to a friend of the need to watch her language—when talking to her middle-class acquaintances. She would shock them by such remarks as that another titled lady had "popped two chicks" before her marriage. *If* Louisa had been suggesting an affair while Browning thought she was proposing marriage they would certainly have been talking at cross purposes. For Browning remained at bottom, as Chesterton has emphasized, a middle-class Englishman, and that class was in

that century hedged in by propriety.

2   It is amusing to note something of the same mentality in the scorn poured on the line "I was ever a fighter." Browning had worn no shining armor, his critics feel, had not even carried a pike or mounted a barricade; he had led the life of a comfortable bourgeois, and had not even fought, like Carlyle and Ruskin, for a better England.

The "Epilogue to Asolando" is distasteful today to most Browning devotees as the boast of an old man, which he would never have uttered in his prime. His own generation, if they cared for his poetry, admired it, perhaps because they recognized its truth. Browning was, like Landor, whom he so much admired, a fighter for his own poetic integrity. When he told Ruskin that he would never change his "point of sight," when he shocked his contemporary world by language considered coarse even by Swinburne, or by views on morality which Julia Wedgwood called his "devil's gospel" he was fighting as resolutely in his own field as were the social reformers in theirs. Like Ruskin, Carlyle, or Morris, he was an anti-Victorian Victorian, and this meant a fighter against the hardest thing there is to fight: an atmosphere.

3   It would be much more possible to treat this question historically if I had been able to see letters from Lady Ashburton to Browning, or from Browning—and Hatty Hosmer —to Lady Ashburton. But unfortunately the letters *to* him must have been among the many destroyed by Browning, while Lady Ashburton's grandson, Lord Northampton, told me he was unable to find any letters *from* Browning to her.

A minor error from the factual

end is the assertion of Gladstone's daughter, Mrs. Drew, that three years *after* the Loch Luichart visit she and Browning were both staying at Belton (Lady Marion Alford's home) "and we all supposed that he was proposing to Lady Ashburton (she was there too) at least she let it be thought so." Mrs. Drew was *not* of the party at Loch Luichart and her letter was written many years after the meeting at Belton. She must have let her imagination get mixed with her memory—for Browning's letter to Edith Story was written before Lady Ashburton arrived at Belton, and on her arrival Browning left!

A full and admirably clear account of all that can be known with certainty has been given by the Canadian Browning scholar, the Rev. William Whitla (author of *The Central Truth; The Incarnation in Browning's Poetry*). In "Browning and the Lady Ashburton Affair" (not yet published as I write) he has assembled all the evidence and given a sketch of Lady Ashburton's character and friendships. To Mr. Whitla I owe also the clarification of the mistake sometimes made that the "proposal" took place at Belton in 1872. He has seen the holographs both of Browning's letters to Edith Story and of Mary Gladstone's.

It may be that the imminence of her coming evoked memories with an acuteness which accounts for the bitter note heard clearly though expressed obscurely, in this much debated letter.

CHAPTER 6   *Mainly   About   the Greeks*

1   *The Swinburne Letters,* edited by Cecil Lang.

2   See Harriet Jay, *Robert Buchanan;* and Hood, *Letters of Robert Browning.*

3   Mrs. Orr quotes Browning on the fever. Browning tells Julia Wedgwood of his talk with Rossetti.

4   In his *History of Greek Literature,* quoted by DeVane in *A Browning Handbook.*

5   Pen Browning declared later that his father had never grasped the Greek accents and he did leave them out when editing William Story's *Roba di Roma.* This might account for Jowett's view that his classical knowledge was "homespun," but not for the lavish praise of other scholars. Maybe Browning despised the accents—after all they only came into the language after the age of Homer (put in no doubt by the Greek copy editors of the era!).

CHAPTER 7   *A Nest of Singing Birds*

1   William DeVane agrees with Rossetti's niece in maintaining that there *was* material enough in the poem as a whole to justify Dante Gabriel's suspicions. But while Helen Rossetti Angeli finds this material in the Epilogue, DeVane finds it in the characters Fifine and Jenny. William Rossetti disbelieves in any basis for Dante Gabriel's feelings other than his own mental state at the time. I cannot but feel that the judgment of an affectionate brother who yet remained on the friendliest terms with Browning is more likely to be correct.

2   Buchanan's letters are in the Alexander Turnbull Library, Wellington, New Zealand. The last one quoted is the last of the collection. Browning's two letters published in *Letters of Robert Browning* are all we possess of his side of the correspondence.

3 From "Under the Microscope." All quotations from Swinburne unless otherwise identified are from *The Swinburne Letters*.

4 Autograph letter: Wellesley College.

5 It is interesting to note that many years earlier Browning had replied to a Mr. Hall, requesting help for a memorial to Moore: "One may be moved to some such project in the case of an undervalued or neglected man of genius: but surely Moore 'in his lifetime received his good things and likewise Lazarus' (I should say Keats) 'his evil things.'" This letter is in the Wellesley College Library.

6 See also Lionel Trilling: *Matthew Arnold*, and *The Portable Matthew Arnold* edited by Lionel Trilling.

7 My attention was drawn to this article ("Tennyson and the Sinful Queen," *The Twentieth Century* CVIII, Oct. 1955) by Freya Stark. The basis for it lies in the change made by Tennyson in the Arthurian legend. But surely Victorian sentiment, which affected him far more than it did Browning (to his good fortune in the Victorian world) sufficiently accounts for these changes.

8 Letter in *Robert Browning and Julia Wedgwood*.

CHAPTER 8 *Two Nations*

1 I have found it impossible in this chapter to keep to chronological order: the encounter with Gladstone and Disraeli, the poetry quoted are of a rather later date than the narrative of Browning's life has yet reached. But the background is that of his world during the whole period covered in this volume.

2 Letter of Mrs. Gaskell quoted by Cecil Woodham Smith in *Florence Nightingale*.

3 Disraeli had indeed always seen that there should be—as in the past there had been—some sort of representation for the "other nation": only he had believed at first that this could be achieved by the press. I cannot help thinking that an element in his curious character made him describe his extension of the franchise of 1867 as a mere political trick. Still more perhaps his reaction to Gladstone's attitude. While "Dizzy," asked by Lord Melbourne at the outset of his career what were his aims, replied cheerfully "to become Prime Minister," Gladstone, his daughter once said in pious tones, "thinks all ambition sinful."

A fascinating review by A. J. P. Taylor in the *Observer* of July 23, 1967, of Maurice Cowling's book *1867 Gladstone and Disraeli: The Passing of the Second Reform Bill* comments on another aspect—the accidental element in this as in so many historical events In a careful analysis of the debates Mr. Cowling shows that "Disraeli had to do so and so because . . . so and so because . . . so and so because." But, says Mr. Taylor, while "There is much to be said for the accidental view of history . . . tendencies cannot be wholly accidental, even though they are composed of accidental details."

And in this particular event we do see two statesmen both concerned in their different ways with social reform, both aware of the demand for it *and* the opposition to it—also both eager to gain votes and "dish" one another. Mr. Taylor holds too that Disraeli was clever enough to realize that a household franchise would affect primarily that middle class whose votes would be heavily Conservative.

4 DeVane's *Parleyings* give an excellent detailed account of George Bubb Dodington. Browning had, he

tells us, two copies of Dodington's *Diary* in his library. See also *The Memoirs of Richard Cumberland*, London, 1856, and Walpole's *Memoirs and Letters*. Lord Chesterfield described him as "Blest Coxcomb!"

5   Robert Blake, in his most interesting *Disraeli*, has shown that this descent was fabulous, but it seems to have been accepted by Disraeli's contemporaries.

6   John Holloway, in *The Victorian Sage*, gives us as sages both Carlyle and Disraeli. His others are George Eliot, Newman, Arnold, and Hardy. For both this chapter and the last, this book is useful reading. The introduction is especially important.

A vivid picture is drawn of *The Victorian Age* in the book of that title admirably compiled and edited by Robert Langbaum. We are given selections from writers of today and of the period itself covering politics and sociology, art and literature, Victorian taste, and finally a brilliant essay of Yeats, "Art and Ideas," which at once links and illuminates the whole.

I would suggest also Chesterton's *The Victorian Age in Literature*. Coming as he did, an eccentric genius, at the end of that age he casts light on the ethos and ideas by which its wheels went around.

For a fuller picture of social conditions Marx, Engels and the two Hammond books are the most vivid and the fullest. See Bibliography.

CHAPTER 9   Red Cotton Night-Cap Country *to* La Saisiaz

1   Letters on the subject of *Red Cotton Night-Cap Country* to George Smith are published in *New Letters of Robert Browning*. Those on *The Inn Album* are in the Murray Collection, mostly unpublished.

2   Appearing originally in *The Nation*, January 20, 1876, this was reprinted in *News and Reviews*.

3   Despite a confusion between the two Chapman brothers the best account of Browning's relations with the firm is that given in an Appendix to *New Letters*.

4   Quoted in *New Letters of Robert Browning*.

5   Autograph letters, Wellesley College Library.

6   Browning's account and Sarianna's differ a little in details.

7   This remark, quoted by Harriet Jay, is typical of the change noted above in Buchanan's attitude to Browning.

CHAPTER 10   *The Public Face*

1   Julian Hawthorne in *Shapes that Pass*, Churton Collins in *Life and Memoirs*, Sidney Colvin in *Memories and Notes of Persons and Places*

2   In G. W. E. Russell's *Portraits of the Seventies*.

3   In *Learned Lady*.

4   David Bispham in *A Quaker Singer's Recollections*, Mrs. Bailey Aldrich in *Crowding Memories*, Mary Anderson in *A Few Memories*, Leslie Stephen in *Studies of a Biographer*.

5   Unpublished letter from Henry James in the Baker Library, Dartmouth College.

6   Boyd Carpenter in *Some Pages of my Life*.

7   *Memoirs and Letters of Sir James Paget*.

CHAPTER 11   *Daily Life in London*

1   Unpublished letter, Baker Library, Dartmouth College.

2 Alfred Domett is an interesting sample of human incoherence. While writing romantic poetry about the Maoris he was defending British settlers (against the efforts of the remote home government) for stealing their lands. A real or pretended misunderstanding of the tribal system was the excuse put forward—an individual with no right to do so having allegedly sold tribally owned acreage to this or that settler. Domett held positions in the newly constituted government, becoming Prime Minister for a few months. But he never became fully a New Zealander, looking forward to his return to England as coming home. It is fortunate that his letters and the copies he made of letters to him have been preserved in Wellington. See also *Robert Browning and Alfred Domett* and *Diary of Alfred Domett*.

3 The two "poetesses" were much sought after for a few years by London intellectuals. George Moore admired their poetry, George Meredith invited them to his cottage on Box Hill, Browning fussed over them. Reading their verse today one can only wonder. But reading *Works and Days* one understands why Oscar Wilde among others was excited over this curious couple.

CHAPTER 13   *Age Not Crabbed but Crowded*

1 *Learned Lady*, June 23, 1888.
2 *Letters to George Barrett*, May 2, 1882.
3 Unpublished journal of W. J. Hoppin quoted by Leon Edel in *The Conquest of London*.
4 *Life of Octavia Hill as told in her Letters*.

5 Orr, *Life and Letters of Robert Browning*.
6 *Charlotte Brontë: The Evolution of Genius*.
7 See Lilian Whiting, *The Brownings: Their Life and Art*, for an account of Professor Corson's memories of his visit to England and of his conversations with Browning.
8 Both *Dearest Isa* and *Learned Lady* are exceptionally well edited by Dr. Edward C. McAleer, with notes containing all relevant and little irrelevant information. Apart from quotations from those to Mrs. Bronson in Lilian Whiting's *The Brownings: Their Life and Art* these remain unpublished, in the possession of the Conte Rucellai by whose kind permission I quote them.

CHAPTER 14   *Browning and the Carlyles*

1 Letters from R. B. to various correspondents, First Series, quoted in DeVane, *Browning's Parleyings*.
2 *New Letters of Thomas Carlyle*.
3 This is quoted with no reference in Henry Jones, *Browning as a Philosopher and Religious Teacher*.
4 The picture of the Carlyle relationship emerges from the Froude publications and the excellent Hanson biography of Jane, *Necessary Evil*, one of Carlyle's names for her. Iris Origo's *A Measure of Love* contains also some excellent insights. The Hansons feel that no certain conclusion can be reached about the question of whether the Carlyle marriage was ever consummated. What seems certain is that when it took place Carlyle *was* very much in love with Jane while she only worshiped his genius and was herself in a state of rebound from an unrequited love.

5   DeVane, reissuing his earlier work, *Browning's Parleyings*, does so rather apologetically. It is worth looking also at his later treatment in the *Handbook*. The earlier book shows him perhaps a little too eager to prove a doubtful point. This Parleying he believed was written chiefly because Browning was personally irritated with Carlyle (on one page there are five suggestions of the kind introduced by "might be," "maybe," "very probably").

6   This interesting record is at Baylor University Armstrong Library. Mr. Curtis declared he had written down the conversations immediately to ensure accuracy.

CHAPTER 15   *Back to Italy*

1   In the *Cornhill Magazine*, Vol. XII (Feb. 1902) pp. 145–71. See also Mrs. Bronson's "Browning in Asolo" *Century Magazine* LIX (1900).

2   Both these letters are in Hood, *Letters of Robert Browning*.

3   A good many letters are published in Hood—and we have also Fannie's little book, *Some Memories of Robert Browning*. Clearly she had an intensely romantic feeling both for Pen's dead mother and his living father.

4   The first of these quotations is from *Letters of Henry James* edited by Percy Lubbock, the second from an unpublished letter at Dartmouth College.

CHAPTER 16   *Two Robert Brownings?*

1 and 2   See Leon Edel: *Henry James, The Conquest of London*, Vol. II, to which I am indebted, both

for quotations and for valuable analysis of Henry James.

3   From *H. G. Wells and Henry James*.

4   Graham Greene from "The Plays of Henry James" in *The Lost Childhood*.

5   The difficulty of the biographer is increased by the existence of two Browning legends: the old one, and the new, which has established itself with amazing rapidity. I have always found reviews valuable, especially when they criticize, but one intelligent review of my first volume was also a little bewildering. The reviewer drew attention to "significant" facts about Browning which I left "unexplained and sometimes even unmentioned." Some of the matters listed I had discussed rather fully. Others were not facts: they belong to the new legend. I take four examples. Browning's father was *not* "passive," but very active; as educator, introducing his son to the classics, to art, to a wide range of reading; himself a collector of rare books; adequate in his profession, very eccentric in daily life.

Browning did *not* avoid "close relationships with his age mates." His greatest friends, Ripert Monclar, Domett, and Joseph Arnould, were all his own age, and a larger surrounding group is indicated in the few letters of his young manhood that are accessible.

Browning did *not* expect his wife to "manage his practical affairs"— the couple would indeed have been sunk if he had; he conducted their very difficult life with astonishing energy and success, carrying on equally well after Elizabeth's death.

I have left to the last the oddest of the "significant facts . . . left unexplained and even unmentioned" in my book—that Browning disliked being portrayed through fear of "exposing the secret of his personality"; when it had to happen, he "surrendered half his face only."

If he did have this neurosis he certainly brought it under control. His son, besides making a bust, painted him at least fourteen times. Browning established his manservant as a photographer and helped his reputation by many sittings. At one moment in his last decade he confesses to weariness when posing for four portraits. Baylor University possesses 160 Browning likenesses and Grace Wilson, in her book *Robert Browning's Portraits, Photographs and Other Likenesses and Their Makers*, declares that despite all her efforts she could not, writing in wartime (1943), make certain she had discovered all that existed in England and Italy, in private families as well as collections.

The largest number of these likenesses belong to the last decade of the poet's life when he was more famous and photography more advanced than in his earlier years. But besides the three likenesses in profile of Browning's twenties (one a daguerreotype, one done by Ripert Monclar), there is Lowes Dickenson's full-face crayon portrait; in his early thirties there is E. Heber Thompson's pen drawing (full face), and the far better one by W. Fisher. At this time the American artist William Page painted him, having fifty-four sittings never less than an hour and a half and generally two hours.

Browning told a friend how much he enjoyed the talk with which these sittings were enlivened, and it is clear from Rossetti's letters that Browning's sittings for him in Paris (1855) were equally good fun. I used this picture as a frontispiece to Vol. I: it is so full of thought and character. About the same time Anne Thackeray drew him (full face) in pen and ink, and three years later we have Talfourd, Lord Leighton, Rudolph Lehmann, and Gordigiani—all of them full face. My own guess is that when we have portraits in profile it was the artist who chose it so—the profile *was* rather notable.

6 Quoted by Robert W. Hartle in "Gide's Interpretation of Browning," Texas University Studies in English, Vol. 28.

CHAPTER 17 *Parleyings with Certain People of Importance in their Day*

1 In some places Mrs. Orr denies that Browning was a Christian—elsewhere she appears only to state the obvious fact that he did not accept everything demanded by orthodoxy. At that date the lines of orthodoxy were in every denomination narrowly drawn.

2 The painter Alma Tadema declared that Browning could with his left eye "read the number of a picture at the end of a long gallery; while with the other, without artificial assistance, he could write an ode of Horace on a piece of paper of the size of a three-penny piece." This was reported by Sir Mountstuart Grant Duff in his *Notes from a Diary* (*1892–1895*), of which there are at least forty volumes recording London gossip. But the keenest sight in the world could not create space on a three-penny piece of that date; more believable is the commoner story that Browning could write the Lord's prayer on a half crown (or the now extinct crown piece?).

3 Told by Boswell in his life of Johnson.

CHAPTER 18   *Death in Venice*

1 These letters to Pen and Fannie are at Balliol College, Oxford; a few are published in Hood, *Letters of Robert Browning*.
2 From *Robert Browning Personalia*.
3 This letter is quoted by Charles Tennyson and was printed in full in *The Times Literary Supplement* of June 3, 1965.
4 Hood, *Letters of Robert Browning*.
5 I am indebted to B. R. Jerman's article in *The University of Toronto Quarterly*, October 1965, for a careful working out of the details of Browning's last days. I am convinced, as is he, "that Miss Barclay is by far the most reliable witness," Pen and Fannie being both confused and confusing. Mr. Jerman also clarifies the order of events in regard to the cemetery at Florence and the Abbey burial and adds many interesting details to the accounts hitherto published. Sarianna's whereabouts remains something of a puzzle. One gathers that at first she was constantly by Browning's bedside but toward the end broke down and remained in her own room.
6 The sequence may be found in *Astrophel and other Poems*. I have changed the order of the two sonnets from which I quote.

EPILOGUE   *Robert Barrett Browning*

1 Michael Field perceived a combination in Pen of a sincere love of his father with "a strain in the relationship." This had certainly existed, and Pen pictures lessons given the morning after his father's good dinners and port wine which had "told on the boy's Greek lessons." Here perhaps Pen's imagination played some part, for the period of frequent dining out coincided not with Browning's tutorial period but with that of Mr. Gillespie. It seems to have been only in one seaside vacation that Browning went back to tutoring his son.
2 The picture of his visit to Asolo given by Phelps in his autobiography is a pleasant one.
3 Unpublished letter of Henry James.
4 I owe the valentine to the kindness of Mrs. Hall Wheelock, grandniece of Mrs. Bronson.

Selective Bibliography

THERE ARE at once too many and too few books about Browning. As Philip Drew has pointed out in his Introduction to *Robert Browning: a Collection of Critical Essays*, "brief unargued rejections" have been "for many years the sole response to Browning by a most influential body of opinion."

On the other hand, there are an enormous number of records contemporary with Browning, and while some of the criticism in them may be outdated, the pictures of the man and his world remain valid. I have tried to choose a cross section of these; there are many others. Books listed in the Bibliography for Volume I reappear here only if they refer to the latter half of Browning's life, work, and the world then surrounding him.

There seems a compulsion in the world of letters to write articles about some aspect of Browning: from his star imagery to the question of whether he whistled or sang, from his religion to his dining out, from his son to his "footman ancestor." Some of these are really valuable, but their name is legion. I decided finally to make no list but to indicate in text or footnote where articles biographically important can be found.

WORKS OF ROBERT BROWNING

Essay on Chatterton. Edited by Donald Smalley. Harvard: Oxford, 1948.
An Essay on Percy Bysshe Shelley. Published for the Shelley Society by Reeves and Turner, 1888.

The Poetical Works of Robert Browning, John Murray, 1951. (First definitive edition, Smith, Elder, 1896.) This one volume edition has been used for all quotations in this book, but for the student of Browning's poetry two larger editions are valuable: *The Florentine* (1898) in twelve volumes and *The Centenary* (1912) in ten volumes.

BIOGRAPHIES

Burdett, Osbert, *The Brownings*. Constable, 1928.

Chesterton, G. K., *Robert Browning*. English Men of Letters Series, Macmillan, 1903.

Dowden, Edward, *The Life of Robert Browning*. Everyman's Library, J. M. Dent, 1904.

Griffin, W. Hall, and Minchin, H. C., *The Life of Robert Browning. With Notices of His Writings, His Family, and His Friends* (revised edition), Archon Books, 1966.

Hovelaque, Henri Léon, *La Jeunesse de Robert Browning*. Les Presses Modernes, 1932.

Miller, Betty, *Robert Browning: A Portrait*. John Murray, 1952.

Orr, Mrs. Sutherland, *Life and Letters of Robert Browning* (1891). New edition, revised and in part rewritten by Frederic G. Kenyon. John Murray, 1908.

Sharp, William, *Life of Robert Browning*. Walter Scott, 1890.

Whiting, Lilian, *The Brownings: Their Life and Art*. Little, Brown, 1911.

LETTERS

The Letters of Robert Browning and Elizabeth Barrett Browning. Smith, Elder, 1899.

Robert Browning and Alfred Domett. Edited by Frederic A. Kenyon. Smith, Elder, 1906.

Letters of Robert Browning. Collected by Thomas J. Wise. Edited, with an Introduction and Notes, by Thurman L. Hood. John Murray, 1933.

Robert Browning and Julia Wedgwood. A Broken Friendship as Revealed in Their Letters. Edited by Richard Curle. John Murray and Jonathan Cape, 1937.

New Letters of Robert Browning. Edited, with Introduction and Notes, by

William Clyde DeVane and Kenneth Leslie Knickerbocker. John Murray, 1951.

Dearest Isa: Robert Browning's Letters to Isabella Blagden. Edited by Edward C. McAleer. University of Texas Press: Nelson, 1951.

Browning to His American Friends: Letters between the Brownings, the Storys, and James Russell Lowell (1841–1890). Bowes and Bowes, 1965.

Learned Lady: Letters from Robert Browning to Mrs. Thomas FitzGerald 1876–1889. Edited by Edward C. McAleer. Harvard University Press: Oxford, 1966.

Letters of the Brownings to George Barrett. Edited by Paul Landis. University of Illinois Press, 1958.

GENERAL

Abbot, Evelyn and Campbell, Lewis, *Life and Letters of Benjamin Jowett.* Dutton, 1897.

Allingham, Helen, and Williams, E. B., editors. *Letters to William Allingham.* Longmans, Green, 1911.

Allingham, William, *A Diary.* Edited by H. Allingham and D. Radford. Macmillan, 1907.

Angeli, Helen Rossetti, *Dante Gabriel Rossetti.* H. Hamilton, 1949.

Armstrong, Dr. A. J., editor. *Intimate Glimpses from Browning's Letter File.* Baylor Bulletin, September 1934.

Arnold, Matthew, *The Letters of Matthew Arnold.* Edited by G. W. E. Russell. Macmillan, 1896. 2 vols.

———, *Unpublished Letters of Matthew Arnold.* Edited by Arnold Whitridge. Yale, 1923.

———, *The Portable Matthew Arnold.* Edited, with Introduction, by Lionel Trilling. Viking Press, 1949.

Austin, Alfred, *The Poetry of the Period.* Richard Bentley, 1870.

Bancroft, Marie and Squire, *Recollections of Sixty Years.* John Murray, 1909.

Bancroft, Squire, *Empty Chairs.* John Murray, 1925.

Barclay, Evelyn (Mrs. D. Giles), *Diary: Telling of the Last Days of Robert Browning,* Presented to Dr. A. J. Armstrong, Torbrugh Brora, Scotland, 1932.

Benson, E. F., *Our Family Affairs.* Cassells, 1920.

Berdoe, Edward, *Browning and the Christian Faith,* G. Allen, 1899.

Browning, Fannie Barrett, *Some Memories of Robert Browning*. Marshall Jones Co., 1928.

Browning, Oscar, *Memories of Sixty Years*. John Lane, 1910.

The Browning Society's Papers. 12 Parts in 3 vols. The Browning Society, 1881–91.

Carlyle, Thomas, *The Diamond Necklace*. Houghton, Mifflin, 1913.

———, *Letters of Carlyle to John Stuart Mill, John Sterling and Robert Browning*. Edited by Alexander Carlyle. Stokes, 1923.

———, *New Letters of Carlyle*. Edited by Alexander Carlyle. John Lane, 1904.

———, *Past and Present*. Everyman's Library, 1912.

———, *Reminiscences of Carlyle*. Edited by J. A. Froude. 1887.

Carter, John and Pollard, Graham, *An Enquiry into the Nature of Certain Nineteenth Century Pamphlets*. Constable, 1936.

Chesterton, G. K., *A Handful of Authors*, Sheed and Ward, 1953.

———, *The Victorian Age in Literature*. Home University Library, 1913.

Collins, John Churton, *Life and Memoirs*. John Lane, 1912.

Colvin, Sidney, *Memories and Notes of Persons and Places*. Edward Arnold, 1921.

Comyns-Carr, J., *Some Eminent Victorians*. Duckworth, 1908.

Cook, Arthur Kemball, *A Commentary upon Browning's The Ring and the Book*. Archon Books, 1966.

Corkran, Henriette, *Celebrities and I*. Hutchinson, 1905.

Cross, J.W., *George Eliot's Life as related in her Letters and Journals*. Blackwood, 1885.

Crowell, Norton B., *The Triple Soul: Browning's Theory of Knowledge*. University of New Mexico Press, 1963.

DeVane, William Clyde, *A Browning Handbook*. Second Edition. Bell, 1956.

———, *Browning's Parleyings: The Autobiography of a Mind*. Yale University Press, 1927.

Disraeli, Benjamin, *Sybil or the Two Nations*. Longmans, Green, 1907.

Domett, Alfred, *The Diary of Alfred Domett (1872–1885)*. Edited by E. A. Horsman. Oxford University Press, 1953.

Drew, Mary Gladstone, *Mary Gladstone (Mrs. Drew): Her Diaries and Letters*. Edited by Lucy Masterman, Methuen, 1930.

Drew, Philip, editor, *Robert Browning: A Collection of Essays*. Methuen, 1966.

Duckworth, F. K. G., *Browning—Background and Conflict*. Ernest Benn, 1931.

Duffy, Sir Charles Gavan, *Conversations with Carlyle*. Low, 1892.

Edel, Leon, *Henry James*. Hart-Davis, 1953-63. 3 vols.

————, editor, *The Diary of Alice James*. With Introduction by the editor. Hart-Davis, 1965.

————, and Ray, Gordon N., editors, *Henry James and H. G. Wells*. University of Illinois Press, 1958.

Engels, Friedrich, *On the Condition of the Working Class in England in 1844*. Translated by Florence Kelley Wischnewetzky. Swan Sonnenschein, 1892.

Faber, Geoffrey, *Jowett: A Portrait with Background*. Faber and Faber, 1957.

Field, Michael (Pseud.), *Works and Days*. Edited by T. and D. C. Sturge Moore, John Murray, 1933.

Froude, James Anthony, *The Earl of Beaconsfield*. Everyman's Library, 1914.

————, *Thomas Carlyle: Story of His Life in London 1834-1881*. Longmans, 1919.

Gardner,W. H., *Gerard Manley Hopkins (1844-1889)*. Oxford University Press, 1958.

Gérin, Winifred, *Charlotte Brontë: The Evolution of Genius*. Oxford, Clarendon Press, 1967.

Gosse, Edmund, *Robert Browning: Personalia*. Fisher Unwin, 1890.

Grant-Duff, Sir Mountstuart, *Leaves from a Diary (1896-1901)*, John Murray, 1905.

Guérard, Albert, *Napoleon III*. Harvard University Press, 1943.

Hammond, Barbara and John Lawrence, *The Town Labourer 1760-1832*. Longmans, Green, 1917.

————, *The Village Labourer, 1760-1832*. Longmans, Green, 1911.

Hancher, Charles M., *The London Browning Society, 1881-1892*. Unpublished dissertation, Yale University, 1967.

Hanson, Lawrence and Elizabeth, *Necessary Evil: The Life of Jane Welsh Carlyle*. Macmillan, 1952.

Hawthorne, Julian, *Shapes That Pass*. Houghton, Mifflin, 1928.

Hawthorne, Nathaniel, *French and Italian Notebooks*. Strahan, 1871.

Hodell, Charles W., *The Old Yellow Book*. Everyman's Library, n.d.

Holloway, John, *The Victorian Sage*. Macmillan, 1953.

Home, Daniel Dunglas, *Incidents in My Life*. Longman's, 1871.

Honan, Park, *Browning's Characters*. Yale University Press, 1961.

James, Henry, *The Aspern Papers*. Collins, 1956 (originally published as a short story in 1888).

————, *Autobiography*. Scribner's, 1917.

————, *Essays in London and Elsewhere.* Harper, 1893.

————, *The Middle Years.* Collins, 1917.

————, "The Novel in *The Ring and the Book*" from *Notes on Novelists.* Scribner's, 1914.

————, *The Private Life and Other Tales.* Harper, 1893.

————, *The Tragic Muse.* Harper, 1960.

————, *William Wetmore Story and His Friends.* Blackwood, 1903.

————, *Views and Reviews.* Ball Co., 1908.

Jay, Harriet, *Robert Buchanan. Some Account of his Life's Work, and His Literary Friendships.* T. Fisher Unwin, 1903.

Jones, Sir Henry, *Browning as a Philosopher and Religious Teacher.* Macmillan, 1891.

Kenyon, F. G., *Robert Browning and Alfred Domett.* Smith, Elder, 1906.

King, Roma, Jr., *The Bow and the Lyre: The Art of Robert Browning.* University of Michigan Press: Cresset Press, 1965.

————, *Browning's Finances from his own Account Book.* Baylor University Browning Interests, 1917.

Kitchel, Anne Theresa, *George Lewes and George Eliot: A Review of Records.* The John Day Company, 1933.

Knight, William, *Retrospects.* First Series. Smith, Elder, 1904.

Langbaum, Robert. *The Poetry of Experience. The Dramatic Monologue in Modern Literary Tradition.* Chatto and Windus, 1957.

————, editor, *The Victorian Age: Essays in history and in social and literary criticism.* Fawcett Publications, 1967.

Lehmann, Rudolph C., *Memories of Half a Century: a record of friendships.* Smith, Elder, 1908.

Leon, Derrick, *Ruskin the Great Victorian.* London, Routledge and Kegan Paul, 1949.

Litzinger, Boyd, and Knickerbocker, K. L., *The Browning Critics.* University of Kentucky Press, 1965.

Luhan, Mabel Dodge, *Intimate Memories.* Vol. II, *European Experiences.* Harcourt Brace, 1935.

Masson, Flora, *Victorians All.* W. & R. Chambers, 1931.

Maurois, André, *Disraeli. A Picture of the Victorian Age.* Translated by Hamish Miles. Bodley Head, 1962.

————, *Prometheus. The Life of Balzac.* Bodley Head, 1965.

Meredith, Owen (Lytton, E. Robert Bulwer), *Letters to Robert and Elizabeth Browning.* Edited by Aurelia B. Harlan and J. Lee Harlan, Jr. Baylor Browning Interests, 1936.

Mill, John Stuart, *Autobiography*. Preface by J. J. Cross. Columbia U. P.: Oxford, 1924.

——, *Essays on Politics and Culture*. Edited by Gertrude Himmelfarb, Doubleday, 1962.

Miller, J. Hillis, *The Disappearance of God*. Harvard U. P. Oxford, 1963.

Minchin, H. C., *Walter Savage Landor: Last Days, Letters and Conversations*. Methuen, 1934.

Moscheles, Felix, *Fragments of an Autobiography*. J. Nisbet Co., 1899.

Munro, John, editor, *Frederick James Furnivall: A Volume of Personal Record*. Oxford University Press, 1911.

Nicoll, Sir William Robertson, and Wise, Thomas, *Literary Anecdotes of the Nineteenth Century*, Vol. I. Dodd, Mead, 1896.

Origo, Iris, *A Measure of Love*. Jonathan Cape, 1957.

Orr, Mrs. Sutherland, *A Handbook to the Works of Robert Browning*. Bell, 1885.

Packe, Michael St. John, *The Life of John Stuart Mill*. Secker and Warburg, 1954.

Paget, S., editor, *Memoirs and Letters of Sir James Paget*. Longman's 1901.

Partington, Wilfred, *Forging Ahead: The True Story of the Upward Progress of Thomas James Wise*. G. F. Putnam's Sons, 1939.

——, *Thomas J. Wise in the Original Cloth*. Robert Hale, 1946.

Phelps, William Lyon, *Autobiography with Letters*. Oxford University Press, 1939.

Pick, John, *A Hopkins Reader*. Oxford University Press, 1953.

Pope-Hennessy, James, *Monckton Milnes. The Flight of Youth*. Constable, 1951.

Pound, Ezra, *The A.B.C. of Reading*. Faber, 1962.

Reid, T. Wemyss, *The Life, Letters and Friendships of Richard Monckton Milnes*. Cassells, 1890.

Renton, H., *John Forster and His Friendships*. Chapman and Hall, 1912.

Ritchie, Anne Thackeray, *Records of Tennyson, Ruskin and Browning*. Harper, 1892.

Rossetti, Dante Gabriel, *Poems*. Roberts Brothers, 1870.

——, *Letters of Dante Gabriel Rossetti to William Allingham*. Edited by George Birkbeck Hill. T. Fisher Unwin, 1897.

Rossetti, William Michael, *Pre-Raphaelite Diaries and Letters*. Hurst and Blackett, 1900.

——, *Rossetti Papers, 1862–70*. Sands, 1903.

——, *Some Reminiscences*. Scribner's, 1906.

St. Helier, Lady Susan, *Memories of Fifty Years*. Arnold, 1909.

Saintsbury, George, *Corrected Impressions*. Dodd, Mead, 1895.

———, *History of English Prosody*, Vol. III. Macmillan, 1906.

Sargent, F. L., *Omar and the Rabbi*. Harvard Cooperative Society, 1909.

Sotheby's Catalogue, "The Browning Collections," 1913.

Stark, Freya, *Traveller's Prelude*. John Murray, 1950.

Stephen, Leslie, *Studies of a Biographer*. Vol. II. Duckworth, 1902.

Strachey, Lytton, *Characters and Commentaries*. Pelham Library, Chatto and Windus, 1941.

———, *Eminent Victorians*. Chatto and Windus, 1918.

Super, R. H., *Walter Savage Landor: A Biography*. Calder, 1957.

Sutherland, Edward H., *Personal Recollections*. Cassells, 1900.

Swinburne, Algernon Charles, *The Age of Shakespeare*. Chatto and Windus, 1908.

———, *Astrophel and other Poems*. Chatto and Windus, 1894.

———, *Contemporaries of Shakespeare*. Edited by Edmund Gosse and Thomas James Wise. Heinemann, 1919.

——, *The Swinburne Letters*. Edited by Cecil Y. Lang. Oxford University Press, 1959.

Symons, Arthur, *An Introduction to the Study of Browning*. Revised edition. J. W. Dent, 1906.

Tennyson, Charles, *Alfred Tennyson, by his Grandson Charles Tennyson*. Macmillan, 1949.

Terhune, Alfred McKinley, *The Life of Edward FitzGerald. Translator of The Rubáiyát of Omar Khayyam*. Oxford University Press, 1947.

Tharp, Louise Hall, *Mrs. Jack: A Biography of Isabella Stewart Gardner*. Little, Brown, 1965.

Trilling, Lionel, *Matthew Arnold*. George Allen and Unwin, 1939.

Troubridge, Lady, *Memories and Reflections*. Heinemann, 1925.

Ward, Wilfrid, *Aubrey de Vere*. Longmans, Green, 1904.

———, *Problems and Persons*. Longmans, Green, 1903.

———, *Ten Personal Studies*. Longmans, Green, 1908.

Waugh, Evelyn, *Rossetti: His Life and Works*. Duckworth, 1928.

Whitla, William, *The Central Truth: The Incarnation in Browning's Poetry*. University of Toronto Press, 1963.

Winwar, Frances, *The Immortal Lovers*. Hamish Hamilton, 1950.

Woodham-Smith, Cecil, *The Great Hunger: Ireland, 1845–49*, Hamish Hamilton, 1962.

Yeats, William Butler, *Essays and Introductions*. Clarendon Press, 1965.

Index